Racism
Postcolonialism
Europe

Postcolonialism across the Disciplines 6

Postcolonialism across the Disciplines

Series Editors
Graham Huggan, University of Leeds
Andrew Thompson, University of Leeds

Postcolonialism across the Disciplines showcases alternative directions for post-colonial studies. It is in part an attempt to counteract the dominance in colonial and postcolonial studies of one particular discipline – English literary/cultural studies – and to make the case for a combination of disciplinary knowledges as the basis for contemporary postcolonial critique. Edited by leading scholars, the series aims to be a seminal contribution to the field, spanning the traditional range of disciplines represented in postcolonial studies but also those less acknowledged. It will also embrace new critical paradigms and examine the relationship between the transnational/cultural, the global and the postcolonial.

Already published
Interdisciplinary Measures: Literature and the Future of Postcolonial Studies
Graham Huggan

Deconstruction and the Postcolonial: At the Limits of Theory
Michael Syrotinski

Friends and Enemies: The Scribal Politics of Post/Colonial Literature
Chris Bongie

Postcolonial Thought in the French-Speaking World
Edited by Charles Forsdick & David Murphy

Black 1919: Riots, Racism and Resistance in Imperial Britain
Jacqueline Jenkinson

Racism
Postcolonialism
Europe

Edited by Graham Huggan
and Ian Law

Liverpool University Press

First published 2009 by
Liverpool University Press
4 Cambridge Street
Liverpool
L69 7ZU

British Library Cataloguing-in-Publication data
A British Library CIP record is available

ISBN 978-1-84631-219-9   *cased*
ISBN 978-1-84631-814-6   *paperback*

Typeset in Amerigo by R. J. Footring Ltd, Derby
Printed and bound by CPI Group (UK) Ltd, Croydon, CR0 4YY

Contents

Contents

Contributors

Philomena Essed is Professor of Critical Race, Gender and Leadership Studies, PhD in Leadership and Change Program, Antioch University, USA. Key works include *Everyday Racism: Reports From Women of Two Cultures* (Hunter House, 1990); *Understanding Everyday Racism: An Interdisciplinary Theory* (Sage, 1991); and *Diversity: Gender, Color and Culture* (University of Massachusetts Press, 1996). Co-edited volumes include *Race Critical Theories* (Blackwell, 2002); *Refugees and the Transformation of Societies: Agency, Policies, Ethics and Politics* (Berghahn, 2004); and *A Companion to Gender Studies* (Blackwell, 2005). Work in progress includes the volumes *Cloning Cultures* and *Dutch Racism*.

Maya García de Vinuesa is Lecturer in English at the Department of Modern Languages of the University of Alcalá, Madrid, Spain. She is editor of the *Journal of Afroeuropean Studies* and key works include *La lengua inglesa en Ghana: léxico y modelos culturales* (*English in Ghana: Lexis and Cultural Models*) (University of Alcalá, 2003) and she co-edited the volume *Migraciones y mutaciones culturales en España* (*Migrations and Cultural Mutations in Spain*) (University of Alcalá, 2007, with L. W. Miampika).

Graham Huggan is Professor of English, Chair of Commonwealth and Postcolonial Literature, and founding Co-Director of the Institute for Colonial and Postcolonial Studies (ICPS) at the University of Leeds, UK. His most recent books are *Australian Literature: Postcolonialism, Racism, Transnationalism* (Oxford University Press, 2007) and *Interdisciplinary Measures: Literature and the Future of Postcolonial Studies* (Liverpool University Press, 2008).

Angéla Kóczé is a PhD candidate at the Central European University, Budapest, Hungary. She is former Director of the European Roma Information Office

(ERIO) in Brussels, as well as the former Director of the Human Rights Education Programme at the European Roma Rights Centre (ERRC) in Budapest, Hungary. She is active in the movement for the emancipation of Roma in Europe, and has a particular interest in issues of women's political representation and social justice.

Ian Law is Founding Director of the Centre for Ethnicity and Racism Studies (CERS) and Reader in the School of Sociology and Social Policy, University of Leeds, UK. Key works include *Racism, Ethnicity and Social Policy* (Harvester, 1996), *Race in the British News* (Palgrave, 2002), *Institutional Racism in Higher Education* (Trentham Press, 2004, with L. Turney and D. Phillips), *Racist Futures* (Ethnic and Racial Studies, 2007, with S. Sayyid) and *Racism and Ethnicity: A Global Analysis* (Pearson, 2009).

Landry-Wilfrid Miampika is Lecturer in Spanish, African and Afro-Caribbean Literatures at the Universidad de Alcalá de Henares, Madrid, Spain, and is the Director of a collection of Francophone literatures in Ediciones del Cobre (Barcelona). Key works include *Voces africanas: Poesía de expresión francesa 1950– 2000/Voix africaines: Poésie d'expression française 1950–2000* (Editorial Verbum, 2000) and *Transculturación y poscolonialismo en el Caribe: versiones y subversiones de Alejo Carpentier* (Editorial Verbum, 2005).

Katarzyna Murawska-Muthesius, formerly Curator of the National Museum in Warsaw, Poland, teaches art history at the Faculty of Lifelong Learning, Birkbeck College, University of London, UK. She has edited *Borders in Art: Revisiting 'Kunstgeographie'* (Institute of Art, Warsaw, 2000) and *National Museum in Warsaw Guide* (National Museum, Warsaw, 2001). Her current research is on cartoons, maps and the representation of east (central) Europe in western visual culture.

Griselda Pollock is Professor of Social and Critical Histories of Art and Director of the Centre for Cultural Analysis, Theory and History at the University of Leeds, UK. Renowned for her feminist, postcolonial theoretical interventions in histories of visual arts and cultural theory, her research focuses on trauma and cultural memory and on aesthetics and psychoanalysis. She is currently Principal Investigator on an AHRC research project Concentrationary Memories: The Politics of Representation (2008–11) and editor (with Max Silverman) of *Concentrationary Cinema: Reading Alain Resnais's Night and Fog* (forthcoming). She is editor of the series 'New Encounters: Arts, Cultures, Concepts' (Macmillan), with recent collections including *Conceptual Odysseys: Passages to Cultural Analysis* (2007), *The Sacred and the Feminine: Imagination and Sexual Difference* (2008), *Bluebeard's Legacy: Death and Secrets from Bartòk to Hitchcock* (2009) and *Digital and Other Virtualities* (2009).

Christoph Ramm is Research Associate in the Department of Southeast European History (Turkish-Ottoman History) at the Ruhr University Bochum, Germany. He has published on Turkey and the European Union, the Cyprus conflict, nationalism and identities in Turkey and Cyprus, and the Turkish community in Germany. Currently he is working in a project funded by the German Research Foundation (DFG) on Turkish Cypriot identity conceptions and transnational migration in northern Cyprus after 1974.

Alex Rotas is Honorary Research Fellow at the School of Journalism, Media and Cultural Studies, Cardiff University, UK. Her research interests include the visual representation of migration, displacement and political asylum and the impact of British migrant artists' work on local understandings of place. She is the co-editor of *Migratory Settings* (Rodopi Press, 2008, with Murat Aydemir).

Ashwani Sharma is Principal Lecturer in Media and Cultural Studies at the University of East London, UK. He is the co-editor of the collection *Dis-Orienting Rhythms: The Politics of the New Asian Dance Music* (Zed Books, 1997, with S. Sharma and J. Hutnyk). He is the co-editor of the online journal *darkmatter* (www.darkmatter101.org) and the editor of the special issue on the television crime series *The Wire* for *darkmatter*. He is currently working on a monograph on media, race and transnational cultural form after 9/11, and researching the racial imaginary of suburbia.

Robert Spencer is Lecturer in Postcolonial Literature and Culture in English and American Studies at the University of Manchester, UK. He is currently working on a book that demonstrates the links between postcolonial literature and the idea of cosmopolitanism.

Nidhi Trehan is an ESRC Postdoctoral Research Fellow at the School of Public Policy/Political Science, University College London, UK. Her research has examined the human rights movement for Romanies in post-socialist Europe. She has long been concerned with human rights issues, as both a practitioner and an academic, and has published in the areas of human rights, identity politics, non-governmental organizations and social movements, and migration.

Michel Wieviorka is Professor at the École des Hautes Études en Sciences Sociales, Paris, France, and Director of CADIS (Centre d'Analyse et d'Intervention Sociologiques). His books in English include *The Making of Terrorism* (University of Chicago Press, new edition 2004), *The Arena of Racism* (Sage, 1995), *The Workers' Movement* (Cambridge University Press, 1987, with Alain Touraine), *The Lure of Antisemitism* (Brill, 2007) and *Violence: A New Approach* (Sage, 2009). He is President of the International Sociological Association (ISA).

Elisabeta Zelinka is Assistant University Lecturer in the Department of Sociology and Psychology, West University, Timisoara, Romania, and a postgraduate student in Women's Studies at the Central European University in Budapest, Hungary. Her research and activism are concerned with issues of human rights, migration and feminism, particularly in eastern Europe.

Acknowledgements

This book is the indirect result of a conference held at the University of Leeds, 15–17 May 2006, though it is hardly that publisher's nightmare, a 'conference volume'. While the conference was co-organized by Ian Law and myself, it could not have happened, still less have been as successful as it was, without the assistance of a small army of postgraduate helpers. Our sincere thanks go out to them all, particularly Senay Kara and Cathy Lean. Many thanks to Alan Ward, who struggled long and hard to get the manuscript into shape, and to our readers at Liverpool University Press, who pointed out weaknesses in the original manuscript. Thanks also to Anthony Cond at Liverpool University Press, who could not have been more helpful. Co-edited volumes are never easy, especially when their contributors come from far and wide, and the contributors themselves should take credit, not least for their patience when being hounded by the likes of myself. Thanks, finally, to Ian: this book is the end product of discussions that began several years ago, and Ian's good sense and organizational experience have been invaluable to me throughout. No doubt our collaborative work will continue; but so, too, unfortunately, will racism, and hopefully the readers of this book will also want to join us in the continuing struggle for a more equitable Europe, and for a more fully decolonized world.

Graham Huggan

CHAPTER 1

Introduction

Graham Huggan

In *Dead Europe* (2005), the Greek Australian writer Christos Tsiolkas's blatantly sexualized and racialized vampire novel, Europe is a place seemingly condemned to repeat its own violently self-destructive history. Haunted by spectres of its own making, it is a deadened – but also deadly – site of corrupt pimps and destitute sex workers, caught in a vicious web of race- and class-based exploitation that eventually threatens to engulf them all. Tsiolkas's Europe, as voraciously predatory as his own undead protagonist, is a far cry from the fount of idealistic humanism dreamed up by generations of both pre- and post-Enlightenment politicians and philosophers, a Europe defined by its durable capacity for civility in an otherwise barbarous world. After all, as the historian J. G. A. Pocock has argued, modern Europe has tended to view itself as a civilized place of liberty and peace, a loose 'republic or confederation … held together by states to which wars were merely auxiliary' (Pocock 2002, p. 64) – this despite the obvious fact that Europeans have proven over time to be 'one of the most belligerent groups of people anywhere in the world' (Pagden 2002, p. 14).

This cosmopolitan idea/ideal of Europe, envisioned perhaps most comprehensively by Kant, has resurfaced more recently as a counterpoint to American neo-imperial aggression, typically repressing the mutually entangled colonial histories that many see as intrinsic to modernity in general and that have been instrumental in making modern Europe what it is (Asad 2002; Mignolo 2000). For most modern European states, this apparent contradiction has created a 'double imposition: the need to repudiate their imperial past while clinging resolutely to the belief that there can be no alternative to the essentially European liberal democratic state' (Pagden 2002, p. 11). A better approach, perhaps, is to recognize, as Talal Asad does, that European civility – the idea of Europe itself – is inextricable from the workings of colonial/imperial history; and that 'Europe's colonial past is not merely an epoch of overseas power that is now decisively over', but also marked 'the beginning of an irreversible global transformation that remains an intrinsic part of "European experience", and is part of the reason that Europe has become what it is today' (Asad 2002, p. 218). It is not possible, Asad argues, 'for Europe to be represented without evoking this history' and without recognizing the diverse ways in which 'its active power has continually constructed its own exclusive boundary – and transgressed it' (218).

To proceed from this recognition is part of the project of a postcolonial Europe that both reviews the legacies of colonial/imperial ways of thinking for contemporary European societies and cultures and simultaneously works towards undoing – or, to use Dipesh Chakrabarty's term, 'provincializing' – those self-privileging ideologies that have supported the ingrained view of Europe as a hub of civilization or a centre, possibly even *the* centre, of the world. As Chakrabarty suggests, 'provincializing Europe is not a project of rejecting or discarding European thought, [which] is indispensable ... in helping us think through the experiences of political modernity in non-Western nations'; however, such experiences must also be 'renewed from and for the margins', creating a series of Europes that necessarily appear different when they are seen from the point of view of those who have historically undergone 'colonization or inferiorization in specific parts of the world' (Chakrabarty 2000, p. 16). The provincialization of Europe thus also implies the disaggregation of a European polity often falsely assumed to be homogeneous or unified in its motives, while at the same time recognizing that 'getting beyond Eurocentric histories remains a shared problem across geographical boundaries' (17) – a problem as likely to be intensified as alleviated by current federalist sympathies for a 'sense of [European] belonging that can perceive diversity while giving allegiance to that which is shared' (Pagden 2002, p. 24).

The chapters in this book variously contribute to this provincializing project while paradoxically performing just the opposite: turning the postcolonial critical gaze, which had previously been most likely to train itself on regions *other* than Europe, and sometimes those perceived to be most culturally or geographically *distant* from Europe, back on Europe itself. The chosen emphasis is on the racial ideologies that have long been central to European social and cultural identities, and that some commentators have seen as being inextricable from the internally differentiated, often directly competing, modernizing and/or civilizing missions that European countries, usually acting in their own national interests, have taken it upon themselves to impart to the world (Lentin 2004; MacMaster 2001). There is a close link here between racism, nationalism and colonialism, whereby 'race' becomes a 'phenomenon of expansive nations' (Nicholson 1999, p. 7) and racism is envisaged as a 'supplement internal to nationalism, always in excess of it, but always indispensable to its constitution' (Balibar 1991, p. 54).

In his overview *Racism in Europe 1870–2000*, Neil MacMaster captures this ideological co-dependency neatly. A 'complex apparatus of institutionalised racism', he says, was needed to back up 'imperial ideologies of [white European] racial superiority', which, while intrinsic to the global civilizing mission, also had a major impact on metropolitan European societies back home (MacMaster

2001, p. 25). Colonial societies, he claims, 'were not only the originators of discriminatory ideologies … but, far more crucially, they provided the context in which racial practices were implemented through tough legal systems, oppressive policing regimes, segregation and a host of other measures' (25). Colonial societies, in other words, were effective laboratories for a modernity based on racial stratifications and exclusions which, in order to be confirmed, needed to be rigorously tested, and which laid new foundations for the global expansion of the (white) European bourgeois order as a whole (25).

To what extent these stratifications and exclusions have been reproduced in contemporary Europe is a matter for debate, dividing those who see 'new' racisms as evolving from recent conditions attached to cultural/economic globalization processes (Castles 1998) from those who see a modified continuation of older patterns of colonial racism in European societies still struggling to come to terms with the internal as well as external consequences of their own imperial pasts (Balibar 2003). There is some agreement that these 'new' racisms – generally defined as being based on culture rather than biology – are manifesting themselves in a variety of western European anti-immigration national-populist movements, in the alarming rise of anti-Semitism in post-communist eastern Europe, and in the exclusionary practices derived from a 'fortress Europe' philosophy in which the politically motivated expansion of the European Union (EU) clashes with the economically motivated expansion of migration flows from beyond Europe's borders. The widening range of ethnic groups now settling in Europe has led not just to a *less* inclusive idea of Europe, but also to a diminished conception of what it means to be European in an increasingly globalized world (MacMaster 2001; Pagden 2002). There is little agreement, however, on anything else, from the question of the historical origins of racism in Europe to the degree to which 'new' forms of cultural differentialism, perhaps most notably multiculturalism, are either overtly or surreptitiously racist in their turn.

The chapters in this book engage with these debates, several of which might be described as taking place under the ambivalent sign of 'postcolonialism', a portmanteau term which – much debated itself – usually involves some recognition that the impulse to decolonization necessarily carries traces of the very processes of colonialism and imperialism it wishes to disavow (Gikandi 1996). Some chapters seek evidence of specific forms of postcolonial racism allied to new or recrudescent modes of cultural nationalism that mistake ethnic particularity for 'ethnic absolutism' (Gilroy 1993), though their practitioners strenuously deny that they are racist. Postcolonial racism can be a racism of *reaction*, based on the perceived threat to traditional social and cultural identities; or a racism of (false) *respect*, based on mainstream liberals' desire to hold at arm's length 'different' cultures they are anxious not to offend. Most of all, postcolonial racism, at least within the contemporary European context, is a racism of *surveillance*, based on what Étienne Balibar calls the strategic transformation of a 'project of inclusion into a program of exclusion', whereby 'foreigners' become 'aliens', 'protection' disguises 'preference' and 'cultural difference' slides into 'racial stigmatization' – all in the interests of representing the European *people*, which is a very different entity to the European *population* as a whole (Balibar 2003, p. 122).

At the heart of this process, claims Balibar controversially, is a structure of European 'apartheid' revolving around both the official treatment and the unofficial perception of migrant workers from Africa, Asia and other, economically disadvantaged parts of Europe. These workers, who '"reproduce" their lives on one side of the border [but] "produce" on the other side', are 'neither insiders nor outsiders'; instead, they are

> insiders officially considered [to be] outsiders, [whose uncertain status] produces a steady increase in the amount and violence of 'security' controls, which spread everywhere in the society and ramify the borderline throughout the 'European' territory, combining modern techniques of identification and recording with good old 'racial profiling'. (Balibar 2003, p. 123)

The discriminatory treatment of such workers, Balibar suggests, indicates that the ideal of a *democratic* Europe does not necessarily imply a *desegregated* Europe, certainly not in terms of the ascription of citizenship and other basic political rights. On the contrary, uneven access to citizenship and nationality has been built into the development of the so-called 'New Europe', and these structures of discrimination, a feature of all the established European states, are one of the most conspicuous inheritances of the colonial past (Balibar 2003; Brah 1996).

Postcolonial criticism, despite appearances, is not best positioned to account for these developments. For, so the argument might run, its emphasis has been on a 'language of hybridity and transnationalism as a means for understanding the changing nature of postcolonial racialised existence', a language that inadvertently 'obscures the roots of racism' and that radically underestimates both the durability of these roots and the tenacity of their hold on contemporary, everyday social life (Lentin 2004, p. 315). For the sociologist Alana Lentin, among others, this has led to a confusion of postcolonial racism with 'post-racism', and to a curious reluctance on the part of many critics, particularly those influenced by poststructuralism, to give due attention to the material conditions surrounding racisms of both the present and the past. These conditions are better dealt with, according to Lentin, in the work of earlier anti-colonial thinkers, from Frantz Fanon's personally experienced 'fact of blackness' to Aimé Césaire's still unrivalled analysis of the racial machinery of colonial/imperial regimes (Lentin 2004, pp. 316–17).

This view is ostensibly linked to a debate long-standing within (and arguably co-terminous with) the history of postcolonial criticism, over the shortcomings implied by its predominantly culturalist approach (Parry 2004; Young 2001). It is also linked to a disciplinary feud that still exists within postcolonial studies, one based on contending perceptions of which discipline or disciplines might most valuably contribute to it, and which of these disciplines or combinations of disciplines might supply the most appropriate methodological approach (Huggan 2002; Quayson 2000). To my mind, the best way of resolving the problem is to see postcolonial studies as a *cross*-disciplinary exercise: one to which a large number of disciplines may profitably contribute, and one in which single disciplines will probably always be found wanting in method and approach. The same goes for studies of racism and, for that matter, studies of Europe, both of which actively solicit a multidisciplinary perspective. To that end, the essays gathered here cover a fairly wide range of different disciplines and methodologies, with sociology, history, art-historical studies and literary/cultural criticism all contributing to a cross-disciplinary dialogue in which no preference is given to any one, nominally 'postcolonial' approach.

The book is broken down into four continuously structured but thematically interrelated parts, through which a complex historical trajectory of colonial/postcolonial racisms in contemporary 'multicultural' Europe is played out. Part I, 'Concentrationary legacies', takes its cue from Griselda Pollock's Holocaust-inspired attack on continuing patterns of state totalitarianism in Europe (Chapter 2). Beginning with the Holocaust makes sense in several ways, not least in order to show the structural links between Islamophobia – analysed in more detail in later chapters – and anti-Semitism, as well as to chart some historical background to the European colonial-racist attitudes and systems that drive them both. Pollock's chapter seeks accordingly to reveal links between what she calls, after Freud, the specific 'racism of minor difference' in the Shoah and the larger histories of racism and colonialism in Europe as a whole. Was the Shoah, she asks, a 'non-colonial form of racism'? Or was it, rather, that 'a convergence of different modes of colonialist and racist ideology and practice overdetermined the event'? In fact it was neither of these, strictly speaking, for, as she goes on to show, 'The trauma of European history is that its most egregious colonial crime … was enacted against its own citizens, who were internally differentiated and marked for eradication from European civil society by [the] newly emerging ideologies of modernity [itself]'. Among these ideologies, and arguably a new political form, was state totalitarianism. Drawing inspiration from Hannah Arendt, Pollock links the Holocaust to the crystallization of a number of events, both more and less recent, that gave rise to a particular, genocidal strain of totalitarianism, both captured and condemned by the 'concentrationary universe' it systematically created (and which it always does create). Totalitarianism, Pollock suggests, is a composite evil greater than both the colonialism and the racism it enfolds; and our greatest task is to resist it, to find alternatives that might allow us to live together in our difference, as Europeans in Europe, but also as human beings in the world.

Chapter 3, by Elisabeta Zelinka, and Chapter 4, by Nidhi Trehan and Angéla Kóczé, both indirectly address the 'concentrationary legacies' of state totalitarianism in Europe, Zelinka in the context of institutionalized anti-Semitism in contemporary Romania, and Trehan and Kóczé in response to continuing patterns and practices of discrimination against Romani peoples in eastern Europe in particular and, indeed, in Europe as a whole. Anti-Semitism in present-day Romania, Zelinka suggests, has not reached the peaks of the 1930s, when it flourished as a direct consequence of Nazi propaganda, but it has yet to be fully contained within mainstream Romanian society, where it resurfaces in a variety of social and political discourses, and in openly discriminatory and/or offensive behaviour that all too often goes unchecked by the authorities and that seems, at times, to be actively encouraged by the press. Zelinka's focus is on attempts, particularly on the part of female Jewish activists, to combat residual or emergent anti-Semitism in Romania, for example by promoting and protecting Jewish culture at national and international levels through the development of educative strategies aimed at addressing the everyday problems facing Jews, especially Jewish women, in Romanian society. However, while she rightly praises these initiatives, she is less sanguine about the possibility of stamping out anti-Semitism in Romania. Romania's recent entry into the EU, she suggests, *may* have the effect of curbing institutionalized racism in accordance with imposed political and economic agendas, but such is the 'deep-rootedness of sexist, homophobic and anti-Semitic discourses in today's Romanian society, it may take years, even decades, to alter the status quo'.

Trehan and Kóczé are concerned, like Zelinka, to examine the impact of institutionalized racism in Romania and elsewhere in eastern Europe, but open the context wider, to consider the so-called 'Gypsy problem' – the continuing vilification of Romani peoples as a criminal subculture – across Europe as a whole. For these co-authors, the discriminatory treatment of the Roma is: (1) an example of internal colonialism both around and within the geopolitical concept of 'eastern Europe', in which colonialism is understood as 'a way of maintaining asymmetrical relations of economic and political power'; and (2) an example of postcolonial racism, in which Romani peoples become subject to new forms of economic dependency, and their political representatives are effectively re-objectified by a variety of well meaning 'human rights entrepreneurs'. Trehan and Kóczé argue powerfully for the need to construct grass-roots alternatives to the dominant, neo-liberal paradigms within which Romani peoples are materially and symbolically captured – paradigms informed both by older, dichotomzed (occidental/oriental) understandings of cultural difference and by newer, EU pressures brought to bear on eastern Europeans to prove their western credentials, which have led at times only to their further separation from the Roma people, or to the consolidation of a racialized social order in which Romani and other travelling peoples are, ironically, fixed in (last) place.

Part II of the book centres on what might loosely be called European racisms of migration, from Alex Rotas's wide-ranging treatment of oppositional refugee/asylum-seeker art (Chapter 5), to Landry-Wilfrid Miampika and Maya García's critical analysis of the cultural dimensions of recent immigration policy in Spain (Chapter 6), to Christoph Ramm's historical overview of mediatized German attitudes to the cultural compatibility of Turks in light of recent EU accession debates (Chapter 7). In all three chapters, characteristic forms of cultural differentialism can be found to rub shoulders with xeno-racisms based on what Rotas calls the fear of 'impoverished strangers', of whatever colour or cultural background, in a postcolonial world 'where it is the interests of capital that ultimately dominate and prevail'. Rotas's chapter is concerned with the various ways in which professional visual artists within Europe's refugee and asylum-seeker populations have incorporated issues of both cultural differentialism and xeno-racism into their work. Some of the images she considers are quite harrowing, while others are more playful; but all show how easily suspicion of refugee and asylum-seekers can slide into more virulent forms of resentment or even hatred. The artists' works can be seen in this context, both as establishing their own agency and as challenging the ingrained prejudices of even their most sympathetic viewers: prejudices mirrored, and often magnified, in society at large.

Miampika and García, like Rotas, look at ways of counteracting continuing racial prejudice in Europe, much of it embedded in colonialist attitudes against refugees and other designated migrant groups. For these contributors, one effective way might be to foster the development of the kind of 'intercultural consciousness' that supports and promotes the idea of a 'reinvigorated multi-cultural society'. To what extent, the co-authors ask, have recent initiatives in Spain been successful in supporting an increasingly diverse population? While educational reforms have gone some way towards correcting jaundiced views of non-European migrants (often automatically seen as 'illegals'), no political consensus exists in Spain as to whether integration – itself a debatable term – 'should be managed according to a French model (assimilation), a British one (communitarianism), or some combination of both'. Similarly, while the increased monitoring of racism in Spain has arguably brought with it a greater public awareness of discriminatory practices and of the need for intercultural dialogue, it has also reconfirmed that rampant discrimination is taking place at all levels, for example within both the labour and the housing markets. Whether Spain is capable of producing a more 'convivial' society (Gilroy's 2004 term) with the potential to transcend 'racialist ideologies and fundamentalist particularisms in the greater service of human cooperation and goodwill' thus remains an open question; certainly, the co-authors' brief survey of recent postcolonial initiatives at Spanish universities, most of them confined to the domain of literary studies, suggests that the greater goal of creating a convivial national society within the context of a radically re-imagined, transnationally articulated Europe is still some way off.

Rounding off Part II ('Racisms of migration'), Christoph Ramm's chapter also provides a segue to the next ('Multiculturalism and its discontents'), which looks at the ways in which strategic misperceptions of 'cultural incompatibility' within the framework of the European nation have been used to question or redirect the project of the 'integrated' multicultural state. Ramm's essay looks accordingly at some of the historical background behind recent European, more specifically German, anxieties about the viability of Turkey as an EU partner, anxieties fuelled by a wide variety of media-driven 'sick man' metaphors and civilizationist discourse about the place, or not, in 'Christian Europe' of a populous 'Muslim state'. In much of this rhetoric, Turkey is identified – whether by history, geography or culture – as a 'non-European' place. In Germany, the recent accession debates have also fed into national-populist concerns about failed multiculturalism and the dangers posed by parallel societies. These concerns, as Ramm shows, have gained strength from the renewed circulation of colonialist myths and racist stereotypes loosely associated with, but nonetheless firmly attached to, the Enlightenment idea/ideal of a self-identical, self-sufficient Europe, the well-being of which is threatened by a collective Muslim 'other': a good example of the coming together of 'sick man' rhetoric in which the 'sick man' that is Turkey is positioned both *outside* Europe's borders and *within* Germany itself.

Rotas, Miampika and García, and Ramm are all concerned directly or indirectly with the policing of cultural difference in national or pan-European contexts in which difference is less likely to be seen as an asset than as a threat. One of the terms under which this management of difference is most frequently encoded is *multiculturalism*: a much-contested term that is seen, sometimes simultaneously, as containing the potential to combat racism and as perpetrating racism in its turn. As Ashwani Sharma puts it in Chapter 8, which outlines several of the issues that go on to dominate Parts III and IV of the book, multiculturalism has become a 'key modality in which race and racist paranoia have been delineated in recent [post 9/11] times'. In particular, he argues, multiculturalism has acted as the cultural front of the global 'war on terror', in which specific racial identities/differences, generally categorized as 'Asian' or 'Muslim', are identi-fied as being antagonistic to ideas of belonging and social cohesion within the nations of western Europe, and as posing a direct threat to western civilization as a whole. Multiculturalism, however, is not necessarily a catalyst for social cohesion; thus, while such reassuring ideas as 'belonging' and 'cohesion' are integral to discourses of multiculturalism – particularly national discourses – they are also effectively challenged by it, insofar as vernacular multiculturalisms reveal, even as their official counterparts seek to disguise, the normative forms of western (European) *whiteness* against which cultural diversity is measured, monitored and controlled.

Multiculturalism thus opens up, in spite of itself, the possibility of address-ing questions of race and ethnicity in a postcolonial Europe where public discussions of racism are either deflected onto designated but usually undif-ferentiated outsiders (refugees, Muslim terrorists, etc.) or are systematically repressed. Why postcolonial? Because, for Sharma, following Homi Bhabha (1994), the word 'multicultural' functions as a floating signifier in the twin contexts of decolonization and globalization: contexts that have made the borders of Europe 'increasingly porous to people and cultures from the formerly colonized worlds'. Multiculturalism, understood this way, becomes a 'specific political model of managing cultural heterogeneity in times of postcolonial "hyper-globalization"', in which 'the demands and movements of capital and labour have brought into crisis the historical colonial divisions', and the for-mer colonial/imperial boundary between 'the racialized white Occident and its [oriental] "others" [is no longer] clearly marked and secured'. What results, at least in part, are what Sharma calls 'mutating forms' of postcolonial racism in which multiculturalism is used either to confront alien ideologies (e.g. Islamic extremism) or to celebrate a postcolonial nation at ease with its own diversity precisely because it can position difference in relation to a racialized (white) norm. Multiculturalism, however, is still far more likely to generate anxiety at a time when differentiating categories of all kinds (white/non-white, Muslim/non-Muslim, etc.) are increasingly questioned, and the most frequent reflex this produces is blame: 'for the end of empire, the decline of the nation and the loss of white identity [itself]'.

In Chapter 9, similar processes are traced by Philomena Essed in the Netherlands, a country known for its tolerant attitudes towards a wide range of criminalized activities, but not averse in turn to criminalizing the (perceived) foreigners in its midst. Essed's focus is on the ways in which tolerance functions as a 'national characteristic, a sign of civilization of enlightenment, generated by those seen as "genuinely" Dutch'. Seen this way, tolerance can easily be used to exclude those (nearly always non-whites) considered to be intolerant, with moral superiority being attributed to those (nearly always whites) considered as matching the cultural norm. Tolerance thus becomes a mechanism for the perpetuation of cultural racism, supplying at worst a moral licence for denigration in a country where 'ethnic minorities, and lately Muslims in particular, are routinely exposed to public scorn'. Such denigration Essed calls 'cultural pain' because, as she says, 'it is pain experienced as a result of the denigration of the culture, religion or ethnicity the targets of humiliation identify with'. Such public humiliations can easily become systemic, being used to anchor notions of a core white culture, and to keep the non-white cultural other in its (subordinate) place.

The paradox of humiliating tolerance, Essed argues, is particularly visible in the contexts of economic decline and 'internal discomposure' that lie behind contemporary 'Europism', a neologism that she distinguishes, as in her earlier work, from 'Eurocentrism', with the latter emerging out of the victories of European imperial conquest and the civilizing mission, and the former being based on a resentful perception of European defeat. For Essed, Europism is at the heart of contemporary racism in the Netherlands, where, much as in other western European countries, cultural and economic insecurities have given rise to the search for new enemies, and blame is most easily laid at the door of 'unassimilable' – and therefore punishable – Muslims and 'welfare-seeking' refugees. This politics of blame, and the ritual humiliations that ensue from it, are sometimes produced in the name of free speech, as in the circumstances surrounding the assassination of the controversial film-maker Theo van Gogh, whose anti-Islamic film *Submission* demonstrates a self-serving ideology of tolerance whereby 'representatives of the dominant [white] culture claim the right to express themselves in any way they wish about Islam, a religion perceived as tolerated only because it does not belong to the Netherlands'. As Essed argues, the film and its reception in the Netherlands and elsewhere only helped perpetuate the stereotype of ethnic minority women as passive victims of their cultures. The right to free speech, Essed insists, is not the same thing as the right to offend in the name of public critique, which may be little more than another demonstration of white (male) European arrogance; thus, while she readily concedes that the 'exposure and public rejection of violence against women in non-dominant communities is a necessary step in the process of ethnic and gender emancipation and integration', she adds the crucial caveat that '[p]ublic critique is most constructive when formulated in ways that are not stigmatizing, criminalizing or otherwise humiliating for the whole ethnic group'.

Perhaps the most conspicuous recent instance of the tensions between free speech and the right to offend are the undeniably racist cartoons which, first appearing in a relatively obscure Danish newspaper in September 2005, came rapidly to inflame the public imagination of Europe as a whole. The 'cartoon war' that evolved was to pit Muslim rage against western defiance in a series of highly mediated gestures that appeared initially to support the 'clash of civilizations' thesis while suggesting how older, orientalist or occidentalist forms of cultural stereotyping have taken on a new lease of life under current conditions of new racism, in which 'the focus has arguably shifted from individual bodies to entire cultures, including their religious affiliations and their socio-cultural taboos'. Katarzyna Murawska-Muthesius's overview of the conflict in Chapter 10 goes beyond the binaries within which it has been customarily framed, in part by showing the ambivalent status of cartoons themselves, which, as artful combinations of 'piercing insight' and 'worn-out cliché', are often perceived as being socially subversive even as they help maintain established boundaries and protect the status quo. The right to offend, Murawska-Muthesius suggests, remains a defining feature of the medium; however, cartoons are not *necessarily* demeaning and may in fact provide opportunities for the diverse forms of positive re-signification that are intrinsic to the resistance struggles of minority communities and groups. Whether cartoons function as vehicles of racism or freedom depends on how their representational codes are manipulated: hence her view that the 'cartoon war' was largely *about* media representation, registering a further 'disastrous episode in the long-running battle for signification itself'. Thus, while the 'war' had obvious real-world consequences, the grounds on which it was fought were largely virtual, with the greatest battlefield of all being that of the World Wide Web. As Murawska-Muthesius points out, a number of cartoons also appeared in the Muslim media, and it would certainly be a mistake to see the conflict in terms of Islamic 'physicality' versus western 'cool media' and 'remote control'. Rather, commentaries from the Muslim world at large, as well as the Muslim minority in Denmark, indicate cartoons' global dimensions and enduringly self-critical potential, even as they continue to operate as instruments of western cultural racism and as part of an 'occidentalist vendetta against the Jews and the "corrupt west"'.

Part IV of the book ('Towards the future?') features chapters by Michel Wieviorka and Robert Spencer, which stand apart from the rest insofar as they offer tangible solutions or at least practical alternatives to the crises they diagnose. For Wieviorka, the French Republic has entered a period of total crisis, exemplified by the French government's hysterical reaction to the outbreaks of violence of October 2005. Although this type of violence was not new – as Wieviorka says, such racially motivated violence has periodically erupted in France since at least the end of the 1970s – the scale and intensity of these outbreaks were unprecedented, prompting rogue intellectuals like Alain Finkielkraut to speak of an 'anti-republican pogrom', and more measured social scientists to stress the successive failures of French governments to address the concerns of a large proportion of urban black youths, who, finding themselves 'rejected by the very society that had ordered them to integrate', turned to violence as a means of expressing their individual frustrations and collective social rage.

For Wieviorka, the vocabulary of crisis is appropriate. The crisis is institutional insofar as the institutions of the Republic tend to reproduce social inequality; it is cultural insofar as the Republic fails to recognize specific, historically marginalized identities now competing for attention in the same public space; it is political insofar as the Republic's political system is increasingly unable to be representative; and it is intellectual insofar as the ideas/ideals of republicanism are perverted when strident calls for immigrants to integrate and 'adopt the values of the Republic' fly in the face of a social/political system in which 'the concrete means towards this integration are effectively being refused'. At the same time, events such as, a few months after the 2005 riots, the Parisian Jewish community's response to the race murder of a young Jewish man, Ilan Halimi, may indicate new forms of social mobilization allied to what Wieviorka calls a 'post-republican' programme in which the aim of socially stigmatized communities is to continue to adhere to the values of the Republic while constituting themselves as 'a [religious] minority in the public sphere'. As Wieviorka suggests, the classical model of republicanism is currently foundering on the contradictions of a race-blind logic that posits all French people as equal citizens and nationals, united under French law. Continuing forms of colonialist discrimination are no longer disguised by the rhetoric of universalism under which this classical model shelters. This has precipitated fresh enquiries into France's role in the slave trade and colonization, and new protests against the neo-liberal machinery which, partly intended to modernize republican principles, has only exacerbated 'a situation that remains socially blocked'. Still, while Wieviorka concludes that France remains 'paralysed by blockages, of which the most obvious are social and political in nature', it is beginning to look forward to a post-republican model that affords a possible way out of these institutional blockages and opens the door to social/political reform.

Part IV ends with a fiery essay by Spencer, who, like Wieviorka, attributes the crisis in contemporary, postcolonial Europe to the global dominance of neo-liberalism but who, more explicitly than Wieviorka, sees the ideology of neo-liberalism as a direct continuation of the principles and practices of colonialism: as imperialism by other means. Spencer's more specific targets are the 'new national, even national*ist* ideology that associates the British state's domestic and foreign policy with values and practices that are made to appear altruistic but are actually parochial', and, lurking behind this ideology, the continuing failure of the British state to come to terms with the consequences of the nation's colonial past. Imperial nostalgia, says Spencer, following Rosaldo and Milne, best describes a current structure of feeling, exemplified in the work of the revisionist historian Niall Ferguson, in which self-interest masquerades as altruism, nationalism as internationalism, and the 'tolerance and fair-mindedness that might previously have been associated with a multicultural challenge to the status quo' are 'appropriated as unchanging attributes of the British state'.

This 'multicultural nationalism' often amounts to little more than token respect, but a more radical version, which Spencer calls 'cosmopolitanism', still has the potential to combat racism in Europe in the name of a 'cosmopolitan consciousness first articulated by minorities and those in solidarity with them'. Cosmopolitanism, he suggests, offers a workable alternative to the false pieties of civilizationism, which, unsurprisingly rampant after 9/11, reaffirms the values of the transatlantic axis while denying its own racial prejudices, holding to the view that it is cultures, not races, that are incompatible and that the western nations have a right to defend their own way of life. Only a critical examination of the history of European imperialism can help counteract these 'new' forms of imperial nostalgia while allowing for the construction of a postcolonial Europe in which more worldly forms of cosmopolitanism substitute for the competing provincialisms arguably built into the idea of Europe itself. This, Spencer suggests, is postcolonial studies' remit, and while the views in this book are sharply differentiated, they all share postcolonial criticism's self-confessedly utopian sympathies for a more fully reflexive attitude to Europe, and its hopes for a more fully decolonized world.

Works cited

Asad, T. (2002) 'Muslims and European Identity: Can Europe Represent Islam?' In: Pagden, A. ed. *The Idea of Europe*. Washington, DC, Woodrow Wilson Center Press, pp. 209–27.

Balibar, É. (1991) 'Racism and Nationalism'. In: Balibar, E. and Wallerstein, I. eds. *Race, Nation, Class: Ambiguous Identities*. London, Verso, pp. 37–68.

—— (2003) *We, the People of Europe? Reflections on Transnational Citizenship*. Translated by J. Swenson. Princeton, MA, Princeton University Press.

Bhabha, H. (1994) *The Location of Culture*. London, Routledge.

Brah, A. (1996) *Cartographies of Diaspora: Contesting Identities*. London, Routledge.

Castles, S. (1998) 'The Racisms of Globalisation'. In: Castles, S. and Vasta, E. eds. *The Teeth Are Smiling: The Persistence of Racism in Multicultural Australia*. Sydney, Allen and Unwin.

Chakrabarty, D. (2000) *Provincializing Europe: Postcolonial Thought and Historical Difference*. Princeton, MA, Princeton University Press.

Gikandi, S. (1996) *Maps of Englishness*. New York, Columbia University Press.

Gilroy, P. (1993) *The Black Atlantic: Modernity and Double Consciousness*. Cambridge, MA, Harvard University Press.

—— (2004) *After Empire: Melancholia or Convivial Culture?* London, Routledge.

Huggan, G. (2002) 'Postcolonial Studies and the Anxiety of Interdisciplinarity'. *Postcolonial Studies*, 5(3), pp. 245–75.

Lentin, A. (2004) *Racism and Anti-racism in Europe*. London, Pluto Press.

MacMaster, N. (2001) *Racism in Europe 1870–2000*. Houndmills, Palgrave.

Mignolo, W. (2000) *Local Histories/Global Designs*. Princeton, MA, Princeton University Press.

Nicholson, P. (1999) *Who Do We Think We Are? Race and Nation in the Modern World*. London, M. E. Sharpe.

Pagden, A. (2002) 'Introduction'. In: Pagden, A. ed. *The Idea of Europe*. Cambridge, Cambridge University Press, pp. 1–33.
Parry, B. (2004) *Postcolonial Studies*. Manchester, Manchester University Press.
Pocock, J. G. A. (2002) 'Some Europes in Their History'. In: Pagden, A. ed. *The Idea of Europe*. Cambridge, Cambridge University Press, pp. 53–71.
Quayson, A. (2000) *Postcolonialism: Theory, Practice or Process?* Cambridge, Polity Press.
Tsiolkas, C. (2005) *Dead Europe*. New York, Random House.
Young, R. (2001) *Postcolonialism: An Historical Introduction*. Oxford, Blackwell.

Part I
Concentrationary legacies

CHAPTER 2

Concentrationary legacies: thinking through the racism of minor differences

Griselda Pollock

In the opening hour of Part Two of the First Era of Claude Lanzmann's nine-hour film *Shoah* (1985), an epic cinematic journey across the faces and places that mark the attempted genocide of two European peoples on European soil in the middle of the twentieth century, there is an interview with Mrs Michelsohn, the Nazi teacher's wife. In a tightly framed close-up, a middle-aged woman's face is set against a dark, heavily wallpapered background, at an angle that creates tension. The viewer thus encounters the face of a former member of the Hitlerjugend, a pioneer who volunteered to 'colonize' for the Third Reich an area of recently conquered Poland that had been renamed Wartheland by the Reich. This region included the village of Chelmno, renamed by the Germans Kulmhof. Its ruined eighteenth-century Schloss and then its church were used in two periods as holding points for the mass murders of Jewish civilians by locking them in vans and piping exhaust fumes into the enclosed loading space until the 'cargo' was asphyxiated. This process marks the beginning of an industrial killing process using gas that was initiated in Chelmno on 7 December 1941. This date marks for Lanzmann the impossible and inconceivable moment with which he had to 'begin' his film. The event marks the rupture in human history towards which – *nach dem* – Lanzmann's nine-hour cinematic journey repeatedly returns us, not as something to be understood or explained, situated in prior events gradually leading to it, but to be known viscerally as pure horror in the collision of human action and human suffering tracked across his relentless recording of faces and places. Here is the transcription (from Lanzmann 1995, pp. 69–72) of parts of that interview conducted by Claude Lanzmann (CL):

Mrs Michelsohn (Germany), wife of a Nazi schoolteacher in Chelmno:
How many German families lived in Chelmno, Kulmhof? Ten or eleven, I'd say. Germans from Wohlnia and two families from the Reich – the Bauers and us.

CL:
And you?
Us, the Michelsohns.
How did you end up in Kulmhof?
I was born in Laage, and I was sent to Kulmhof. They were looking for volunteer settlers, and I signed up. That's how I got there. First in Warthbrücken (Kolo), then Chelmno. Kulmhof.
Did you opt to go to Kulmhof?
No, I asked for Wartheland.
Why?
A pioneering spirit.
You were young?
Oh, yes, I was young.
You wanted to be useful?
Yes.
What was your first impression?
It was primitive. Super-primitive.
Meaning?
Even worse, worse than primitive.
Difficult to understand, right? But why?
The sanitary facilities were disastrous. The only toilet was in Warthbrücken, in the town hall; you had to go there. The rest was a disaster.
Why a disaster?
There were no toilets at all. There were privies. I can't tell you how primitive it was.
…
How far was your house from the church?
It was just opposite – 150 feet.
Did you see the gas vans?
No…. Yes, from the outside. They shuttled back and forth. I never looked inside; I didn't see Jews in them. I only saw things from the outside – the Jews' arrival, their disposition, how they were loaded aboard. Since World War I the castle had been in ruins. Only part of it could be used. That's where the Jews were taken.
The ruined castle was used…
For housing and delousing the Poles, and so on.
The Jews!
Yes, the Jews.
Why do you call them Poles and not Jews?
Sometimes I get them mixed up.
There's a difference between Poles and Jews?
Oh yes!
What's the difference?
The Poles were not exterminated, and the Jews were. That's the difference.
An external difference, right?
And the inner difference?
I cannot assess that. I do not know enough about psychology and anthropology. The difference between the Poles and the Jews? Anyway, they could not stand each other.

By the time we arrive at the encounter with Mrs Michelsohn in the film, we have already spent about three hours getting to know a range of Polish agricultural and railway workers in the villages around Treblinka and Sobibor, where extermination camps were built after 1941. We have also met: the only two survivors of Chelmno, Simon Srebnik and Mordechai Podchlebnik; one from Treblinka, Richard Glazar; and two men who escaped from the burning pits in the forest of Ponari, where the bodies of those murdered in the Vilna Ghetto were cremated, Motke Zaidl and Itzhak Dugin (Pollock 1996). The film carefully recreates the mix of populations in the relatively unchanged Polish countryside where the Polish contemporaries of these men still live. The film works by visually and linguistically registering different social and economic conditions of existence, appearance and sound – and the ways each of the different communities appeared to the other. What the episode with Mrs Michelsohn, the German colonizer, exposes so skilfully through a series of perfectly calibrated edits and intervening montages of scenes that reflect back upon what she is saying by touring contemporary Poland, is what might appear to us now as the strangeness of a European world of the *intense racism of minor differences*, which were, nonetheless, the basis for an egregious crime against humanity, racism turned truly annihilatory. The interview with Mrs Michelsohn, a figure caught between her status as a bystander and as a perpetrator, writes into this film the point at which different economies, histories and narratives collide: anti-Semitism, colonialism, racism, and on European soil.

In these interfaces, caught in the tight close-up interview with an ageing Nazi, a colonial imaginary appears to be at work without any movement between continents, or without showing us what we now consider to be major ethnic/cultural differences, and without those now highly visible markers of skin colour that are the axis of north/south racism; what, following Frantz Fanon, Homi Bhabha will call the 'epidermal racial schema' (Bhabha 1983). European to European, the Reichsdeutsch Mrs Michelsohn expresses her embarrassed contempt for her poorer, rural Slavic neighbours, whose historically conditioned economic under-development is represented by her as if it were an indelible racial trait. Mrs Michelsohn describes her horror on arriving in the village of Chelmno with the remark: 'It was primitive. Super-primitive.' *Meaning?* 'Even worse, worse than primitive.' Pressed by Lanzmann, we discover she is complaining about the lack of flushing toilets. The country people's use of what today we might call their eco-friendly soil arrangements appeared, to a metropolitan German used to a different regime of personal hygiene, as a pure and racial sign – a stereotype – of genetic backwardness, reminding us of the immense power within racial discourse of these bodily connoters of clean or proper bodies versus the dirty or the imperfectly policed (Gilman 1985, 1992).

For Mrs Michelsohn, however, there is an englobing of *all* others into this primitivization. She mentions the castle but in a slip of the tongue refers to its use for delousing the *Poles*. Lanzmann corrects her: the Jews, surely? Yes. Why does she say Poles not Jews? She gets them mixed up. What is the difference? 'The Poles were not exterminated, and the Jews were.' This is a blunt external –

and we should add *political* – difference. Lanzmann pushes her to identify an *internal* difference. Mrs Michelsohn cannot do this – she says she does not know enough psychology or anthropology. These are the sciences by means of which we might know cultural difference. Is there a difference? 'Anyway, they could not stand each other' (Lanzmann 1995, pp. 71–72).

From a colonial vantage point, her lazy confusion already exposes her contempt for local Polish people; the outsider, however, asserts the fact of mutual dislike between those she almost cannot be bothered to distinguish. Whose anti-Semitism is at work here? At the same time, the nature of the difference (as opposed to behavioural opposition) is seemingly intellectually posited: what makes Jews and Poles really different needs science. It is to be ascertained only by the social and cultural sciences, such as anthropology and psychology – indicating paradoxically that 'difference' may be both difficult to discern and due to cultural factors that are not, therefore, purely genetic, as racist discourse claims and as her own presentation uncritically presumes.

Lanzmann edits into this interview a montage of other interviews that enables him to test out Mrs Michelsohn's propositions about mutual dislike of the two local co-habiting communities, and the nature of the Polish perceptions of their Jewish former compatriots. The film thus uses its own cinematic means to examine the nature of this racism of minor differences – only from the perspective of the local inhabitants surrounding the now removed Mrs Michelsohn, interviewed in her German home far away from the site of their continuing lives in that place. Lanzmann intercuts his interview with Mrs Michelsohn with his talk to a man outside a house once owned by Jewish people in the nearby village of Grabow, some of whom were the man's now regretted classmates at school. The man and his wife do not speak with hatred, even as it slowly emerges that they are living in a house that once belonged to extinguished Jewish fellow citizens. Into this scene Lanzmann also weaves an interview with a group of older Polish women standing outside another house in this village. The film records the spontaneous responses of the local working women, one of whom tells us matter of factly that she has not been to school (i.e., does not know anthropology or psychology, let alone sociology or economics), but feels that she is better off now. She used to pick potatoes (physically stressful work); now she sells eggs (and is thus a petit bourgeois trader). Lanzmann asks whether such social and economic improvement is a result of socialism or the disappearance of the Jews; the woman responds that she does not know anything except that she is better off now. The women also speak of their relief that there are no longer beautiful Jewish women to share the men with. In a sense, this exchange functions precisely as an exercise of anthropological, and even psychological, research, testing the thesis that 'they' – the Poles and the Jews – could not stand each other, as so casually affirmed by Mrs Michelsohn. The conversations with Polish locals reveals, as one might expect from any anthropological investigation, two grounds for social tension between coexisting communities living on the economic edge: sexuality and economics. These, like the privies in Mrs Michelsohn's narrative, all too easily translate the historically contingent materiality of social living into fixed, reiterated racial stereotypes – *la belle juive* and the rich Jew, the latter fantasy introduced in yet another of these intervening discussions with local Polish workers, where, following a discussion of former Jewish workers in the tanning industry, which made them 'smell', we have the assertion that, before socialism, 'the Jews ran Poland' (Lanzmann 1995, p. 78). Only after these inserted explorations of the complex relations between the Polish-Catholic and the Polish-Jewish inhabitants of the backwaters of rural Poland does the film then return to Mrs Michelsohn, who once lived in the house opposite the Schloss at Chelmno – the place where the whole film started – telling us with a long textual preface that it was here, on 7 December 1941, that Jewish people were first gassed by use of carbon monoxide piped from a truck's engine back into its locked loading space. We are thus returned by cinematic movement to the place of the radical caesura – only two and a half years on from the Evian conference, in which European powers, failing to come up with any solution to the forced exile of Jewish-Austrians following the Anschluss in 1938, effectively opened the door to what was hitherto inconceivable: mass annihilation. How do we get from Mrs Michelsohn's easy-going colonial mentality and the ambivalences of local class rivalries to this unspeakable act? This is Lanzmann's perpetual probe into racism and colonialism in Europe.

Mrs Michelsohn speaks of what happened at Chelmno in a way that reveals a combination of knowledge and wilful misinformation. Beyond the initially exposed colonial disdain for lesser versions of the human species, the Poles, emerges the complete absence of acknowledgement of the humanness of yet others, the Jews, who were being systematically massacred day after day, hour after hour, just a stone's throw from the teacher's home.

> 'Get's on your nerves, seeing that everyday…. And the screams. It was frightful. Depressing. Day after day, the same spectacle! It was terrible. A sad sight. They screamed. They knew what was happening. At first the Jews thought they were going to be deloused. But they soon understood. Their screams grew wilder and wilder. Horrifying screams. Screams of terror! Because they knew what has happening to them.' (Lanzmann 1995, p. 83)

Mrs Michelsohn's testimony thus quite simply, as does so much of this film, belies the claim that no one saw or knew. Visible, proximate and now revealed as clearly and painfully audible, the screams of agonized and terrified people were 'frightful'. 'Day after day': the machinery works relentlessly, the factory of death is already present. Yet this merely registers as an irritating noise-off that tries the nerves of Mrs Michelsohn, that obliges her to bear this nuisance of tortured people's terror before death without her being required to do anything to respond to their pleas for mercy. It is this breach, too, that Lanzmann's film captures in the unobtrusive appearance of a documentary interview with a German bystander.

The event of racism, therefore, occurs on screen, not in the past, not then and there, but here and now, as we watch and see its delineation in the facial expressions of Mrs Michelsohn, her pursed mouth, her emotional indifference and self-betraying banality – exhibiting precisely a lack of depth and thoughtfulness appropriate to the enormity of the events she witnessed that formed for Hannah Arendt the shocking banality of this evil (Arendt 1963). Lanzmann asks if Mrs Michelsohn knows how many were murdered. 'Four something … 400,000 or 40,000.' This vast numerical difference holds no memorable significance for her. The lower figure already marks a massacre of incredible proportions; the higher figure staggers us, and links back to the film's discovery of the only two survivors of Chelmno. Simon Srebnik was one of the last child workers in Chelmno's killing fields. When the camp was liquidated and all traces erased, the remaining work details were shot. Srebnik was shot in the head, but not mortally wounded. Restored to health by local farmers, he ultimately made his home in Israel, from whence he was returned by Lanzmann to the village to wander the now grassy field and tell us: 'It's hard to recognize, but it was here. They burned people. A lot of people were burned here. Yes, this is the place. No one ever left here again' (Lanzmann 1995, p. 3).

In the long penultimate scene at the end of the film's First Era, Simon Srebnik is welcomed by the Polish villagers of contemporary Chelmno, who remember the young boy who was obliged to sing as he was rowed up the river in chains to collect food for the camp rabbits. He is placed among the Polish workers once again outside the very church, next to the Schloss, used as the holding bay in the second period of Chelmno's history as a killing field. At first, there is warm camaraderie and genuine welcome of the well-remembered singing boy. The locals are keen to speak to Lanzmann and his crew about the past, what they saw, what they tried to do to help, all the while standing directly outside the church, itself filled with celebrants of a Catholic festival. When asked, however, why 'this' happened to the Jews, unlike Mrs Michelsohn's evasive reference to anthropology and psychology, the villagers *know*. The Christian story of deicide and Pontius Pilate washing his hands comes tumbling out with sudden and disconcerting intensity and with a virulence of expression. As that old tale fills the soundtrack, the almost smiling face of Simon Srebnik loses all expression; it literally dies again before our eyes. As the camera relentlessly turns, his face returns to the empty deadness that it held when first he found himself again in 'the place': Chelmno camp. The past, a moment before merely the recalled story of a remembered event, happens again in the present before our eyes. Cinematic anthropology loses its distance and makes the viewer witness to the very experience of how representation and killing could coincide.

In a collection of studies on racism and postcolonialism in Europe, it is perhaps obvious and yet surprising to introduce *Shoah* (1985) and hence the Shoah, more often known by that most inappropriate of Greek terms *holocauston,* which refers to a sacrifice entirely consumed by fire: *burnt whole.* The Holocaust is not to be measured comparatively in a scale of racist horrors. It must, however, be located as one of the defining historical breaches after which we now live, the imaginative possibilities of racist horror forever shaped by the utter novelty of that realized, enacted and murderous totalitarianism named by David Rousset, a French political prisoner in a German concentration camp (not a Polish extermination camp – the distinctions are significant) in 1946 as 'the concentrationary universe' and called by Jean Cayrol in 1955 'the concentrationary disease' (Rousset 1946; Cayrol in *Night and Fog*, Resnais, 1955). Yet how do the incidents of internal European colonialism and the deep structures of European racism within its longstanding mixed populations relate to current debates about racism and colonialism, debates framed through the lens of postcolonial critique and hence with reference to geographically and territorially dispersed European–'other' relations after 1600?

Some years ago, I invited to talk at a seminar entitled 'From Trauma to Cultural Memory: The Unfinished Business of Representation and the Holocaust' a Holocaust survivor from Konin – a town in the Wartheland, not far from Chelmno. He came from a working-class background and had lost his entire family. He survived Auschwitz as a still young boy having witnessed unspeakable horrors and emotional trauma over six years. At the end of his talk to my students, he made a comment to underline the extreme sadism of what he had witnessed and suffered: he declared that it was not as if this had happened among 'the savages of Africa', but in Europe. As leader of the class, I felt obliged immediately to challenge a potentially 'racist' remark, to remind the students that this assumption of violence among African peoples and a propensity to atrocity as a natural occurrence of that continent was neither historically accurate nor politically sustainable. Indeed, one might say that this particular colonial nonsense represents not only a misrepresentation of African societies and cultures in general, but also works to disavow Europe's historically leading role in inventiveness with regard to human atrocity. The Holocaust happened between Europeans in the middle of the twentieth century using all the mechanics of industrial modernity. This remains a knot of difficulty in understanding Europe's responsibility for concentrationary legacies.

It is this problem I wish to explore: Europeans' difficulty in facing up to their leading role in what still has to be considered philosophically and politically the novel extremity of the systematic state-administered crime of genocide. Frankfurt School philosopher Jürgen Habermas defines the crime and its effects thus:

> There in Auschwitz something happened, that up to now nobody considered as even possible. There one touched on something which represents the deep layer of solidarity among all that wears a human face; notwithstanding all the usual acts of beastliness of human history, the integrity of this common layer had been taken for granted.... Auschwitz has changed the basis for the continuity of life within history. (Habermas quoted in Friedländer 1992, p. 3)

Habermas here echoes Frankfurt School founder Theodor Adorno, whose reflections on metaphysics 'after Auschwitz' also stressed the novel horror of a non-human death that was the death of humanity: 'That in the concentration camps it was no longer an individual who died but a specimen' (Adorno 1990, p. 371). Sarah Kofman parses Adorno: 'Since Auschwitz, all men, Jews and non-Jews, die differently; they do not really die; they survive death, because what took place – back there – without taking place, death in Auschwitz, was worse than death' (Kofman 1998, p. 9).

One of the deep problems of fully grasping the impact of the Shoah lies in the fact that this crime, which suspended utterly the deep solidarity between all who wear the human face, was perpetrated against Europeans. Does this mean that the Shoah was a non-colonial form of racism? Or was it, rather, that a convergence of different modes of colonialist and racist ideology and practice overdetermined the event? It was enacted against Europeans who had been marked off, however, as *Jews* and *Gypsies,* in a novel, racializing *language* in which ethnic, religious and cultural specificity was turned into a signifier for the right to live – or rather its suspension. The power and importance of fascist language work during the Third Reich has been studied by Victor Klemperer (1957). For Klemperer, the two groups designated for what was named a *final solution* – a construct that, of course, itself presumes/produces a problem to be finally solved – might be said to share a singularity: while socially present in Europe for more than ten centuries, they were, by choice or by historical accident and political persecution, deterritorialized peoples. Denied rights to land in earlier centuries because of the Christianity that underpinned the feudal system of sworn service, European Jewish communities had until the late sixteenth century been subject to arbitrary expulsion and forced mobility. After 1570, fixed settlement in designated areas, known as ghettos, became the norm but a price of exorbitant taxes was usually exacted for such residence and for any other movement beyond its enclosure. Periodic pogroms of extreme violence were regular occurrences between spectacular massacres. Just when these restrictions were removed, at the beginning of the modern period, and civil 'emancipation' allowed western European Jewish communities access to education, urban living, economic freedom and the professions, a new discourse, anti-Semitism, emerged to posit essentialist nationalism against the stillborn universal citizenship of the original Enlightenment vision. During the most intensive period of modern nationalism, millennia-old European Jewish communities were newly imagined as unassimilable 'strangers', hence figures of what modernity found so problematic for the emerging culture of nationalism: ambivalence (Bauman 1992). The mobilizing ideologies of this new racism called upon impersonal and absolute forces, nature and history, in order to rewrite the contingencies of actual historical processes in which Europe, marked by various imperia from Christendom to the Holy Roman Empire to the Austro-Hungarian Empire, had been home to a variety of peoples, cultures, ethnicities, religions, languages and histories. Nature (race) and history (invented tradition based on language, blood and long-term territorial occupation) were now to found indefatigable laws that must be obeyed for the truth and safety of those selectively allowed national identity, as opposed to those on whom was merely conferred legal citizenship by birth. Ties to nationality were forged exclusively by (and fantasmatic connections were articulated through) the intimacy between *Blut und Boden*: blood and soil. The trauma of European history is that its most egregious colonial crime – born inside this nationalism turned into imperialism that would bring its member states to two of the most violent and technologically devastating of wars within a half century – was enacted against its own citizens, who were internally differentiated and marked for eradication from European civil society by newly emerging ideologies of modernity (Bauman 1989).

The slow and delayed history of European confrontation with, commemoration of and analysis of what only in the 1970s acquired a generally used but contested name – the Holocaust (itself a linguistically fascinating fact, since we do not give Srebinica or Rwanda a non-descriptive name; we simply and descriptively use place and act: the Rwandan genocide, for instance) – can be understood in terms of the psychological features of trauma. Trauma is an event so extreme that it overwhelms consciousness; it shatters the means we have to register the event, which, nonetheless, lodges its wound – trauma meaning a wound that pierces – within the psyche. Its affective impact, unknown, nonetheless leaks slowly into memory from the place where it was not forgotten, since it was not remembered in the first place, having not been registered through the usual conscious processes. Although scholars are often anxious about extending analyses of individual psychological processes such as trauma to cultures and collectivities, I think it is possible to use the concept of trauma culturally as a metaphorical diagnosis of the cultural symptoms of delay in recognition of what had happened, which has wounded our world beyond any reprieve. The delay reveals itself in the discontinuous, fragmentary, uneven and often perverse trajectory of the entry of the Shoah/Holocaust into cultural memory (indicated by publications, or lack thereof, of its histories, a literature of memoirs and testimonies, films, museum installations of pedagogic and memorial projects, days of remembrance, political and philosophical analysis and so forth) between 1945 and 1995, with its long silences, active repressions and passive disinterest, and belated breakthrough into being recognized as a key event for philosophy, historiography, sociology, aesthetics, ethics, literature and cultural theory only around 1989.[1] We are still part of that process – a process itself consistently marked by the political unconscious that makes it so difficult for Europe, now politically speakable as a post-national and post-imperial economic and political world force in terms of the European Union, to grasp its unique responsibility for creating a form of modern political violence that seeps, like the undesired memories of the Holocaust, into the world of political possibility.

Let me illustrate these claims by considering briefly the critical and negative reception of two quite different projects that could be considered the first attempts at cultural commemoration of the Holocaust in European culture. They both occurred in 1955, at the tenth anniversary of the liberation of the concentration camps, and thus the documented and witnessed revelation of reports

---

1 Although, at present, it seems as if there is a massive amount of research into and discussion of the Holocaust, a survey of the dates of publication of a developing body of major scholarship reveals the key moment to be around 1989 for research and 1993 for public visibility – the year in which the opening of the US Holocaust Memorial Museum coincided with the release of a highly successful Hollywood film, *Schindler's List*.

that had been widely circulating but remained beyond imagining, nonetheless. The first project I wish to discuss is the film *Nuit et Brouillard* (*Night and Fog*), directed by Alain Resnais, who used archive footage from 1945 and a script specially written to accompany his montage of images by a concentration-camp survivor, the political deportee and surrealist poet Jean Cayrol (Silverman 2006). Politically funded and motivated, this French film has been hailed as the most important film ever made on this topic (van der Knaap 2006). The other project is a stage play, which then became a Hollywood film directed by George Stevens in 1959, based on the diaries of a young German-Jewish adolescent in hiding in Holland who died in Bergen-Belsen in 1945: *The Diary of Anne Frank*. The stage play was based on the English translation of the *Diary*, published only in 1952, after much pressure and with great reluctance, and was written by two leading American playwrights, Frances Goodrich and Albert Hackett (Kushner 1997).

Seemingly incommensurate as cultural products, both films received intense criticism for the manner of their representation of the events: in different ways, both films (and the screenplay for *The Diary of Anne Frank*) universalized and thus depoliticized what was a particular and racist horror perpetrated against Jewish Europeans. The American playwrights were accused of de-judaizing Anna Frank (significantly anglicized by being named Anne) and her family to make the characters more acceptable to the American audience, itself convulsed at the time with a paranoia that managed to combine anti-communism and anti-Semitism during the early 1950s (Doneson 2002). *Night and Fog* speaks only of 'deportees', naming among the unsuspecting targets Jewish students or book-keepers who are Jewish only if the viewer can recognize Jewish as opposed to Christian French, German or Polish surnames. Lanzmann's *Shoah* was perhaps a response to this former moment's rendering invisible of the heart of the concen-trationary project – annihilation of ethnicized groups of Europeans – although Lanzmann would not himself acknowledge the attempted extermination of the Roma and Sinti, against whom a proposed final solution was less systematically but still tragically pursued (Lewy 1999). Thinking once again about the non-specification in *Night and Fog* and *The Diary of Anne Frank*, we need to ask if their strategies of imprecise representation signify a craven fear of continuing anti-Semitism, or even their own unconscious brand of it, which could not equate a specifically Jewish representation with that which might appeal to and instruct a larger non-Jewish world about the very racism they sought to condemn. What is the nature of this anxiety – or rather what is its history? How modern is it?

So, we have these two vastly different projects but a common complaint. Is totalitarianism, the concentrationary disease, synonymous with racism and colonialism, or is it something distinct? I think the question remains unresolved as to whether or not it matters that we specify the identity of the victims of genocide in distinction from those persecuted for political resistance, sexuality, health or criminality, or distinguish the precise nature of the process, for example by focusing on the suffering of the annihilated Jewish victims in extermina-tion camps or on the emergence of the possibility of fascist totalitarianism. Emotionally, it is very difficult not to be called into human compassion for suffering and the resulting terrorization that continues to have its negative effects. That is a work of commemoration. Politically and theoretically, however, we need to recognize that in whatever historical costume it first emerged – Nazism versus the Jews, Stalinism versus everyone including the Jews (Stalin had his own plans for a local final solution) – the totalitarian possibility is now available for any group anywhere in the world to think and act with: wherever absolutes of faith, history and destiny are called upon to be obeyed. Such calls for total obedience to a transcendent absolute can involve the arbitrary suspension of other human beings' right to life. Terrorism may well be the home-kit version of state totalitarianism, one as promiscuously available as are the technologies of destruction. The irony of Iraq may be that the war was waged against someone presented as a Hitler figure, a head of a fascist regime, who, once toppled, would be succeeded by an Iraqi Adenhauer – only to find that Saddam Hussein's actual legacy was already globally entrenched and up for independent deployment, irrespective of the state machinery that once defined totalitarianism.

It is in response to these difficult questions that I return to one of the first major political-historical analyses of the events of the mid-twentieth century, which appeared in 1951, under what the author, Hannah Arendt, admitted was the unsatisfactory title of *The Origins of Totalitarianism* (Arendt 1951). The year 2006 marked the centenary of the birth of this major political thinker, whose daring and unsentimental address to the intersection of Europe's newest form of racism, anti-Semitism – which, of course, postdates the emergence of its racist constructions of Africans, Indians and others Europe had colonized – with Europe's post-nationalist colonialist imperialism and with the emergence of a new political form, totalitarianism, deserves to be read in the context of our present perplexity. The early twentieth-first century has opened with our having little to guide us through its ever-increasing spirals of difference-inspired violence.

Like Lanzmann, who pursued the question not of why but of what happened, relentlessly pushing his witnesses, brilliantly trapping the bystanders, suavely betraying the perpetrators, gently cajoling the survivors into sharing the horror whose speaking could still wrack their bodies with its pain, Hannah Arendt set herself in the immediate aftermath of 1945 to think about what she declared was now the question of the rest of the century: evil. If this is the question, what is the meaning of the architecture of the book written and presented in three parts: Anti-Semitism, Imperialism, Totalitarianism? What are the relations between the parts that combine to produce an analysis that required two elements to be identified and distinguished and then knotted together in their conjunction as the ground for the novel form of total domination: totalitarianism? What is the novelty that Arendt brought to this analysis as a European political theorist confronted with the most challenging question ever faced by political theory, a question that exceeded the limits of political theorization's prior models of power, violence, rule? In the year of her centenary, the significance and legacy of her political theory were widely reviewed and argued, and here I cannot do it justice. I want to draw out just one thin thread of her tripartite argument that specifically contributes to the core discussions of this volume: racism, postcolonialism, Europe.

Within a book bursting with original and disturbing insights in almost every paragraph, one of her most novel approaches arises with her question: why did something so slight as the Jewish question, which was well on the road to increasing insignificance, become the cause of something so extreme and atrocious that human polity is forever changed by a truly racist and purely racist crime that goes beyond all others in quite a solid catalogue of human beastliness?

> Twentieth century political developments have driven the Jewish people into the storm center of events; the Jewish question and anti-semitism, *relatively unimportant phenomena in terms of world politics*, became the catalytic agent first for the rise of the Nazi movement and the establishment of an organisational structure of the Third Reich, in which every citizen had to prove he was *not* a Jew, then for a world war of unparalleled ferocity, and finally for the emergence of the unprecedented crime of genocide in the heart of Occidental civilisation. That this called for not only lamentation and denunciation but for comprehension seemed to me obvious. This book is an attempt at understanding what at first and second glance seemed simply outrageous. (Arendt 1951; quoted from Arendt 1994, Preface to Part One, p. xiiv, emphasis added)

Challenged to explain her method, Arendt revealed that she was not writing a history of either anti-Semitism or imperialism but rather aiming to analyse the elements of Jew hatred and expansionism as they became visible and active in the making of the totalitarian phenomenon itself. Arendt studied what she called their 'crystallization into totalitarianism'. In so many forms of cultural commemoration and didactic pedagogy of the Holocaust, the trend is to lead the student or visitor towards the 'final solution' through the logical and chronological plaiting together of the rise of fascism in Germany and a history of anti-Semitism. This has, however, the effect of naturalizing the very convergence that Arendt identifies as remarkable, and hence in need of careful analysis. It is against this trend, which gives to the Holocaust a logic in what preceded it, that Lanzmann identified 7 December 1941, in Chelmno, as the 'beginning' of his film about the absolute rupture. Refusing the false comfort of a pre-known and pre-destined historical narrative ensures that we do not fall prey to the illusion that totalitarianism was historically inevitable. Rather, it is the *crystallization* of unexpected factors that produces and defines the novelty Arendt seeks to elucidate; but for us, now, once this possibility, hitherto unimaginable by existing historical-political configurations, has become possible, it falls into our perpetual reality. Arendt explains the difference between plotting a historical event as a narrative, and discovering its formation because of the event itself:

> Whenever an event occurs which is great enough to illuminate its own past, history comes into being. Only then does the chaotic maze of the past happenings emerge as a story which can be told, because it has a beginning and an end. (Arendt 1994, p. 319)

Political analysis is inevitably non-narrative and retrospective; its possibility is conditioned by the historical event itself. Only that which has happened can make clear, in a moment of illumination, what was invisibly moving towards this event's becoming in its still undetermined pre-history. In this sense, Arendt radically deconstructs the comforting explanations of the Nazi genocide of the Jews of Europe. For instance, one such explanation is that there has always been Jew hatred or anti-Semitism, and that the Holocaust was but a singularly egregious chapter, or even epitome, of the 'longest hatred' (Wistrich 1992). The witness of the peasants of Chelmno outside their church in Lanzmann's film, who suddenly vent the Gospel story of the murderous Jews delivering Jesus to the Romans and calling for a death the guilt for which they are then said to accept lies on their own heads, might be proof of the persistence of deep-seated anti-Semitism inherent in the Christian Gospels, which induct every Christian into a belief that the Jews called for, were paid for, the murder of the son of God. As Hyam Maccoby's work has shown, we can track an anthropology of generic anti-Semitism that placed the Jews as a 'pariah people' across a long history of the mutual encounter of Christianity and Judaism (Maccoby 1973, 1996). Maccoby's anthropology of religious ideas also reveals a deeper mythic narrative at work, in the form of the concept of the 'sacred executioner', a figure required by its culture to perform a necessary human sacrifice, for which the executioner then receives the obloquy of the very people he served. The Gospels place the Jews, an oppressed people under the boot of a cruel Roman occupation, as those who called for and delivered Jesus to die, placing the rabble and the individuated representative, Judas, in the role of sacred executioner (Maccoby 1982). Such studies might take us back to the grounds of conflict between Christians and Jews considered anthropological by Mrs Michelsohn. But while the peasants of Chelmno stood by under the duress of their vicious German occupiers, drove trains, and switched tracks and operated signals, they neither conceived nor enacted what the terrorizing colonial Reich planned and systematically executed at great cost and in the midst of a territorial war. Stories of deicide may have risen to the surface, to be shrieked in the town square. Janina Bauman's own testimony in her memoir of her survival in the Warsaw Ghetto and later in the Polish countryside, *Winter in the Morning* (1991), counters this trend with a story of the Catholic peasant woman who gave her, along with her mother and sister, unquestioned refuge for the same reasons that she demanded, at the end of the war, that Janina herself take a bowl of soup and a piece of bread to a fleeing German soldier hiding in her barn. When implicitly questioned by a confused Janina, she declared that whoever came needing her help, received it without question (Bauman 1991, p. 190). This is just as much a version of a Catholic faith that ignored difference and that vies with the representations of the Jews as sacred executioners in the Gospels. Yet even here there is further complexity in terms of theologies. Both European Catholics and European Protestants believed that the Jews must survive in order to bear witness to their own blindness, and that only their conversion to Christianity would ensure the coming of the Messiah. The year 2006 was also the 350th anniversary of another myth: that of Cromwell's benign readmittance of Jews to England after their expulsion in 1290 by Edward I. Negotiations were held with the Puritan republic around 1656. The Puritans, however, swayed between violent hatred of the Jews for their crime and a messianic concern to have Jews convert, so as to hasten the return of the Messiah. Nothing was decided; no edict was ever revoked. Slowly and without formal acknowledgement, the re-immigration began and was not legally or violently opposed.

The arguments for a persistent and continuous persecution of the Jews, which is part of the self-defining myth of contemporary Jewish culture, does not stand up to historical inspection as the grounds for the emergence of genocide in industrial modern Europe in 1941. Studying the persistence of myths and narratives remains critical but cannot be used alone as explanation of a singular historical event, however much that event draws its ideological support promiscuously, from all resources in culture. Arendt's research as the political scientist she, the trained philosopher, was forced to become because of the rise of fascism and its Holocaust, points to another and different feature: the vulnerability of the Jewish world in the twentieth century because it had no political consciousness of the new forces threatening it, nor means of organizing itself politically to counter them. Arendt argues that within modernity, post-emancipation, the Jewish world was caught between two competing identities: *parvenu* and *pariah*. The parvenu wishes, and hence always fails, to achieve integration into a host culture, despite cultural and religious difference. Or, by means of attempting to erase it, the parvenu can only advertise his or her otherness through such yearning for integration which is unknown to those who experience themselves centred in the norm, bolstered by fictions of immemorial national or class belonging. On the other hand, the pariah accepts otherness, making of the condition an imaginative home which can, and did, foster significant aspects of modernist culture that could make of 'the Jew' – for Jews and non-Jews alike – a metaphorical figure for general aesthetic alienation or philosophical exile from bourgeois society. Critical pariah status, however, is for Arendt a more active thinking-machine for understanding the impossibility of inhabiting either space without awareness of its utter unreality. What Arendt manages to create in, and precisely *through*, her writing – through language as the only instrument of dialogical, self-reflecting thought – is the defiant sense of writing in this historical juncture and of this historical event *as a Jewish subject*, while this is neither an identity imposed on her from outside, nor a condition derived from some essence within. It is a political position created in and by a specific history that she felt she had to assume as a necessity in the face of a fascism that saw her only as a Jew. This was an act against her, one in which she could change the terms – not necessarily ensuring her survival – of the relations implied by the fascist designation of her as a 'Jew', meaning someone exiled from human polity (Bernstein 1996). To respond is to act as a subject of human polity in the name of the negative marking which conditions fascism's assault on her. In her famous televised interview with Günter Gaus in 1964,[2] Arendt tells

---

2   Hannah Arendt, 'What Remains? The Language Remains', interviewed by Günter Gaus on the German television programme *Zur Person*.

of her own upbringing in a secular and intellectual household, one susceptible, nonetheless, to both the casual anti-Semitism of street kids' name-calling and the formal enunciation of racist ideologies by teachers at her school. The former, her mother told her to deal with in street fashion by herself; the latter was to be dealt with by leaving the class on the instant, coming home and reporting verbatim the insult. A letter of protest would be written by her irreligious and communally unaffiliated mother, whose lesson to her was that you must resist *as a Jew* since you have been attacked *as a Jew*. The dialectic of radically different ways in which one would cognitively experience such 'as a Jew'-ness resulting from acts of linguistic resistance to the othering projected against you by a racist and hence racializing community cannot be sufficiently stressed: it does not imply tit-for-tat or escalating retaliation so much as the specific exercise of reasoned thought through challenges in language, the promise of exchange between mutuals of different perspectives and positions precisely denied by the racist deployment of ideological violence in stereotyped name-calling or formal racist pedagogy aimed at eradicating the very existence of troubling difference and ambivalence.

But the Jewishness that Arendt explores across literature, notably in her lengthy studies of Proust and other figures articulating symbolically what Kristeva will name *judaicité* (Kristeva 1996) as opposed to Judaism, is not sentimental attachment. Rather, this Jewishness formulates a self-reflecting understanding of the intimate connection between human dignity and citizenship. The racist's attempt to impugn the former by denying the latter must be resisted politically through piercing the crystallization of elements, ancient and modern, certainly overdetermined by tradition but also novel, that are the form in which the crisis immediately and actually confronted her. The difficulty I am using Arendt to articulate is summed up in those pathetic (that is, both deeply affecting but nonetheless demoralizing) phrases used when the subjects of racist attack pitifully declare: 'But I am human too' or ask 'Are we not human beings also?' It seems so obvious and compelling to appeal to a shared humanity. Yet when and how did such a commonness come into being, to be called upon except in the extremity of its breaching? It seems to me that history has taught us this: that the concept of a common humanity came into consciousness and linguistic use only at the point of its extreme betrayal, only in those social and political experiments so extreme in their suspension of the very basics of another's humanity that the response had to be in kind: at a level that should never need saying. In European chattel slavery, the resisting African subject called for slavery's abolition by having to articulate what was most egregiously denied in this cruellest and most modern version of slavery (Blackburn 1989). This is also at the heart of the genocidal assault on the Jews of Europe: to be persecuted religiously is one thing; to become the object of social suspicion is another; but to be denied human life as a group, to be reduced to species being, to 'bare life', is without precedence.

In the final hours of the Second Era of Lanzmann's *Shoah*, two Jewish leaders, from opposing Bundist and Zionist groups, appeal to a former courier for the

Polish government in exile, Jan Karski, who has agreed to take messages from them to the Allies and world Jewish leaders. In their emotional appeal, which Karski seems still able to repeat verbatim in its affective intensity, they say: 'We are humans, Do you understand it? Do you understand it? Never happened before in History what is happening to our people now' (Lanzmann 1995, p. 156). Compare this with the angry simplicity of Primo Levi's poem 'Shema' (which translates as the order 'Hear!') (1947), where he inverts such appeals and commands the readers he summons to 'consider whether this is a man':

> You who live secure
> In your warm houses
> Who return at evening to find
> Hot food and friendly faces:
>
> Consider whether this is a man,
> Who labours in the mud
> Who knows no peace
> Who fights for a crust of bread
> Who dies at a yes or a no.
> Consider whether this is a woman,
> Without hair or name
> With no more strength to remember
> Eyes empty and womb cold
> As a frog in winter.
>
> Consider that this has been:
> I commend these words to you.
> Engrave them on your hearts
> When you are in your house, when you walk on your way,
> When you go to bed, when you rise.
> Repeat them to your children.
> Or may your house crumble,
> Disease render you powerless,
> Your offspring avert their faces from you.
> (Levi 1988, p. 9)

The pathos of these pleas and Levi's fierce anger at those who are indifferent to their grounds should not blind us to the novelty of anyone having to make them. Nor should it blind us the fact that the distillation of people, in all their diversity, diversity being synonymous with the condition of being people, down to a common ground of merely and then barely being human, and thus having now to spell out and demand *human* rights, such as rights to life and safety, is the product of an event that involved both the novelty of genocide – the killing of a human group defined as a genus within the species – and the specific insignificance of its target. Jews, Roma and Sinti are, and even were then, a minute percentage of the population of Europe. In Germany, in 1933, its Jewish citizens formed less than 1 per cent of the population, a mere half a million souls.

Arendt argues that the essence of totalitarianism is that 'everything is possible'. This not only overrode the existing conventions regarding violence against others, but also eradicated the until then unspoken condition of what she will argue is in fact the condition of *human* being: plurality and spontaneity.

> The concentration and extermination camps of totalitarian regimes serve as the laboratories in which the fundamental belief that everything is possible is being verified. Compared with this, all other experiments are secondary in importance – including those in the field of medicine whose horrors are recorded in detail in the trials against the physicians of the Third Reich…. Total domination, which strives to organize the infinite plurality and differentiation of human beings as if all of humanity were just one individual, is possible only if each and every person is reduced to a never-changing identity of reactions, so that each of these bundles of reactions can be exchanged at random for any other. The problem is to fabricate something that does not exist, namely, a kind of human species resembling other animal species whose only 'freedom' would consist in 'preserving the species'. Totalitarian domination attempts to achieve this goal both through ideological indoctrination of the elite formations and through absolute terror in the camps; and the atrocities for which the elite formations are ruthlessly used become, as it were, the practical application of the ideological indoctrination … while the appalling spectacle of the camps themselves is supposed to furnish the theoretical verification of this ideology.
>
> The camps are meant not only to exterminate people and degrade human beings but they also serve the ghastly experiment of eliminating, under scientifically controlled conditions, spontaneity itself as an expression of human behaviour and of the transforming of the human personality into a mere thing, into something that even animals are not; for Pavlov's dog, which, as we know, was trained to eat not when it was hungry, but when a bell rang, was a perverted animal…. It is only in the concentration camps that such an experiment is at all possible and therefore they are not only *'la société la plus totalitaire encore realisée'* (David Rousset) but the guiding ideal of total domination in general. (Arendt 1951, pp. 437–38)

Drawing on the immediate post-war literature of the French political deportees who survived to bear witness to the concentrationary universe they experienced at Buchenwald and Mauthausen (rather than Chelmno or Treblinka, which were temporary but dedicated extermination centres), Arendt is talking about the concentration camp, not the extermination camp. Unlike Buchenwald on one side and Chelmno or Treblinka on the other, Auschwitz was a hybrid, where those who were forced to live and not die immediately in the gas chambers experienced the concentrationary universe – which is why the testimony of survivors is the testimony to this laboratory of human annihilation rather than to genocidal extermination, which is the focus of Lanzmann's film. Only Simon Srebnik and the handful of others Lanzmann tracked down or the survivor of the *Sonderkommando* at Auschwitz, Filip Muller, can testify to that (Muller 1979).

One more element of Arendt's analysis needs to be put in place before I conclude. The book begins with her novel and heretical interpretation of modern anti-Semitism in the context of a failure of Jewish culture to generate its own political analysis of the dangers that would arise precisely in the modern situation of apparent social equality. She seems to be arguing that the purely cultural or acculturated identity sought by the parvenu was insufficient and, worse, dangerously deluding. Although Arendt endorsed some aspects of Zionist aspirations, as the one political response that did emerge to the novel conditions of Jewish life in nationalist times, she did not simply endorse Jewish nationalism, as she was afraid of all the ordinary mistakes and cruelties that every state ends up performing when constituted on nationalist lines. The general lack of real political analysis of the situation in Europe is set against the other force mobilizing itself at the same time. Going beyond an almost out-of-date mid-nineteenth-century nationalism and colonial expansionism, transmogrifying into a modern and different form of imperialism (she points to the difference between Rome, where everyone works for the Empire, and colonialism, where everyone works for you), made the colonies the laboratories for this process itself. In a sense, Third Reich Germany brought the colonial process back, to expand it upon Europe. In its own ideological conception of its very modern imperium, the Third Reich perceived itself in universal terms – building beyond local nationalist ideologies, Nazi ideology produced for Germany a world destiny that would overrun all boundaries and dominate all Europe. Precisely in their real insignificance and self-torturing pursuit of assimilation or nationalist localization in response to older, nineteenth-century European configurations, the Jews, nonetheless, figuratively represented for the imperialist fascist dream a negative fantasy as their only contesting other. The Jews were not merely a local population, like the Slavs or the French, to be colonized, ruled and worked. The Jews were the only other people with a comparable vision of a universal identity beyond nations and localities. Why else would anyone *believe* such fictions as the *Protocols of the Elders of Zion*, which allege a world Jewish conspiracy for domination? It is worth noting that these forgeries are again being used in Arab countries to vilify this surprisingly resilient remnant of an ancient culture with the same accusation of a secret conspiracy of world domination. Given that the vast majority of Europe's Jews in 1933 lived in poverty so extreme that they were leaking out of Europe in their millions to make better lives in the United States, France and Britain, that the majority were rural people living subsistence lives in the backwaters of Carpathia and the Ukraine, or in the slums of European cities as tailors, peddlers or factory workers, why the potency of the recurring image of the rich Jew, the capitalist, the materialist – 'running Poland' as Lanzmann captures in his conversations around Chelmno?

Arendt argues that anti-semitism (she always used a lower case) grew in direct proportion to which nationalism *declined*. The linkage of Nazism to anti-Semitism cannot be explained as mere ideological bribery of the Germans' nationalist xenophobia. Arendt also rails against those misguided folk who believe that anti-Semitism is good for the Jews, as it keeps an otherwise disintegrating community together in a defensive solidarity. She insists on the full realization of the meaning that anti-Semitism is genocidal now. In fact, over three decades since her death in 1975, we hear it in the speeches of those whose solution to a violent and horrifying territorial dispute that is the unresolved product of late colonial nationalism in the Middle East is a second annihilation of the tenuous Jewish state and, we suppose, its populations. That this is the political position freely spoken by existing and elected political representatives of countries in that region, however much people might hate or be ashamed of what is being done to the Palestinian people in the name of Israeli self-defence, is a mark of the normalization of the totalitarian disease in our world. The laboratory experiment does not need camps to be repeated for its findings to be deployed as a substitute for politics.

For Arendt, the issue is how to reground the possibility of the political, which she understands as the living together of peoples in the creative and necessary human conditions of plurality and spontaneity – the very conditions of human life that totalitarianism negates. Her conclusion is hopeful. She saw the point of her work as being to arrive at a condition in which we can imagine a rebirth of plural and spontaneous concepts of humanity after its annihilation and in the shadow of the twin examples of mid-twentieth-century totalitarianism: Stalinism and Nazism. These were, of course, for a political theorist, specific instances of modern forms of governmentality. While it is all too tempting to ask what Arendt's relevance or message is for our times of postcolonial racism, post-1989 and the end of the Cold War, and with it the long legacy of Stalinism, we must be wary and learn her lessons of acute analysis of specific conditions of political novelty. We love to use old tools to discern comfortingly familiar patterns in conditions that scare us with their originality and defy incorporation into pre-existing narrative. Instead of politically judicious analysis, we are too often offered by politicians on all sides only mythically overloaded rhetoric.

In a passage, in her conclusion, about loneliness, Arendt sketches a picture of what happens when we fail to provide for groups which, in their cultural and even religious identity, form part of a general plurality, but still find no form of political involvement and recognition. We might identify these groups as the internal exiles of the minorities in postcolonial societies. For an Arendtian, therefore, multiculturalism – the cultural solution – is not the answer because the fostering of cultural difference, without the political framing of plurality, could easily exacerbate the fine line between equally sharing space and total alienation, within a loneliness that results from the deep contradiction between apparent equality and real diversity. If anything, the study of modern Jewish experience and anti-Semitism is the case study for this failure to conjugate politics and culture for the benefit of minorities; and look how that ended: in state-managed genocide. The powerless in local, national or geographical worlds will borrow its rhetorics – there is a world conspiracy: maybe all Christians, all westerners, all Americans, all non-*x,y,z* are to blame. Blaming – projecting onto a persecutory other what is experienced as one's own frayed and collapsing sense of a full self – allows the victims to escape their own implication and political responsibility and to avoid the need for political analysis of the stalemate in which they feel enclosed. Let me offer a final passage from Arendt, with its suggestiveness for current discussions of how we create future societies on the ruins of our own making – neither blaming nor avoiding – but realizing that the historical conditions that crystallized in Europe in the mid-twentieth century define the very conditions of human social survival. What we are looking for is not old explanations but honest research, such as Hannah Arendt dared to undertake as she responded to the necessity to think as a Jew about that which had encompassed her destruction as a human being:

> What prepares men for totalitarian domination in a non-totalitarian world is in fact that loneliness, once a borderline experience usually suffered in certain marginal social conditions like old age, has become the everyday experience of the ever growing masses of our century. The merciless process into which totalitarianism drives and organizes the masses looks like a suicidal escape from this reality. The 'ice-cold' reasoning and the 'mighty tentacle' of dialectics which 'seizes you as in a vise' appears like a last resort in a world where nobody is reliable and nothing can be relied upon. It is the inner coercion whose only content is the strict avoidance of contradictions that seems to confirm a man's identity outside of all relationships with others. It fits him into the iron band of terror even when he is alone, and totalitarian domination tries never to leave him alone except in the extreme condition of solitary confinement. By destroying all space between men and pressing men against each other, even the productive potentialities of isolation are annihilated; by teaching and glorifying the logical reasoning of loneliness where man knows he will be utterly lost if he ever lets go of the first premise from which the whole process is being started, even the slim chances that *loneliness may be translated into solitude and logic into thought* are obliterated. If this practice is compared with tyranny, it seems as if a way has been found to set the desert itself into motion, to let loose a sandstorm that could cover all the parts of the inhabited earth. The conditions under which we exist today in the field of politics are indeed threatened by these devastating sandstorms. (Arendt 1951, p. 478, emphasis added)

To grasp the implications of this passage, I need to stress Arendt's distinction between loneliness and solitude: the former emerges only in company. Solitude requires being alone, but in that solitude one is not lonely because it offers the dialogue with oneself, 'where all thinking is done':

> All thinking, strictly speaking, is done in solitude and is a dialogue between me and myself; but this dialogue of the two-in-one does not lose contact with the world of my fellow-men because they are represented in the self with whom I lead the dialogue of thought. (Arendt 1951, p. 476)

For Arendt, isolation, however, is the precondition of terror's rule; it is the political complement of loneliness 'in the sphere of social intercourse'. I see in the passage above an important moment when Arendt links her distinction between loneliness and solitude with the difference between logic and thought, logic being a blind obedience to an absolute such as history, nature or a religious doctrine: the dominative effect of 'the logicality of ideological thinking' and its cold reasoning.

There is no danger of a permanently totalitarian world, argues Arendt, for each regime carries within it the seeds of its own destruction. But organized loneliness is more dangerous than unorganized impotence because it can ravage the world. I wonder if this concept of organized loneliness – the rupture of any possibility of political relations between conflicting or merely co-habiting peoples, where cold and blind logics displace equivocal but social thought, and particularity becomes loneliness rather than creative solitude, the creativity of the margin that is not brutalized materially and spiritually by poverty and despair – can be mobilized in our present crisis.

The point of starting with what I called the racism of minor differences, of the in-house spats among long co-habiting Europeans that outraged common sense in becoming the grounds of the egregious crime of twentieth-century totalitarianism, is to get us beyond our own fixed logics, in which racism is seen in terms of cultures, colours and beliefs. Mrs Michelsohn's social sciences, anthropology and psychology, can help to explain why people make so much of utterly insignificant pluralities, which are, after all, our treasure house as people. But political thought, which I also find explored in both Arendt and Lanzmann in their different orientations, asks us to think about *people living together in their difference*, recognizing that my uniqueness depends on the preservation of every other's comparable particularity, whether I know them, like them, understand them, appreciate them or not. Most of our experiments in attempting to 'live together' are failing to provide safety and to avoid loneliness, in which the totalitarian disease can prey. In 1951, Arendt was waiting for the new birth. It did not come. She went on to write *The Human Condition* in 1958, which was a manual for life on the planet newly challenged by the new colonialism: the space race, a vision not realized in history yet but fantasized endlessly in science fiction. Ridley Scott's epoch-defining film *Blade Runner* (1983) is perhaps the most exemplary work to fulfil Arendt's darkest vision of the concentrationary legacy alive and well, the premise for the action film being that the job of the human agent is to hunt and destroy the lonely and desiring 'replicant', built to serve the off-world colonists and never allowed to inhabit this planet with its industrial manufacturers. In a total perversion of Philip K. Dick's profound story about human empathy and otherness vis-à-vis the animal world, Scott's film makes popular culture out of the direst episode of world history, an event that was sadly Europe's gift to the world. This fact also makes it Europe's specific responsibility to work politically towards the repairing of the conditions of human life as it encounters new and as yet unplotted challenges around plurality, difference and the co-habiting of shared space.

Works cited

Adorno, T. (1990) *Negative Dialectics*. London, Routledge.
Arendt, H. (1951) *The Origins of Totalitarianism*. New York, Harcourt, Brace & Co.
—— (1963) *Eichmann in Jerusalem: A Report on the Banality of Evil*. New York, Viking Press.

—— (1994) *Essays in Understanding 1930–54* (ed. J. Kohn). New York, Harcourt, Brace & Co.

Bauman, J. (1991) *Winter in the Morning: A Young Girl's Life in the Warsaw Ghetto and Beyond.* London, Virago Books.

Bauman, Z. (1989) *Modernity and the Holocaust.* Cambridge, Polity Press.

—— (1992) *Modernity and Ambivalence.* Cambridge, Polity Press.

Bernstein, R. J. (1996) *Hannah Arendt and the Jewish Question.* Cambridge, Polity Press.

Bhabha, H. (1983) 'The Other Question – The Stereotype and Colonial Discourse'. *Screen,* 24(6), pp. 18–36.

Blackburn, R. (1989) *The Overthrow of Colonial Slavery.* London, Verso Books.

Doneson, J. (2002) *The Holocaust in American Film* (new edition). Syracuse, NY, Syracuse University Press.

Friedländer, S. (1992) *Probing the Limits of Representation: Nazism and the 'Final Solution'.* Cambridge, MA, Harvard University Press.

Gilman, S. L. (1985) *Difference and Pathology: Stereotypes of Sexuality, Race and Madness.* Ithaca, NY, Cornell University Press.

—— (1992) *The Jew's Body.* London, Routledge.

Habermas, J. (1989) *The New Conservatism: Cultural Criticism and the Historians' Debate.* Cambridge, MA, Harvard University Press.

Klemperer, V. (1957) *Lingua Tertii Imperii* [*The Language of the Third Reich*]. Translated by M. Brady. London, Continuum Books.

Kofman, S. (1998) *Smothered Words.* Translated by M. Doby. Chicago, IL, Northwestern University Press.

Kristeva, J. (1996) *Time and Sense: Proust and the Experience of Literature.* New York, Columbia University Press.

Kushner, T. (1997) 'The Memory of Anne Frank'. In: Evans, M. and Lunn, K. eds. *War and Memory in the Twentieth Century.* Oxford, Berg, pp. 3–26.

Lanzmann, C. (1995) *Shoah: The Complete Text of the Acclaimed Film.* New York, Da Capo Press.

Levi, P. (1988) *Collected Poems.* Translated by R. Feldman and B. Swann. London, Faber and Faber.

Lewy, G., ed. (1999) *The Nazi Persecution of the Gypsies.* Oxford, Oxford University Press.

Maccoby, H. (1973) *Revolution in Judea: Jesus and the Jewish Resistance.* New York, Taplinger Publishing.

—— (1982) *The Sacred Executioner: Human Sacrifice and the Legacy of Guilt.* London, Thames and Hudson.

—— (1996) *A Pariah People: The Anthropology of Anti-Semitism.* London, Constable.

Muller, F. (1979) *Auschwitz Inferno: Testimony of a Sonderkommando.* London, Routledge.

Pollock, G. (1996) '*Dangerous Places: Ponar* – An Installation by Pam Skelton'. *Third Text,* 36, pp. 45–54.

Resnais, A. (1955) *Nuit et Brouillard* [*Night and Fog*]. Paris, Argos Films.

Rousset, D. (1946) *L'Univers concentrationnaire* [*The Other Kingdom*]. Translated by R. Guthrie. New York, Reynal and Hitchcock (1947).

Silverman, M. (2006) 'Horror and the Everyday: *Nuit et Brouillard* and Concentrationary Art'. *French Cultural Studies,* 17(1), pp. 5–18.

van der Knaap, E. (2006) *Uncovering the Holocaust: The International Reception of Night and Fog.* London, Wallflower Press.

Wistrich, R. (1992) *Antisemitism: The Longest Hatred.* New York, Schocken Books.

CHAPTER 3

Xenophobia, anti-Semitism and feminist activism in eastern Europe: a case study of Romania[1]

Elisabeta Zelinka

There is no place for racism or anti-Semitism in the European Union. (Romano Prodi, President of the European Commission, 19 February 2004[2])

Although anti-Semitism in contemporary Romania is radically being curbed by a variety of legislative and political measures, it is still present within Romanian society and occasionally flares up in a number of subversive contexts, including extremist right-wing political discourse and street graffiti, for example those inscribed on the Jewish Theatre in the Romanian capital, Bucharest, in the late 1990s and early 2000s. In the first main part of this chapter, some of the different forms of contemporary anti-Semitic mainstream discourse in Romania are identified; in the second part, the relationship between Jewish female activism in Romania and feminist academia is examined.

Much of the activism against anti-Semitism in contemporary Romania is female activism, which intersects with that of Romanian Jewish feminist academics, the two involving women who see themselves as having broadly similar goals. Leading female figures in resisting anti-Semitism have become role models for the Romanian Jewish diaspora. It is true that men are involved as well, largely

---

1   Given the state of flux that has characterized Romanian society over the last decade, it is pertinent to point out that the present chapter was substantially drafted in 2007. The situation regarding anti-Semitism in Romania has since improved considerably.

2   Romano Prodi, then President of the European Commission, at the European Jewish Congress and the Congress of European Rabbis, Brussels, 19 February 2004, as a response to a controversial *Eurobarometer* survey according to which Israel was rated 'the greatest threat to world peace'. See 'No Place for Anti-Semitism in Europe'. *Europa Newsletter*, issue 28, 24 February 2004. Available from http://europa.eu/newsletter/archives2004/issue28/index_en.htm#antisemit (accessed 31 January 2009).

in relation to the politics of Romania's accession to the European Union (EU) in January 2007, but then, after all, it is men who control all the high political and legislative positions.

Within female activism in contemporary Romania, we can discern two major strands. First, there are the Jewish non-governmental organizations (NGOs), whose activism mainly consists of assisting the Jewish community and helping to consolidate its identity. The second type of activism, the one performed by feminist academics, moulds itself on similar purposes: supporting (Jewish) women's equal rights, furthering their self-sufficiency and empowerment, as well as lobbying against their marginalization and loss of identity. This is the crucial intersection between Jewishness – Jewish activism in this particular case – and feminism, as both promote the same values: equality, social welfare, human dignity and identity (Lewitt 1997, pp. 103, 108–9; Miller 1991, pp. 72–100). However, little attention has been given to the relationship between Jewish activism and feminism in each of these fields, even though they have evolved in parallel over the last three or four decades (Tirosh-Rotshield 1994, pp. 84–86), and none at all has been given to the more particular case of Romania.

Anti-Semitism

The peaceful co-habitation of Jews and Romanians in the territory of Romania is attested to by documents that date back to the seventeenth and eighteenth centuries, especially in the eastern part of Romania (Moldavia) and in the capital, Bucharest. Jews were usually recognized as excellent merchants and bankers, people with capital, guild membership and good cross-border commercial relations. They were acknowledged as living according to different, but accepted, traditions. Hatred and stigmatization of Jews were no greater than were suffered by any other ethnic minority. Indeed, quite often, Jews enjoyed some protection within the Wallachian fiefs, because of the economic and related socio-political power that their capital provided (Manascu and Leib 2006). Anti-Semitism in Romania rose sharply in the 1930s, influenced strongly by Hitler and the rise of Nazi propaganda, which was to shape general sentiment against the Jews all over Europe for years to come. Soaring hatred and anti-Semitism in Romania and associated murder and emigration reduced the number of Jews living in Romania by half (from 800,000 to 400,000). The politics of Romania's political leader, General Ion Antonescu, who saw himself as Hitler's loyal subject, was central to this process. Of the 400,000 Jews who survived the pogroms in Romania, over 350,000 performed Aliyah (emigration to Israel) between 1950 and 1960, a period of hard-core communist rule in Romania. Jews have continued their emigration to the United States, western Europe and Canada up to the present day. Now, there are as few as 7,000–9,000 Jews in Romania, most of them elderly, living in scattered small communities, especially in and around Bucharest.

It is vital to highlight the significance of the Second World War and fifty years of communism, which both fed quite different, but equally durable, forms of hatred and xenophobia. These elements played a central role in the construction of contemporary Romanian psychosocial identities. As late as the 1990s and early 2000s, extremist politicians still presented a xenophobic social and political discourse, not only against Jews but against 'others' in general: all types of minorities, including lesbians, gays, bisexuals and transsexuals (LGBT), the Roma and women as a secondary sex/gender – in short, all those who are perceived to be 'different' from the Orthodox, white, Romanian heterosexual male. Romanians seem particularly susceptible to this binary hierarchical opposition of 'us' versus 'them', and to inferiorizing the 'other' as a result of this pattern of procedural memory (de Beauvoir 1988, pp. xxi, xxii–xxiii). They seem to suffer from 'the otherness syndrome', which spontaneously erupts in expressions of homophobia and anti-Semitism, even in places where such attitudes have been dormant for some time.

One of the most typical and dangerous forms of Romanian anti-Semitism can be traced back to mainstream political discourse, for example that of the (former) Iliescu government (2000–4). It was not until 13 October 2004 that the then Romanian President, Ion Iliescu, acknowledged that during the Second World War there indeed *were* deportations and abuses of the Jews in Romania. For the first time in history, the Romanian political apparatus openly acknowledged its Jewish pogroms but, at the same time, this move was hardly a self-imposed change in the mainstream political discourse. Rather, it was imposed by the EU, by the Council of Europe and by different transnational NGOs, in the context of Romania's ardent wish to join the EU. The joining procedure was conditional on Romanian recognition of certain basic human rights, with implementation of the appropriate legislation. That is why Iliescu was keen on declaring 9 October to be Holocaust Day in Romania, shortly before he stepped down from office. Nonetheless, by the time Iliescu and his government did step down in January 2005, they had done little to curb anti-Semitism among the Romanian people, which can still be identified in other elements of Romanian political and social discourse: for example in the openly anti-Semitic and homophobic speeches of Romanian politicians like Corneliu Vadim Tudor (see below) or the lurid rants of Gigi Becali, owner of the Steaua Bucuresti football club.

Such continuing hostility is unsurprising given that the few democratic steps the Iliescu government took in the late 1990s did *not* stem from its own progressive convictions. As indicated above, they did not come from within the Romanian political class, but were imposed externally by the more powerful international socio-political and military institutions (principally the EU and NATO) in what Kornelia Slavova (2006) calls a 'top-down policy': a type of policy that usually bears little fruit in terms of real change, precisely because it is imposed.

The most blatant example of the strength of political anti-Semitism in Romania was the 2000 presidential electoral support for Corneliu Vadim Tudor, MP, the president of the right-wing, anti-Semitic Greater Romania Party (Partidul Romania Mare, PRM). This is another dangerous form of contemporary Romanian anti-Semitism: one that is subversively uncensored, and adopted by charismatic, extreme right-wing Romanian politicians. On air, on a private television channel called OTV, Tudor (who came second behind Iliescu in the 2000 presidential elections) warned that 'we [the Romanian people] are not at their [the world-wide Jewish mafia's] mercy, and we are not one of their colonies'. Nor was he alone; in a further remark, at a conference organized by the Romanian Academy of Sciences in late June 2002, entitled 'The Holocaust and Its Implications for Romania', Minister of Culture Razvan Theodorescu stated that 'Romania had nothing to do with the Holocaust'.[3]

Moreover, as a direct consequence of the present mainstream political discourse, there were several attempts during 2002–3 to organize meetings and public discussions over the fate of the Romanian fascist Iron Guard movement.[4] Posters with pictures of its founder, Corneliu Zelea Codreanu, in central Bucharest in summer 2000 to commemorate '75 years of suffering and sacrifice' were still visible in 2002–3, along with pro-Iron Guard publications, as well as various anti-Semitic texts. This form of contemporary anti-Semitism in Romania is subversive, veiled, sporadic, but still present and even public. Here, Jan Burkitt's theory of the 'inscription of the habitus' is applicable (Burkitt 1999, pp. 87–88). Burkitt argues that dominant socio-political subjects can use their own power to 'inscribe' onto the grass-roots their norms of thinking, talking and acting. Applying Burkitt's theory to the Romanian authorities, we can conclude that anti-Semitic, Romanian (political) discourses routinely inscribed their own xenophobia onto everyday popular culture and contemporary social attitudes. Thus, mainstream political discourse can be effective in spreading hatred and allowing it to thrive.

Various channels and methods are employed in this process. Education, or indoctrination, may prove one dangerous and effective means of spreading anti-Semitism in Romania. The Ministry of Education has allowed biased history schoolbooks to be printed and to be used in class. History teachers sometimes informed their students that there were no real pogroms in Romania during the Second World War, and that the political leadership of the country did its best to avoid any deportations of Jews. When youngsters receive such a biased education in school, one can hardly be surprised that instances of the vandalization of synagogues have been reported. In 2002, for example, major incidents of an anti-Semitic character were reported: a synagogue (in Falticeni) was desecrated, another in Vatra Dornei was broken into, and hateful anti-Semitic graffiti were written on condominiums in Cluj, the third largest city in Romania. Also, on the night of 11–12 October 2002, well known Nazi slogans were etched on the walls of the Jewish Theatre in Bucharest, recalling those at Auschwitz (Katz

---

3   Both quotes taken from the Website of the Stephen Roth Institute for the Study of Contemporary Anti-Semitism and Racism, Romanian country report, at www.tau.ac.il/Anti-Semitism/asw2002-3/romania.htm (accessed 13 March 2006).
4   The Iron Guard was the ultra-nationalist, anti-Semitic, fascist movement and political party in Romania in existence from 1927 into the early part of the Second World War. It was founded by Corneliu Zelea Codreanu. As well as being responsible for a long series of political assassinations, it was also notorious for mass murder of Jews.

2002). What is alarming is that, to date, there is little or no information on any police investigations into these incidents (Katz 2002). Thus, a further 'tool' that the state is using, consciously or not, to 'permit' the dissemination of anti-Semitism is still inadequate policing and prosecution when existing legislation on anti-Semitism is broken. Among the most important pieces of legislation in this respect are Emergency Ordinance No. 31/2002 'regarding the prohibition of organizations and symbols with a fascist, racial or xenophobic character' (Katz 2002) and the 2004 Law Against All Forms of Discrimination[5] (as well as that establishing the National Council for Combating Discrimination). In addition, the Center for Monitoring and Combating Anti-Semitism in Romania (MCA Romania) reported a rise in anti-Semitism in its 2004 report.[6]

Finally, the government provides no substantial financial support for the promotion of Jewish culture and patrimony, such as rehabilitating deteriorated and desecrated synagogues (many of which are UNESCO heritage sites), financing Jewish cultural publications, or supporting NGOs and community organizations. In 2007, the novel *Fateless*, by Imre Kertész, a winner of the Nobel Prize for Literature, had still not been published in Romania, although, as a Hungarian novelist, he is a neighbour. Nor can one easily buy reliable documentation on the Romanian Jewish Shoah.

To conclude, considering all these forms of contemporary anti-Semitism and related channels of cultural reproduction, it is not surprising that the Romanian non-Jewish younger generation still holds anti-Semitic views, despite the fact that the country aspires to occidental democratic values and institutions. Romania's accession to the EU has, though, diminished its anti-Semitic discourses and it is to be hoped that it will continue this alignment to occidental official discourse and legislature.

It is also interesting to note that Romanian Jewish youth, similar for example to their counterparts in Germany, are almost all secular (Kaplan 1994, pp. 77–88). They mainly neglect their Jewishness or, even if they identify with it, tend not to take it seriously. They often lack basic knowledge of traditional Jewish cultural practices, religion and customs. This may become a serious socio-cultural issue concerning not only the Jewish community but also Romanian society at large. This loss of cultural identity by the younger generation indicates that the Romanian Jewish community is in danger of slowly dying out or, much the same thing, of acculturating, losing its cultural roots, traditions and identity as it does. The hostile socio-political context facilitates this process of loss and marginalization, but also, as we shall see in the next section of this chapter, gives rise to opposition and activism.

---

5   Available (in Romanian) in pdf format online from www.cdep.ro/proiecte/2003/400/90/5/leg_pl495_03.pdf (accessed 31 January 2009).
6   See 'Romania 2004' on the Website of the Stephen Roth Institute for the Study of Contemporary Anti-semitism and Racism, www.tau.ac.il/Anti-Semitism/asw2004/romania.html (accessed 31 January 2009).

Female Jewish activism and feminist academia

In this section, Jewish women's activism and its relationship to female feminist academia are examined. These two groupings intersect and overlap, as both promote the same values of equal rights, support, self-consciousness, group consciousness and the demarginalization of the Jewish diaspora in Romania. I also focus on one particular academic personality in Romania, Professor Laura Grünberg, well known for her feminist activism. At the outset, it is worth recalling bell hooks's theory that in every society the marginalized (in this case, the Jewish community in Romania) can use the space of marginalization as a site of 'oppositional political struggle' (hooks 2004, p. 153). Marginal positions within a society can be used as a space for gathering strength of mind and for acting against mainstream discourse. Marginality thus becomes a symbolic site for retaliation, a place from which to fight for freedom. Applying hooks's theory raises the question: in what way do Jewish women in Romania use their marginal socio-cultural location as a space of opposition? How do they carry out their roles as advocates of Jewish identity and of the Jewish community within the diaspora (Kaye 1998, p. 241)? I also investigate how they use this space of marginalization, not to commiserate with each other passively, but to unite and take steps against anti-Semitic discourse, both in Romania and elsewhere.

Diaspora and Romanian Jewish women, after the fall of communism, took steps to strengthen and consolidate the Romanian Jewish community. These women were members of the JDC (American Jewish Joint Distribution Committee). They organized a conference in October 2002, the first ever Jewish women's conference in Romania. Owing to the success of this first event, held for women under the age of thirty-five, another women's seminar was held in May 2003 that included middle-aged women. The themes of the two conferences were rebuilding and strengthening the Jewish (female) community, as well as Jewish identities, traditions and culture, which had been smothered during fifty years of communist rule. The second conference was also a great success and the women who participated learned a great deal, not just about Judaism but also about themselves. According to one of the participants:

> As an active Jewish feminist, I personally feel that many modern Jewish women have a hard time finding a place in a male centered Jewish community. By attending the Women's Seminar, many of these women had their first opportunity to spend a weekend free from the stresses of daily life as a modern middle-aged Jewish woman in Romania.[7]

The JDC continues to work together with FEDROM (the Federation of Jewish Communities in Romania) in order to create a transnational network of Jewish

---

7 'The Many Faces of the Modern Jewish Woman in Romania', on the Website of the American Jewish Joint Distribution Committee, at www.jdc.org/p_ee_rom_ps_build_seminar. html (accessed 11 March 2006 but since removed).

communities. Their common goal is to unite these diaspora communities, helping them interrelate and communicate through well organized, targeted actions: Jewish women's seminars, female counselling groups, and anti-Semitism seminars and conferences, as well as lobbying and discourse challenging anti-Semitism, for example through publications. By organizing these seminars, the women of the JDC, a foreign NGO, have succeeded in creating an expansive network of communication and mutual support between the forty-five Romanian Jewish communities and the worldwide diaspora.

Melanie Kaye argues that it is primarily Jewish women, not men, who support Jewish identity and culture within the diaspora, key concepts in their success being multiculturalism (Kaye 1998, pp. 245–46), transnationalism and connectedness (251). It is these women who have a direct and unmediated connection to everyday reality and its issues; it is they who try to address the issues faced by Jewish women, by building a network at both national and international levels. Such networking helps women preserve and promote their Jewishness by comparing and sharing different cultural and multicultural (international) inputs, issue solutions and experiences. By communicating among themselves, women have the chance to share different experiences and to gain new knowledge from them. Following Kaye's theory, we may conclude that this is exactly what Jewish activist women in Romania have succeeded in building: a network of interconnectedness that strengthens Jewish communities on both a national and a multicultural/transnational/global scale. Furthermore, Jewish women are central in providing support for marginalized, vulnerable social groups such as the aged and the sick, children in orphanages and elderly people in care centres.

The activism of Jewish women's NGOs helps to promote and develop Jewish heritage and culture among both younger and older generations. Through women's seminars, conferences and workshops, through the creation of Websites and the publicizing of their own activities, through care for abandoned children and the sick, and through the organization of special Jewish holiday events, these women build and strengthen Jewish identity and cultural inheritance in Romania. In their seminars, they teach Romanian Jewish women (in particular, mothers) how they can and should face the main issues of anti-Semitism, how they can address the problems of marginalization and, most importantly, how they can educate their own children in the spirit of Jewish identity and traditions.

Initiatives such as these are attempts to (re)discover and preserve Jewishness in the context of an anti-Semitic society. Female Jewish activism in Romania has proved to be an effective tool in fighting mainstream anti-Semitic discourse and related forms of political mobilization. As previously suggested, extreme right-wing parties such as the Greater Romania Party vilify Jewish networks as being a serious threat to the national identity of the Romanian people, and they seek to humiliate and marginalize Jewish people. Nevertheless, these marginalized Jews have found the tools to fight back and to foster and secure their own culture and identity.

A leading figure in the context of this activism is Laura Grünberg. She is the most influential avant-garde figure in Romanian (Jewish) feminism and a leading voice in human rights and women's rights, as well as a advocate powerful on behalf of oppressed women in all walks of life. President of one of the most active feminist NGOs in Romania, AnA, the Society for Feminist Analysis, founded in 1993, and editor of this NGO's journal, *Analyze: Journal for Feminist Studies*, she represents a key link between Jewish female activism and feminist activism in Romanian academia.

As argued above, these forms of activism have common goals and methods of combating discrimination, agitating for equal rights, for equal gender opportunities in all fields, for social and cultural demarginalization, and for the promotion of culture and gender-sensitive education. Laura Grünberg joined UNESCO–CEPES[8] in 1993 and is still an active member of this organization. Since 2004, she has been involved in the organization of a series of international conferences and seminars on topics concerning the establishment in Romanian higher education of a curriculum that is more sensitive to gender issues and human rights, as well as equal employment opportunities in the Balkans. These conferences and seminars have also covered issues of key concern to Jewish feminist activists, for example those from JDC and FEDROM: uniting and strengthening marginalized communities, encouraging self-identity and group identity, promoting culture, and challenging mainstream anti-Semitic discourse.

A second strand of activism consists of the multiculturalism, transnationalism and interconnectedness that Kaye highlights as being vital elements in the overlapping of female Jewish activism and feminist activism at large (Kaye 1998, pp. 245–46). Here, feminist activism spills over the borders of Romania and of Romanian culture, to reach out to the entire central eastern European region, and aiming to create a wide network of multicultural and transnational feminist communities, NGOs and academia as a whole.

The work of UNESCO–CEPES on developing the curriculum within Romanian higher education is relevant here. Grünberg's activism illustrates the need for close cooperation between governmental organizations and NGOs working on human rights and education issues in order to reform higher education in Romania. For UNESCO–CEPES, and for Grünberg's work as an anti-marginalization activist, such reforms include the introduction of online courses on information and communications technology and distance education in all major university centres. Here, government support for the reform of higher education and for the implementation of an adequate legislative framework to support this process is urgently required. It is imperative that the Romanian government agrees, first, that greater sensitivity to human rights is needed in producing the curriculum. Second, financial support is needed for specialists to complete fieldwork on abuses of human rights within contemporary Romanian experience and to present, interpret and disseminate the findings across a range of schoolbooks, university courses and teachers' publications. Third, there is a pressing need

---

8   The United Nations Educational, Scientific and Cultural Organization's European Centre for Higher Education, based in Bucharest.

for training workshops and seminars aimed at advising the designers of school and university curricula how to produce a more inclusive curriculum. This is a relatively novel and unexplored field among Romanian academics, especially in the domain of human rights and gender studies. Most of the time, the salaries of these Romanian specialists do not permit them to cover the accommodation and travel costs involved in attending foreign seminars. These are occasions when the financial support of the Romanian government, or of governmental institutions, would be an extremely useful investment.

Laura Grünberg argues (as does bell hooks) that marginalized, peripheral spaces can and should be used as sites from within which to counteract centralized policy. Whether anti-Semitic, misogynist, homophobic, xenophobic or some combination of all of these, dominant political discourses can be effectively challenged. Success here depends on building unity and forging key alliances. The non-governmental sector can be highly effective in lobbying and influencing political parties, the mass media and legislative debates. Collaborative work by human rights organizations strengthens civil society in Romania and helps to counter xenophobia through the shaping of strong social, political and intellectual communities.

Education is a key institution that needs to be democratized, updated and rethought in Romania, with attention to elaborating a demarginalized curriculum that is sensitive to gender issues and human rights. Education shapes the minds of the younger generation, and this generation, in turn, will be key to building a more democratic future for Romania. Grünberg argues that through education we can rebuild the younger generation, instilling pride in their individual and communal identity, as well as shaping a more progressive, democratic system of common values that challenges hostility and prejudice. These arguments are elaborated in the output of UNESCO–CEPES, such as *Good Practice in Promoting Gender Equality in Higher Education in Central and Eastern Europe* (Grünberg 2001). Grünberg has also published a series of articles and studies focused on human rights and educational issues, most importantly the study entitled *(R)evolutions in Feminist Sociology: Theoretical Perspectives, Romanian Contexts* (Grünberg 2002). This study espouses similar goals to those of Jewish women's organizations in Romania (human rights, pride in identity and culture, demarginalization). Lastly, Grünberg calls for political involvement and activism on the part of the public as a whole.

Conclusion

The intersection between Jewish female activism and feminist academia in Romania is clear. The two have similar agendas: lobbying against marginalization, supporting equal rights, self-sufficiency and empowerment, social welfare and human dignity. It is alarming, though, that the Jewish community is diminishing and possibly dying out in Romania, not only demographically but also culturally. Jewish young people are giving up their culture and, because of the hostile atmosphere in Romania, many Jews are emigrating. Will the foreign and national NGOs be able to halt these processes? Will the Jewish community be able to rebuild and maintain its cultural identity, in spite of the so-called 'dissident' younger generation? Will they be able to rediscover, keep and promote their rich culture and traditions in the anti-Semitic atmosphere of present-day Romania? Or will in fact the general homophobia and anti-Semitism decline now that Romania has joined the EU? Political discourses, after all, may change abruptly in order to conform to imposed agendas (such as that of the EU).

However, the evidence suggests that deep convictions and the genuine socio-political and legislative change they should trigger will probably fail to materialize, even though Romania has joined the EU. At most, a gradual change will occur, but owing to the deep-rootedness of sexist, homophobic and anti-Semitic discourses in today's Romanian society, it may take years, even decades, to alter the status quo. Jewish female activists face huge challenges. Still, their deep determination and mutual support, together with pressure from the 'top-down policy' of international and pan-European institutions, may well prove effective in shifting entrenched Romanian attitudes. Continued action by these marginalized socio-cultural communities, and continued anti-Semitism, are certain to remain key features of Romanian society in the future.

Works cited

Burkitt, J. (1999) *Bodies of Thought: Embodiment, Identity and Modernity*. London, Sage.

de Beauvoir, S. (1988) *The Second Sex*. London, Picador.

Grünberg, L. (2001) *Studies on Higher Education: Good Practice in Promoting Gender Equality in Higher Education in Central and Eastern Europe*. Bucharest, UNESCO–CEPES. Available at www.cepes.ro/publications/pdf/good_practice.pdf (accessed 31 January 2009).

—— (2002) *(R)evolutions in Feminist Sociology: Theoretical Perspectives, Romanian Contexts*. Bucharest, Polirom.

hooks, b. (2004) 'Choosing the Margin as a Space of Radical Openness'. In: Harding, S. ed. *The Feminist Standpoint Theory Reader: Intellectual and Political Controversies*. New York, Routledge, pp. 153–59.

Kaplan, M. (1994) 'What Is "Religion" among Jews in Contemporary Germany'. In: Gilman, S. L. and Remmler, K. eds. *Jewish Culture in Germany: Life and Literature since 1989*. New York, New York University Press.

Katz, M. M. (2002) *Anti-Semitism in Romania. 2002 Report*. Bucharest, Romanian Jewish Community. Available at http://www.romanianjewish.org/en/antisemitism_in_romania_02.html#i1 (accessed 31 January 2009).

Kaye, M. (1998) 'Diasporism, Feminism and Coalition'. In: Swartz, S. S. and Wolfe, M. eds. *From Memory to Transformation: Jewish Women's Voices*. London, Second Story Press.

Lewitt, L. (1997) *Jews and Feminism: The Ambivalent Search for Home*. New York, Routledge.

Manascu, C. and Leib, M. (2006) *6 secole de convietuire. Din istoria comunitatilor evreiesti din Romania* [*6 Centuries of Coexistence. Pages from the History of the Jewish Communities in Romania*]. Bucharest, Romanian Jewish Community. Available at www.romanianjewish. org/ro/fedrom_02.html (accessed 13 March 2006).

Miller, N. K. (1991) 'Dreaming, Dancing and the Changing Locations of Feminist Criticism'. In: Miller, N. K. *Getting Personal: Feminist Occasions and Other Autobiographical Acts*. New York, Routledge.

Slavova, K. (2006) 'After the Future: The Paradoxes of Communism and Postfeminism'. Proceedings of the conference Migrating Feminisms (unpublished), Central European University, Budapest, 27 January.
Tirosh-Rotshield, H. (1994) '"Dare to Know": Feminism and the Discipline of Jewish Philosophy'. In: Davidman, L. and Tenenbaum, S. eds. *Feminist Perspectives on Jewish Studies*. New Haven. CT, Yale University Press.

CHAPTER 4

Racism, (neo-)colonialism and social justice: the struggle for the soul of the Romani movement in post-socialist Europe

Nidhi Trehan and Angéla Kóczé

'It's not of air and eternity, evil isn't; it's of earth; it's physical, a disjointedness between our bodies and our souls. Evil is inanely corporeal, humans causing one another pain, no more no less....'

'The real thing about evil,' said the Witch at the doorway, 'isn't any of what you said. You figure out one side of it – the human side, say – and the eternal side goes into the shadow. Or vice versa. It's like the old saw: What does a dragon in its shell look like? Well no one can ever tell, for as you break the shell to see, the dragon is no longer in its shell. The real disaster of this inquiry is that it is the nature of evil to be secret.' (Maguire, *Wicked*, 1995)

What can the critical-theoretical framework of postcolonial studies offer to the study of contemporary Romani oppression, especially the study of oppression *within* the 'movement' for the equal rights of Romani Europeans? In this chapter, we employ the works of a number of critics, many of them influenced by postcolonial theories, in order to interrogate the diffuse forces of power and to show how these operate within the 'Roma rights' movement as a means of explaining the presence of racialized hierarchies and neo-colonial dynamics. In focusing on the repercussions for legitimacy, representation and autonomy in the movement, empirical data from post-socialist Europe[1] are combined with original theoretical insights about 'whiteness' and 'race' to offer a deeper understanding of the complexities of Romani emancipation in the multiply colonized space of the region.

---

1 In this chapter, we define 'post-socialist Europe' as consisting of those central and eastern European countries that have joined the European Union (EU) or are currently seeking membership. These countries all practised diverse forms of socialism prior to the 'transition' beginning in the late 1980s and early 1990s.

Romani subalterity: the burden of being the 'other'

The complexity and range of racism that Romani people, or, more importantly, people *perceived* to be Roma, face in contemporary Europe have begun to be critically explored in recent years. From the British Isles to the Balkans, if you are marked as being Romani (or 'Gypsy'), there is little respite from the violence that envelops you – physical, symbolic, epistemic – as a consequence of persistent and deeply embedded anti-Gypsyism within European cultural enclaves (Clark 2004; Hancock 2002; Heuss 2000; Trehan 2009; Zoltan 2006). Although anti-Gypsyism is persistent in both eastern and western Europe, there are significant differences in how Romani populations have been 'constructed', with the result that policy trajectories themselves reflect this separation.[2] For the purposes of this chapter, which focuses on paradoxical developments in the movement for the rights of Romanies, we restrict ourselves to discussing phenomena affecting post-socialist European states, since it is in this region that the confluence of demographics (large, concentrated Romani communities), the influence of established human rights non-governmental organizations (NGOs) and the large number of official projects (including public–private partnerships) targeting Romani communities, like the Decade of Roma Inclusion, have become most salient.[3]

The Romani subaltern – still to be fully acknowledged in Europe – has been subjected to the disciplinary exigencies of 'infra-humanity':[4] in this particular case, Romanies and their sheer invisibility *as humans* within European discursive and social fabrics, from history books to everyday workplaces. Instead, where you will find Romani people, real or fictitious, will be in the minds of Europeans who have 'othered' them, proffering them a kind of distorted visibility (Clark 2004; Hancock 1997; Heuss 2000).[5] In today's Europe (both 'western' and

---

2 For an excellent piece on how discourses on Roma can be dissonant (as well as deceptive) within the contemporary EU context, see Simhandl (2006). Simhandl suggests that the dichotomy within EU member states between 'western Gypsies and travellers' and 'eastern Roma' enables Romani populations residing in the '"old" Member States to be rendered invisible' and, moreover, reduces Roma to mere political objects. She exhorts European policy-makers to undergo critical self-reflection as a prerequisite to future shifts in discursive practices and policies (109–10).
3 The key institutional founders of the Decade of Romani Inclusion (2005–15), which covers nine countries in central and eastern Europe, are the Open Society Institute, the EU, the World Bank, and the United Nations Development Programme; in addition, affiliated NGOs participate in the implementation of the Decade's programmes, whose express purpose is to foster 'Romani integration' into mainstream European society through an ambitious array of initiatives in the fields of education, employment, health and housing, thus committing 'governments to take into account the other core issues of poverty, discrimination, and gender mainstreaming'. For further details, see www.romadecade.org.
4 Social theorist Paul Gilroy has used this term in reference to both the black Atlantic diaspora and the 'enemy' detainees in Guantanamo Bay (Cuba) at the US military base (Gilroy 2004).
5 The 'banality of racism' towards Roma is ubiquitous in contemporary 'postmodern', 'postcolonial' Europe. A white European academic who completed a doctorate from the University

'eastern' halves), and within this falsely constructed and vigorously recycled *imaginarium*, Romani people occupy varying paradoxical positions, ranging from exotic dancers and wedding musicians to 'annoying' beggars, welfare dependants, prostitutes and thieves.

Within the previously socialist east European countries, this essentialized iconography of deviance and otherness was contained to some extent by an all-pervasive state which disavowed open displays of ethnicity, and which celebrated 'workers' solidarity' – at least rhetorically – across ethnic lines. By minimizing various cultural markers such as language, clothing and even seasonal economic migration, the state offered possibilities for 'proletarianization' through socio-economic integration. You could be a good Bulgarian, a good Hungarian, a good Slovak, a good comrade – even if you were an 'inferior Gypsy'. There was a place for you at the common table, although your seat might be a bit rickety and your cloth napkin tattered beyond repair.

The 'civilizing mission' of the Habsburgs

Attempts to assimilate Romani communities in central Europe date back to the times of the Habsburg Empire's dual monarchy. The Austro-Hungarian Empire in the late eighteenth century covered present-day Austria, Hungary, parts of Italy, the Czech Republic, Slovakia, southern Poland and Ukraine, the Banat and Transylvania (Romania), Slovenia, Croatia, Bosnia and northern Serbia: huge swathes of territory, in which many Romani communities lived. However, the 'civilizing mission' of Empress Maria Theresa and her son, Emperor Joseph II, referred to as an 'enlightened absolutist' by some historians, resulted in far more draconian measures towards her Romani subjects than the communist state enacted. The Habsburgs' experiments with assimilating Roma were essentially a series of regulatory decrees over the thirty years from 1753 to 1783. Initially, these measures appeared inclusive in nature, for example the provision of land for Romani settlement, the permission to conduct artisan trades and the opening up of guild membership to Roma. In addition, Romanies were to be called 'new Hungarians' or 'new peasants', the use of the term 'Gypsy' being discouraged. Nonetheless, the decrees became progressively harsher and, in 1772, mandatory military service was enacted for all Romani males above the age of sixteen, while Romanes, the mother tongue, was prohibited, along with the wearing of traditional dress, marriage among Roma and even the custody of children (Kállai

---

of London, and a person who specializes in gender studies, told one of the co-authors of this chapter that 'Gypsies are dirty and disgusting', thus not only denigrating the very people whose movement she was researching, but further confirming how deeply entrenched and common these biases are, even within 'progressive' intellectual circles, in contemporary Europe. Another colleague, a white doctoral student from south-eastern Europe, made an ironic 'joke' about the recent accession to the EU of two new Balkan countries, commenting dryly, 'well, of course I know about Gypsies in the Balkans – my research focuses on crime!'

and Törzsök 2000, pp. 9–11; Kemény 2005, pp. 15–17).[6] Thus, a conscious effort was made on the part of the Habsburgs to eliminate Romani identity from Austro-Hungarian lands, even as the Romani body was 'salvaged' and became a site of colonization.[7] This 'civilizing mission' has strong resonances with the British colonial mindset in such places as the United States and New South Wales (Australia), where indigenous children underwent forcible removal from their families and were placed in foster care (usually day and boarding schools) for the express purpose of 'becoming civilized', with emphasis being placed on their becoming 'good Christians', but without concern for the corresponding negation of their core identity and beliefs (Buti 2004).[8] Fortunately for some Romani families living under Habsburg rule, the local authorities responsible for the implementation of the decrees did not fully comply with the new regulations. Investing in Romani settlement was not necessarily felt to be a desirable objective, guild membership for Roma was rejected by members who feared competition from Romani artisans, and the social conflicts and financial costs surrounding the removal of Romani children from their families and placement in foster homes proved to be a significant deterrent. The royal courts verified these resolutions, but governing councils simply chose not to implement them in their local areas. Thus, Romani assimilation and cultural negation remained a 'failed experiment', mired at the level of legislative declaration: by the late 1780s, the 'Romani issue' was no longer of official interest to the Habsburgs and it disappeared from the imperial agenda with the closure of the Department of Gypsy Affairs in 1787 (Kemény 2005, pp. 15–17). Nonetheless, the policies of the time reflected the pervasive belief in Romani 'deviance' and 'inferiority' within Austro-Hungarian society, a belief that continues to have repercussions for Romani communities as pernicious narratives of 'Gypsy otherness' reproduce themselves in contemporary European society.[9] These 'civilizing' impulses towards Romanies have historically been coupled with broader and diffuse relations of neo-colonialism with respect to the central east European region, relations that are covered in further detail later in this chapter; first, however, some insight is needed into the contemporary realities of Romani life.

6　Romani children were to be placed in foster homes with peasant families from the age of four, and the counties would pay the farmers directly for their maintenance costs. Many Romani children ran away and ultimately found their way back to their own families.

7　In some areas of Europe, it was a crime merely to be a Gypsy/Romani, and there harsh punishments were put in place (including the death penalty) in order to dissuade Roma from even entering these lands. Thus, the Habsburgs were perhaps relatively 'enlightened' among their contemporaries, as they at least accepted the corporeal humanity of Roma, despite Romani culture being viewed as alien, deeply flawed and in need of 'civilizing'.

8　Boarding schools for Native American children had become more common in the United States by the late 1870s, ensuring the children's isolation from the 'contaminating' influences of their own peoples (Buti 2004).

9　In Hungary today, less than 15 per cent of Romanies speak a dialect of the Romani language, which can be attributed in part to the antipathy towards that language during the time of the Habsburgs.

The post-socialist setting in Europe

There are an estimated six million citizens of Romani ethnicity in the post-socialist countries of Europe today.[10] These Romani communities are highly diverse, both linguistically and culturally, as a result of different historical narratives. The levels of assimilation or integration within eastern European societies also vary according to community background and state policies directed at them. Nonetheless, taken as a whole, Romani citizens of these states comprise the most marginalized peoples in the region: more than 50 per cent are officially unemployed, and in some so-called 'compact communities' – a polite socio-logical euphemism for segregated settlements – the proportion hovers at around 99 per cent. By contrast, under state socialist regimes, Romanies had relative income security and by the 1980s, in countries such as Hungary, employment rates for Romani men were nearing ratios comparable to those of other citizens. As John Wrench of the European Union's Monitoring Centre on Racism and Xenophobia (EUMC) has noted, the integration of Romanies into the larger social fabric – primarily through educational integration – has become an avowed priority for successive governments throughout the region (Wrench 2006).

One response to rising hostility and xenophobia in the region, both officially and in public discourse, has been the formation of a collective political consciousness among diverse groups of Roma. Let us take the example here of post-socialist Hungary, widely recognized among European policy-makers for its liberal and enlightened policies on minorities. The myriad number of Romani cultural associations (some of them active since the 1980s) and of development and human rights NGOs (primarily launched in the mid-1990s), the many media initiatives whose purpose it has been to raise the visibility of the Romani community, as well as the vast network of bureaucratic institutions resulting from Hungary's 'pro-minorities' legislation in the early 1990s – all of this has meant that the socio-political activities surrounding Romani Hungarians has generated an elite class of Hungarians, some of whom are Romanies themselves, whose primary task has been to govern and manage the growing Romani minority (Kovats 1998, 2003; Trehan 2006b).

---

10   This figure is based on data gathered primarily from NGOs, and does not represent official government statistics on the Romani population, which are considerably lower, as a result of strong stigma (including internalized stigmatization) attached to Romani identity. Romani ethnicity is a complex construction and, like other ethnicities, a fluid phenomenon. Moreover, people with just one Romani parent may self-identify in complex ways, depending on various factors, including age (generational belonging) and community setting. For example, a popular female rap singer in Hungary, Fatima, of the band Fekete Vonat ('Black Train'), has an Arab (Egyptian) father and a Romani mother. Few studies have been done in this area; suffice to say that, contrary to popular mythology, Romani communities are not hermetically sealed, despite the fact that spatial segregation is pronounced (and, indeed, has been on the rise since the collapse of the eastern European socialist regimes).

The emergence of the 'Roma rights movement' and ideology

In the early days of 'transition', in the late 1980s, Romani activists, along with liberal dissidents in the newly emerging civil rights movement for Roma, began to challenge the vilification of Roma as belonging to a 'criminal subculture' and to contest the prevalent 'Gypsy problem' discourse by exposing discrimination and racism on the part of both private actors and the state. While the 'Gypsy problem' discourse tends to construct the problems that Roma experience (unemployment, poverty and other manifestations of social exclusion) as essentialized by-products of their own culture (e.g. Romanies are inherently 'socially unadaptable' and intellectually deficient), the 'Roma rights' discourse challenges this characterization by identifying racism and discrimination as being at the root of the problems Roma face (Kohn 1995; Trehan 2009). Furthermore, the 'Roma rights' movement, similar to other movements for the rights of subaltern communities, seeks to ameliorate these negative social phenomena, primarily, though not exclusively, through legal means (Bukovská 2006; Trehan 2006b; Woodiwiss 2006). Issues of socio-economic justice, if addressed at all, are generally marginal to this discourse, though in the late 1990s an emphasis on the 'extreme poverty'[11] of Romani communities surfaced, resulting in a greater appreciation of the need to advance their socio-economic rights. More recently, this has translated into an emphasis on housing rights as a result of the Romani evictions crisis.[12] It is worth noting that the housing rights agenda among Romani activists is not a new phenomenon, being one of the key issues around which early indigenous formations for social justice were developed, in the 1980s (for example, the Anti-Ghetto Committee, led by Hungarian Romani activist Aladár Horváth in the north-east of the country), nearly a decade before the emergence of western 'human rights entrepreneurs'.[13] Nonetheless, rarely do Romani NGO activists make explicit the underlying connection between the embrace of neo-liberal policies in post-socialist Europe since the late 1980s, including various forms of economic 'shock therapies', and increasing rates of housing evictions, which have deepened social exclusion (Trehan 2009).

Viewing the 'movement' as similar to the black civil rights movement in the United States or the anti-apartheid movement in South Africa is potentially misleading. This has to do with several factors relating to the specific nature of power and political organization in contemporary Europe, particularly in

---

11   This is a term used by international multilateral institutions such as the United Nations and the Council of Europe. International financial institutions such as the World Bank and the International Bank for Reconstruction and Development have begun to take an active interest in European Roma. See, for example, Ringold *et al.* (2003). In 2005, several multilateral institutions began the joint initiative Decade of Roma Inclusion (see note 3, p. 51) and devised national action programmes.
12   See 'Roma and Travellers Project', on the Website of the Centre on Housing Rights and Evictions (COHRE), www.cohre.org/view_page.php?page_id=191 (accessed 20 January 2009).
13   This is a term adopted from H. Becker's concept of the 'moral entrepreneur'. See Trehan (2009).

post-socialist countries, which have connections to global forces that inevitably impinge on the current trajectory of the transnational movement for Roma rights (Guilhot 2005; Ost 2005; Trehan 2001). Unlike these other movements, the Roma rights movement emerged at a time of overwhelming neo-liberal policy consensus in post-socialist Europe, and one corollary of this development, as we will show, has been the *marketization* of human rights, through the interventions of human rights entrepreneurs, particularly those affiliated with George Soros's Open Society Institute.

(Neo-)colonialism, east European 'backwardness' and Romani emancipation?

> The essence of neo-colonialism is that the State which is subject to it is, in theory, independent and has all the outward trappings of international sovereignty. In reality its economic system and thus its political policy is directed from the outside. (Nkrumah 1965)

Post-socialist central and eastern Europe as a region can be viewed as a colonized space marked by the profound influence of global capitalist forces based in western capitals, and by the academic and institutional hegemony of the west. This dominance is replicated in the movement for the human rights of Roma, which has been overrun by the influence of neo-liberal policy regimes over the past decade (Chen and Churchill 2005; Gowan 1996; Wessely 1996). Furthermore, neo-colonial forces operate at the macro-institutional level of society: academia, law, policy-making. In this context, the region is often conceived of as being implicitly 'backward' and in need of assistance by western countries.[14] Wessely cites Norbert Elias's path-breaking 1978 study *The Civilizing Process*, in which Elias asserts that the concept of civilization 'sums up everything in which Western society of the last two or three centuries believes itself superior to earlier societies or "more primitive" contemporary ones' (Elias 1978, quoted in Wessely 1996, p. 13). Moreover, Elias points out the divergence in the notion of 'civilization', used by western nations such as France and Britain, as a self-confident appellation for their national identity, and

---

14 Within Britain itself, the (post)imperial landscape is marked by a curious imperial legacy, an almost incontrovertible belief that Britain 'has got multiculturalism right'. Particularly in comparison with continental Europe, liberal British policy-makers and intellectuals emphasize this aspect of contemporary (read 'progressive') Britishness, which they imply is superior to that on the continent (in terms of integration of immigrants). Furthermore, continental Europeans, particularly those who reside in south-eastern Europe, are framed as people suffering from an atavistic 'backwardness', or what the historian Maria Todorova (1997) has termed 'Balkanism'. It remains to be explored how the orientalist view of Romanies (what some prominent Romani scholars such as Ian Hancock and Ken Lee have termed 'Gypsylorism') and Balkanism are interwoven, and to what extent this creates a double burden of 'otherness' for Romani subjects.

that of *Kultur*, used initially in Germany and then subsequently adopted by all central European peoples 'to define and assert the identity of nations lacking stable boundaries and the institutions of civil society' (Wessely 1996, p. 13). This dichotomy between civilization and *Kultur* offers an intriguing clue as to why Romanies themselves have been perceived differently in various parts of the region, and as to how state policy continues to reflect these differences at the national level, despite the 'civilizing' tendencies vis-à-vis Roma that are pervasive throughout Europe today.

It is also important to contextualize the terms 'colonialism' and 'post-colonialism' with regard to the Romani movement. The application of the term 'colonialism' can be understood in a broader sense, not just as a specific conquest or event in the past, but as an ongoing exercise of economic, military and political power by stronger states and groups over weaker ones. The 'colony' as such is internal to the state, comprising subaltern classes and those human subjects perceived to be 'infrahuman'. Furthermore, if we view colonialism as a way of maintaining asymmetrical relations of economic and political power (in the same way as Edward Said talks about 'Orientalism' as deploying a variety of strategies whose common factor is the resultant position of superiority for westerners vis-à-vis the 'Orient'), then there can be no doubting the existence of a neo-colonialist attitude in relation to Romani activism within the European political landscape today.

In subsequent sections of this chapter, the political conditions of Romani communities will be explored, along with their complex, intertwined and symbiotic relationship with the human rights elite. We aim to interrogate the postcolonial realities of Romani advocacy, realities characterized by increasingly problematic questions of agency, subjectivity and the commodification of Romani culture, along with core issues of power and justice. Adopting Spivak's classic language, we will ask: can the Romani subaltern speak? Can the Romani subject finally create a reality for herself, and can she speak on her own behalf?

Romani subalterity –
objectification and racialized hierarchies within the movement

A discussion of postcolonial racism and social justice *within* the Romani civil rights arena entails a meticulous engagement with various taboos that are characteristic of internal oppression mechanisms within the movement – with the 'silences' that permeate its discourse, much of which is exercised by non-Romani human rights entrepreneurs, but also by those Roma who hold power and who, in many cases, have been installed in these power positions by their non-Romani patrons. Several aspects critical to the internal power dynamics within the Romani movement have not been exposed and are clearly being neglected by a self-perpetuating power structure. Many non-Romani human rights advocates working in the sphere of 'Roma rights' are convinced that they are not racist. Applying Frantz Fanon's approach to racism in our research, we might ask the same question as he did:

what does racism do to people? Fanon's own answer was brief: racism objectifies (Fanon 1965). Here, he was following Aimé Césaire, who had previously equated colonialism with what he called 'thingification': the process by which the subjects of colonialism are reduced over time to the status of mere objects (Césaire 2000, p. 21). This concept of objectification is a more complex process than merely conceiving of someone as an object. As Richard Schmitt argues:

> *Objectification* is not best understood either as turning persons into things, or as depriving them of their freedom, but as a carefully orchestrated and systemic refusal of genuinely human relationship. (Schmitt 1996, p. 36)

Objectification is visible and pervasive in Romani affairs, and is further intensified by the dispossessed economic status of Roma and the asymmetrical relations within broader society that are its result. And, as we shall see, diffuse and pernicious racist practices, at least some of which can be viewed as colonial techniques, can be identified even within the Romani civil rights movement and have emerged over the course of our research.

One of the unintentional outcomes of the work of pro-Roma human rights organizations, we want to suggest, has been the objectification of Romani representatives by human rights entrepreneurs. Romani critics claim that rather than being received as active participants in the human rights movement, they have become subjects for the human rights work of others – a tiny number of Romani elites notwithstanding – and have frequently been treated as 'experiments' in the hands of legal professionals and international human rights entrepreneurs. Put succinctly by Blanka Kozma, 'we are nothing but a project to them'.[15] In a rare reflexive piece on the interventions of legal professionals in the arena, human rights lawyer Barbora Bukovská (2006) notes that:

> litigation concentrates [the] agenda in the hands of elites – lawyers; victims [who] are often uneducated with little or no understanding of the law assume a subordinated position with regard to tactics and strategy after human rights advocates decide on litigation. Once victims are confronted with a mysterious legal procedure and complicated legal language, their 'fate is no longer in their hands' as advocates as specialists automatically take over their problems. (Quoted in Trehan 2009, p. 208)

The above insight about the imbalance of power in the relationship between (usually non-Romani) lawyers and their Romani clients emphasizes the subaltern position of Romani human rights victims,[16] who, from the outset of

---

15   Blanka Kozma, interview material from 1999, quoted in Trehan (2009, p. 178). She also mentioned how difficult it was for Roma in Hungary to assess 'who are our genuine friends, and who are the parasites'.

16   The term 'victim' can be problematized; however, it is used here generically in reference to a person suffering from a human rights abuse. There is a large literature on the subject of 'victims' and victims' agency, but this is beyond the scope of this chapter.

legal procedures taken up on their behalf, often initiated by an NGO lawyer or researcher seeking out a victim for a specific test case for 'impact litigation' purposes, exercise little control over the outcome of proceedings, after which time many will continue to live their lives in extreme poverty and exclusion. Indeed, some Romanies even risk becoming local or national scapegoats if there is a backlash as a result of litigation procedures. This is another area where, as Bukovská (2006) correctly points out, there is a current lack of ethical responsibility on the part of human rights entrepreneurs in the region, since even basic respect for the victims is often missing during case proceedings, and very little follow-up is conducted afterwards.

Two characteristic practices of objectification mentioned by Fanon (1965) from his own experience in colonial French Algeria are worth mentioning here in relation to the Romani movement:

(1) *Infantilization.* Roma are perceived to be, and are thus treated as, children. Fanon refers to the example of the black French: it was assumed by the dominant (white) group that they would be incapable of gaining mastery of the French language. Similarly, many Romani activists are patronized by non-Roma in the movement, who assume that the former are not as capable as the latter of professional work. Even the co-author of this chapter, Angéla Kóczé, who has worked in the past for the Brussels-based NGO the European Roma Information Office (ERIO), has experienced the same kind of infantilization by non-Roma working on Romani issues. If we take a closer look at the staff composition of leading development or human rights organizations working in the sphere of Romani interests, it is still rare, well over a decade since the movement was first established, for a Romani person to be in a senior management position. This is the proverbial elephant in the drawing room: the one everyone notices, but also the one we are all careful to ignore.

(2) *Denigration.* As Fanon indicated in his research, it is nearly always assumed that members of various colonized groups are 'defective'. Likewise, leading members of the Romani community who have fallen out of favour with the established power structure have been accused of being criminals or thieves, sometimes with the assistance of the same Roma who are beneficiaries of their patronage. Postcolonial theorist Leela Gandhi (1998), among others, has referred to the existence of a tension between colonizer and colonized and to the mutual dependency and desire contained within this relationship; this tension surely merits further exploration in connection to Romani 'yes men' or 'uncle Toms'. Further, since the funding for Romani projects generally rests in the hands of philanthropic benefactors and governments, there is a tendency not to raise public dissent. The aforementioned character attacks on outspoken Roma who have crossed this invisible line serve to marginalize them within the movement, similarly serving to stifle dissent. In short, there continues to be a deep denial of these 'silenced' narratives and insights, as well as a surreptitious process of auto-censorship, and both of these deserve further analysis in order to better our understanding of the dynamics of internalized oppression within the movement itself.

The story of Melinda

We offer the narrative here of a Romani NGO executive, 'Melinda',[17] who was confronted directly with the (neo-)colonial dynamics of the NGO sector as she sought to advance the rights and visibility of her people. Although the experience damaged her life, perhaps irreparably, it enabled her to understand the colonial structure which is generated around the lives of Romani subalterns, and which serves to prove their 'incapacity', thereby making them fulfil their 'inferior fate' in a way that is scripted by a broader white power structure.

Melinda began her work as the executive director of a newly founded strategic organization in the Romani civil rights movement, and very soon began to confront the forces of structural exclusion. In the first place, she was hired with a lower starting salary than other directors of similar advocacy-type organizations. When she mentioned this to her superiors, she was told by one of the key non-Romani funders that she should be happy that, as an east European Romani woman, she was selected to work for such an organization. The message was clear: she should 'know her place' and not create such a fuss; moreover, she should appreciate their enormous efforts to provide her with such an opportunity in the first place. Secondly, the founders of the organization and financiers designed an organizational structure which resulted in corrosive relations among the staff. By offering two full-time positions within a small office – the executive and the deputy director positions, along with a part-time administrator – they laid the ground for a strong rivalry between the two key NGO staff, both of whom were Roma. In organizations of this size, having two directorial posts tends to generate conflict rather than cooperation, and the case of this particular NGO was not an exception. Melinda believed there were certain intentions behind this, but could not fully comprehend why she did not revolt against it at the time. As she informed one co-author of this chapter, 'my tragedy was paved structurally and very little effort was needed to destroy me'.

Melinda's problems at work were compounded by a relatively low salary. Basically, by the end of every month, she scarcely had money for food or medicine for her family (she was the main breadwinner); moreover, she was working in a city (indeed country) where she had no relatives or friends, and therefore no support network. Nonetheless, when viewed from the outside, Melinda was a high-profile professional employed by an international NGO, and presumably had enough financial means to maintain her family life. She worked on a daily basis with high-ranking officers and politicians in order to persuade them to work on the issue of the social and economic integration of Roma. She was careful to demonstrate articulacy in both oral and written presentation skills and, in addition, ensure that her physical appearance and style were sophisticated enough to challenge the various biases and prejudices towards Roma. In the meantime, she sacrificed her family's happiness to a large degree, as she took

---

17 'Melinda' is a pseudonym.

them to an alien environment where they did not speak the local language; her spouse was unable to obtain work and her son was unable to enjoy spending significant time with her.

Under these circumstances, she needed to take out some money (€50–€100) at the end of each month from the organization's budget in order to survive and to pay for regular childcare. This money was accounted for in bookkeeping, although she admitted she was rather ashamed to report this to the board (she did inform one member of the board whom she trusted, and he was made aware of these ongoing transactions). She used to travel and attend conferences on the weekends without financial compensation.

One summer, when her son needed to have surgery, she decided to take him to her home country in order have the operation, as the medical fees were far more affordable. While in the hospital, she rang her colleagues in the office, and they began to berate her, talking to her as if she was a criminal: they demanded that she stop using the office telephone and bank card. They informed her that, in her absence, they had gone through the office bookkeeping and scrutinized all her expense receipts and bills, and had come to the conclusion that she had misused office money. Subsequently, it emerged that they had prepared an internal report, which they sent to donors, board members and other influential actors in order to destroy her professional reputation and place doubts on her integrity, thereby engineering her dismissal from the post. Needless to say, she was shocked by this attack and became psychologically shattered. Instead of hiring a lawyer to start a legal procedure against her colleagues for violating her personal integrity, she began to internalize – as many subalterns do – all the accusations levelled against her. For its part, the board did not recognize the complex nature of the case, with all the mitigating circumstances mentioned above. On the one hand, it was an underhanded attempt to overtake the directorship from her at a time when she was in a vulnerable position and, indeed, not even in the country. On the other hand, besides her own administrative failures, she was embedded in a colonial organizational structure without adequate administrative and financial support, and this only served to solidify the power structure's own expectation of a subaltern unable to accomplish a professional job.

These unconscious and sometimes unspoken assumptions by colonizers can devastate the life of subalterns and work as powerful 'self-fulfilling prophecies'. It took her over five months to be able to talk about the events to her close friends and family members. She did not retain enough self-esteem and mental strength to challenge the organization legally and the people who had worked behind her back to destroy her professional standing. After she left the organization, the board hired a Romani man to be her successor. He was offered a significantly higher salary than she had received and, in addition, the organizational structure of the office was modified. While, on the one hand, she takes comfort in the fact that the board eventually recognized some structural issues which were internally divisive, Melinda feels that she has 'paid' for this belated acknowledgement with her own dignity, which has been damaged and for which she has never been compensated. The case of Melinda, as with other Romani NGO workers, has been instructive in pointing out how broader ideological agendas obscure the reality of (neo-)colonial relations within the movement for the civil rights of Roma.

The hegemony of human rights entrepreneurs and the rise of neo-liberal agendas

In attempting to make sense of and explain the 'neo-liberal human rights' approach to the contemporary Romani rights movement in post-socialist Europe, the following questions need to be addressed.

- How is the neo-liberal human rights approach manifested in the 'Romani rights' movement?
- What order is it (re)producing and whose interests does it reflect?
- What are its consequences, and are there alternatives to its current trajectory?

In employing the term 'neo-liberal human rights', we refer to the phenomenon whereby human rights concerns and campaigning operate within a global capitalist system, and thus – perhaps unwittingly – become an appendage of the global neo-liberal economic order (Chen and Churchill 2005; Guilhot 2005; Trehan 2009). More than any other single philanthropist, Hungarian-American billionaire George Soros has been responsible for the support and promotion of Romani NGO initiatives through the work of the Open Society Institute (OSI), a global network of foundations.[18] The organizations funded and supported by the OSI currently form the backbone of the 'movement' for the rights of Romani peoples in post-socialist Europe. Notwithstanding the OSI's generous support of numerous progressive campaigns globally, including HIV/AIDS prevention and the rebuilding of democracy in the United States, we would suggest that the Romani civil rights struggle to date has tended to reveal unintended consequences – in this particular case, the creation of hierarchies and divisiveness within the movement – that are characteristic of utopian approaches within the global NGO sphere today. We want to argue (and other scholars concur) that the OSI, in attempting to create an 'open society' in post-socialist Europe, in fact promotes a policy agenda based on particular ideological frameworks that have had a powerful impact on civil society in the region (Guilhot 2005; Trehan 2009). This is all the more evident in the OSI's activities, which focus on the human rights and development of subaltern Romani communities in post-socialist Europe precisely because of the asymmetrical relations of power between Roma and non-Roma.

To a large extent, the neo-liberal approach works hand in glove with the dominant discourse on 'civil society' in eastern Europe, which began to permeate the

---

18   The writings of Popper and Hayek were strong influences upon Soros, who was a student of Popper's at the London School of Economics. See Guilhot (2005) for further details on Soros's ideological development. See www.soros.org for further details on the work of the Open Society Institute and its affiliates.

NGO sector in the early 1990s.[19] The notable absence of alternative trajectories to this approach has been a result of the ideological and material dominance of American epistemic communities and human rights networks in the region throughout the 1990s (Trehan 2006a). There were several cogent reasons why the former dissidents of post-socialist states believed they were compelled to adopt a language and philosophy of human rights commensurate with their Euro-Atlantic donor networks – and why they did so, even when they had grave doubts about the motives of their western benefactors, with only minimal resistance to the prevalent neo-liberal paradigm of human rights. Dimitrina Petrova, a Bulgarian philosopher and human rights advocate, was the director of the European Roma Rights Centre – the pre-eminent NGO in the field – for over a decade from its inception from 1996 until December 2006. She accounts for the relative silence of eastern European human rights activists during the time of the NATO bombing campaign in Kosovo[20] with the following rationale:

> three additional factors overwhelmed the judgment of human rights organiza-tions in eastern Europe. First, eastern European states had opted for NATO membership. The human rights community in these countries was therefore afraid of compromising their respective national chances of being admitted to the alliance if they criticized NATO. Second, *the very status and jobs of most human rights activists were made possible by the generous support of Western, par-ticularly American, donors. Without their continued support, the future of the human rights movement would be uncertain.* Third, the human rights community in our region was caught in the sinking ship of cold war logic. Human rights activists feared that whatever they said would immediately place them in one of two camps – for or against NATO. If one is against NATO, one sides with Russia and China and therefore is an enemy to democracy. (Petrova 1999, quoted in Trehan 2009, p. 201, emphasis added)

Petrova notes the 'lack of leadership' from established NGOs in the west, whose response to the bombing campaign was muted at best (Petrova 1999). Thus, the feeling of powerlessness and lack of agency on the part of eastern European activists, as well as their inability to construct alternative discourses and practices of human rights, have resulted in an implicit acceptance of the model of human rights informed by the contemporary neo-liberal ethos (Trehan 2006a). Aware of their financial dependence on American-based foundations whose political

---

19   'Civil society' generally incorporates NGOs and non-profit organizations, and broadly encompasses political parties, labour unions, workers' cooperatives, business associations, membership-serving organizations and religious bodies, among other actors in society.

20   One of the unintended consequences of this 'humanitarian intervention' by Euro-Atlantic military powers was the 'ethnic cleansing' and/or forcible internal displacement of approxi-mately 75 per cent of Kosovo's pre-war Gypsy population. These included Ashkali, Egyptians and Romanies numbering close to an estimated 90,000 citizens before the NATO military inter-vention. See the Website of the European Roma and Travellers Forum (ERTF), www.ertf.org. For information on lead poisoning within camps in Kosovo for Romani internally displaced persons (IDPs), see http://krrf.tripod.com.

orientations tend to be limited to one particular variant of 'democratization' – to wit, pro-free market and procedural democratic considerations (constitutional reform, elections, etc.) – activists in eastern Europe have seemed unable to devise more radical means for their human rights advocacy, alternative means and methods that are not reliant on the dominant model of corporatist human rights.[21] The movements for reforms of the legal/juridical structures of the past decade in the region have been partly based on the strategic adoption of liberal 'rule of law' and 'democratization' concepts, as formulated by influential NGOs such as the OSI and its affiliates. These principles are in no way incommensurate with the neo-liberal project, according to its prevailing logic (Harvey 2005).

All of this has had profound implications for the trajectory of Romani projects and initiatives throughout the region. It has resulted in an interesting collaboration between the World Bank and the OSI, with the ongoing Decade of Romani Inclusion: 2005–15, which was launched with a donors' conference in Budapest in 2004. The politics surrounding this Decade initiative are instructive. Many grass-roots Romani NGOs were not invited, and participation was based on selective criteria, ensuring that the 'multiplicity' of human rights perspectives would remain altogether 'manageable' by its sponsors (Vesely 2005). The lack of effective resistance to the status quo also characterizes the Romani leadership – both traditional community leaders and those who represent NGOs – engaged in the human rights movement for Roma. Acton and Gheorghe offer one compelling explanation for this:

> in seeking legitimacy for their struggle, Roma politicians have no choice but to lock onto the same concepts of human rights and anti-racism that operate in international organizations and relations between existing states. (Acton and Gheorghe 2001, p. 57)

Alternatives to the current order have yet to be explored because of the stranglehold of neo-liberal human rights, which inhibits the rethinking of Romani grass-roots advocacy and emancipatory politics. Part of the reason for this is the dismissal of Romani agency and resistance by elites within the movement (Bukovská 2006; Oprea 2005; Trehan 2001). This latter point is connected to another aspect of the neo-colonial process – the internalization of domination by oppressed groups, as suggested by C. Wright Mills in his classic 1959 study *The Power Elite*.

Romani subalterity in the NGO sector

> [T]he metaphor of the [human rights] 'box' encompasses a set of historical and structural circumstances that allow the human rights framework to gain

---

21   As Canadian political scientist Richard Cox asserts, 'Corporatism left those who are relatively powerless in society out of account; but being powerless and unorganized they could hardly be considered part of civil society' (Cox 1999, p. 7).

currency among elites while limiting advances, and even creating setbacks, for the awareness and acceptance of human rights among the general population. (Carnegie Council on Ethics and International Affairs, 2000)

Well funded organizations whose work focuses on the diverse Romani communities in the region generally lack grass-roots constituencies and, in many cases, cooperate only superficially with local and national NGOs. In place of a grass-roots constituency for these NGOs, an elite constituency has become established, comprising national and international policy-makers, academics and coalitions of activists (Trehan 2001). In addition, white privilege is also prevalent in the NGO world, for the organizations that comprise Romani civil society are themselves not immune to racialized hierarchies.[22] As one prominent Romani activist has suggested, 'one of biggest challenges facing the non-Roma who work with us is how to work for Roma rights without controlling the movement' (Kóczé 1999, p. 69).

The elite composition of NGO circles also influences the construction of priorities within the movement. Blanka Kozma, the director of the Romani Women's Association in Hungary, and one of the few Romani members of the Budapest city council, offers the following insights in relation to the planning of Roma-related NGO projects:

> these projects were not designed from our perspective, it's not about our survival, it's not about our development ... their main aim is not to help Romani society or to develop the situation, but to *prevent them [Roma] from going to England or America so that we are not a danger to the EU* ... this was the motivation [in the past], and it continues to be to this day. (Kozma, interview material from 1999, quoted in Trehan 2009, emphasis added)

This type of radical critique rarely surfaces in the mainstream literature on Roma, nor is it likely to be found in the plethora of NGO publications. Nevertheless, in various discussions with Romani leaders, we have found this to be one of their foremost concerns about the movement. A concomitant development is that, once elite NGOs have established their dominant position within the 'Romani rights industry', they then seek to legitimate this position by reaching out to community-based organizations and by forming alliances and 'strategic' partnerships. These partnerships are generally on an unequal footing, as the grass-roots NGOs often have a dependency funding relationship with the elite NGOs. This then exacerbates existing asymmetries within the sector as a whole, particularly in relation to Romani development or human rights projects.

In the early days of post-socialism, NGO entrepreneurs in the region and abroad believed that recruitment efforts were critical to attract people to the field of development and human rights. The objective was to enhance professionalism in the field, and offering generous salaries was seen as an effective

---

22 Strategic management posts are disproportionately granted to non-Romani professionals in the field of 'Roma rights'. For a further discussion of white privilege, see McIntosh (1988).

way to achieve this. One result has been that the salaries of NGO workers in the region, especially within NGOs sponsored directly by international private foundations, are likely to be several times higher than those of local professionals, and higher still if one is a foreign worker (Trehan 2001).[23] By the late 1990s, this had had the effect of attracting a large number of degreed professionals into the NGO sector who would otherwise have joined the private sector, government or academia, as the 'Romani rights' sector was a field with good 'career potential'. This has been one of the corrosive impacts of the marketization of human rights, whereby the core ethos of human rights work becomes eroded and transmogrifies from an ideal of solidarity and social justice into one in favour of technocratic skill and loyalty to the established neo-liberal human rights order. Thus, the generous influx of money into the region through the auspices of western private foundations has led to an adjoining, perhaps dysfunctional phenomenon: what many Romani intellectuals cynically refer to as 'ethno-business' or the 'Gypsy industry'.[24] While one should certainly not lament increasing professionalism within the field of human rights, serious questions must be asked when actors within the movement, and the strategies they adopt, begin to manifest the imperatives of a neo-liberal economic order, losing sight of the priorities of the communities and people they are meant to serve. Indeed, prominent American human rights lawyer and scholar David Kennedy has suggested that reflexivity within the 'human rights community' is imperative (Kennedy 2004). The above section has raised issues associated with the growing institutionalization and marketization of human rights work in post-socialist Europe. We now continue this enquiry below by looking further at the hierarchical dynamics of NGOs working in the area.

Relations between elite NGOs and Romani communities

Some scholars have suggested that the complex of projects related to Roma is part of an important survival strategy within Romani communities, an avenue for strengthening these communities' prospects for the future by offering spaces of resistance to non-Romani notions of 'integration' (Pinnock 1998, 1999). With due

---

23 For example, in Hungary, a teacher employed by the state in 2000 earned on average $150 a month; a full-time Hungarian NGO worker based in Budapest could earn over $500 a month. The salaries within some international NGOs in the region are higher, after taking into account the cost of living and purchasing power parity, than for those working in New York or London in similar positions.
24 Monika Horaková, a Romani Czech MP, claims that 'there is too much paternalism … with too many Czechs who speak no Romani making a living by helping a people they do not understand, while Gypsies themselves go jobless' (see Erlanger 2000). The 'Gypsy industry' is not solely a phenomenon of the third sector, but also encompasses the growing number of Romani-related offices and programmes, from culture to education, to minority rights in the state sector as well. Indeed, the EU Phare programmes in the region have funding earmarked for the 'development of civil society', which includes many Romani-related projects.

respect to the fields of human rights and development, we take a more critical view of the proliferation of the NGO sector, or what some scholars have called 'NGO-ization' (Stubbs 2007). For one thing, there is increasing resignation on the part of older Romani activists (those in their forties and above) and a tacit acceptance or even eager acceptance by the younger generation (those in their twenties or thirties) of the inequalities within the NGO sector as it has evolved. In our view, the profound deterioration of the socio-economic circumstances of the majority of Roma resulting from the transition to a market economy based on neo-liberal principles has forced many Roma to 'clutch at straws', leading to their participation in a wide range of 'paper NGOs' and projects in order to get a much-needed piece of the NGO funding pie (Kovats 2001; Trehan 2001, 2006a).

Donor dependency – ideological and structural control

If Romani leaders and politicians have historically been dependent on state structures for financial support, so too, in post-socialist times, have Romani actors within the NGO sector become dependent on major philanthropic donors for continuing their work. A pecking order of dependency has emerged in which elite NGOs and international NGOs in particular are reliant on western philanthropy via private foundations, and local Romani NGOs then rely in turn, for their own survival, on these elite NGOs. As explained earlier, most NGOs working in the field are not sustainable without foreign assistance, and membership-funded organizations are virtually non-existent, the majority of projects being necessarily donor driven.[25] Donor dependency undermines the autonomy of local NGOs and initiatives, as donors subscribing to neo-liberal agendas may have different priorities from local, economically depressed communities (Trehan 2001).

Some advocates for the Roma in Europe have drawn parallels between their Romani communities and those in the so-called Third World (Biró 1995). Nevertheless, these same advocates tend to overlook the power dynamics and distortions that result from their well meaning interventions in Romani communities. Even active Romani advocates and intellectuals within civil society are comparable to those in the Third World in terms of both their relatively isolated position globally and their subalternity. Their common struggle as double minorities in the region – both dissidents and Roma – takes place on several fronts simultaneously: not only against the state, but now increasingly against structures that inhibit Romani participation in the achievement of their

---

25   The lack of voluntary membership of these organizations was explained away in the early days of post-socialism, for example in the 1990 annual report of the Autonómia Foundation, by the 'legitimate suspicion against voluntary action, as during 40 years [under communism] there was the practice of compulsory "volunteering", and membership fees were deducted from salaries'.

own emancipation, including those within civil society at large.[26] This polemic raises serious ethical questions that Romani activists have now begun to ask. To whom are Romani and non-Romani NGOs ultimately responsible – to their donors, to the Romani communities they seek to assist, or to the general public? Who decides, and who should decide, what the priorities are for the development and emancipation of Roma within the NGO sector?

Bukovská (2006) raises an interesting point with regard to the question of legitimacy, noting that many elite human rights NGOs have been accepted as legitimate 'partners' by governments and intergovernmental organizations such as the Organization for Security and Co-operation in Europe (OSCE), the Council of Europe and the EU. One result is that Romani voices at the local or national level have been largely usurped by the power of elite human rights entrepreneurs, who have superior networking skills and easier access to global human rights sponsorship. At times, Romani representatives have publicly aired their increasing frustration with the monopoly these entrepreneurs wield within the human rights sector. In one particular forum at the Central European University in Budapest in 2001, Aladár Horváth, then director of Roma Polgarjógi Alapitvány (Roma Civil Rights Foundation), a national NGO in Hungary, suggested a colonizing role in the movement was indeed being played by elite human rights entrepreneurs, most of whom were not Romani:

> The Romani Movement has a long way to go. This present discussion itself illustrates how far we are from a normal situation: we have several non-Roma experts discussing the future of the movement, while we Roma get to say something in the end. I will offer some conclusions about the background of this development by quoting Malcolm X, who after his trip from Mecca once asked, 'If you drink coffee which is too strong, too black, what do you do with it? Well, you put some cream … but if you put too much cream, it no longer tastes like coffee'. This is a lesson from the Black civil rights movement, which offers us a strong critique of black integration. (Quoted in Trehan 2009)

Horváth was irritated because the non-Romani human rights entrepreneurs had been asked to speak first; by invoking Malcolm X, he was seeking to emphasize his own marginal position, even within a social field that was supposedly representing the emancipatory interests of his own community.

Of equal importance is that, inside these institutional circles, human rights elites use their personal leverage to promote the careers of friends and family members, many of whom reappear on various boards and/or act as trustees of

---

26   Aladár Horváth, Rudko Kawczyinski and Blanka Kozma are a few of the many Romani intellectuals in the region who believe that the hierarchical structure of the NGO sector today inhibits Romani people from participating fully in the decision-making process. Certainly, the burden most Romani intellectuals carry in their attempt to represent themselves, their families, their communities and, indeed, their whole people – if this is even conceivable, let alone possible – is tremendous. See Kawczynski (1997). Rudko Kawczynski was at that time director of the Regional Roma Participation Program within the Budapest branch of the OSI, as well as on the board of directors of the European Roma Rights Centre.

domestic NGOs and international NGOs as well as members of their legal advisory committees. Those of Romani origin are few and far between. Retrospectively, we can see that the 1990s were characterized by the American human rights establishment's controlling stake in the 'Roma rights' cause in Europe. By contrast, German, French or British human rights advocacy networks have only recently become active in this area, propelled by the EU accession of post-socialist states (Trehan 2009).

As shown above, the proliferation of US-funded NGOs – whose ideological orientations are usually burdened with preconceptions drawn from the neo-liberal paradigm, for instance 'law as salvation'[27] – reflects the interests of those Euro-Atlantic elites who are attempting to manage – or pacify – Romani communities perceived to be dangerously marginalized and potentially unstable. This 'management of Roma' appears to be concealed within a broader framework in which progressive agendas of integration and civil rights are espoused.

However, despite the increasing number of civil rights lawsuits brought before the courts on behalf of Romani plaintiffs, the seeming rise in rights awareness in the public sphere and the media, and the launch of ambitious programmes for the integration of Roma over the past decade, the fundamental oversights and weaknesses of these approaches are now becoming clear. For example, the social distance between Roma and the majority population is actually on the rise. Legal interventions do not always obtain desired results for the victims, and in many cases prove to be harmful for local Romani–majority relations. Nor do court trials always result in justice *per se*, since a primarily litigious approach does not address the roots of popular prejudice or the structural inequalities embedded in society. In many cases, litigation does not even help Romani victims to regain their dignity (Zoltan 2006). Moreover, with regard to 'Romani-specific' initiatives for integration, post-socialist societies have begun to react negatively, either by suggesting that Roma are now being favoured by government programmes at the expense of their non-Roma counterparts, or by implying that policies of the 'affirmative action' type are unwarranted in the first place, with the Roma being considered a particularly undeserving group.

The two faces of the Romani civil rights movement: emancipation and exploitation

For central and eastern European countries, the disintegration of the diverse ideologies of state socialism (and subsequent membership of the EU) created a space for liberal human rights discourses and concomitant socio-legal prac-tices. We have suggested in this chapter that these discursive human rights practices were then subsumed within a global hegemonic neo-liberal political

---

27   This is the model espoused by the European Roma Rights Centre's former director Dimitrina Petrova (2003), and one of the legacies of international human rights NGOs such as Human Rights Watch, which is closely affiliated with the OSI.

order, thereby relegating issues of egalitarianism and social justice within civil society to the periphery. This has been particularly marked in the case of the Romani civil rights movement. In exploring an emerging hierarchy of 'post-imperial' privilege within the movement for the empowerment of Romanies in central and eastern Europe today, which is labelled the 'Roma industry' by some activists, we have offered a critique of the broader marketization of human rights. The collapse of socialist state structures resulted in the re-emergence of a full-blown nationalism as well as the rise of ethnic visibility in the region. One casualty of the 'transition' has been the incipient and fragile social solidarity between Romani and non-Romani communities that had accrued under successive socialist regimes in eastern Europe. The resurgence of nationalism has been linked to the rise of extreme violence, both physical and symbolic, towards a number of visible minority groups, including Romanies, while the rise of 'ethnicization' – in one of its most liberal variants – has taken the shape of a 'celebration and preservation of cultural difference' (cf. Kovats 1998). This latter view is supported by extensive state institutional machineries, including state institutional frameworks for minorities, offices for ethnic and national minorities, and various ministerial departments that specialize in social policy issues linked to Romani citizens. Although these may appear to be sites of well meaning initiatives for social inclusion, one inadvertent result has been the consolidation of a status quo which obscures the ongoing marginalization and 'infra-humanity' of Romani Europeans, who continue to occupy the bottom rung of a racialized hierarchy, even in seemingly progressive social spaces such as the contemporary 'human rights community'.[28]

More specifically, within the movement today, the advocacy elites at the very top of the ladder tend to be western (primarily American) human rights entrepreneurs, followed by eastern European 'white' (or non-Romani) elites; the order then moves down to include Romani elites (urban, educated Roma), and, finally, local Romani communities and their representatives (usually rural and semi-literate). Moreover, EU accession for the post-socialist countries has resulted in a *de facto* centre and periphery within Europe itself, thus exacerbating the already marginal economic and political position of Roma, whose communities continue to subsist as internal colonies within Europe. The multiple levels of visible neo-colonialism – for example, western Europe's economic stranglehold over eastern European polities – propels eastern Europeans to show their 'western credentials' by separating themselves from their Romani neighbours, which only 'others' them further, and reinforces the racialized social pecking order that is already set in place (Trehan 2006b).

As we have shown, this racialized hierarchy is not hermetically sealed, as there is considerable differentiation and fluidity within it, but the basic contours of its structure have continued to remain recognizable along these lines for more

---

28   The expanding institutionalization of minority policies in post-socialist Europe is akin to what Stuart Hall (1999) has termed 'multicultural drift' in Britain.

than twenty years, ever since the first Romani civil rights organizations were formed. We have suggested, further, that the autonomy of these indigenous Romani organizations has now been usurped by the powerful interventions of neo-liberal human rights entrepreneurs. The postcolonial racism embedded within this hierarchy is a result not just of material resource advantages (e.g. the dominance of those American philanthropists who have taken up the Romani cause), but also of symbolic power configurations that have their roots in 'eastern otherness' and, in contradistinction to it, 'western normality'. This chapter has attempted to make sociological sense of the above developments, in many cases paradoxical, within the contemporary human rights movement for Roma today.

The struggle for the soul of the Romani movement is currently being waged on multiple fronts. One crucial task over the next century for Europeans living side by side with their Romani neighbours will be to acknowledge and humanize their common lives and realities, for entrenched mutual apprehensions and suspicions urgently need to be overcome. For Romani Europeans, this task will be achieved only when they begin to acknowledge and challenge the neo-colonial relations they encounter as subalterns, thereby empowering themselves in the diversity of contexts that encompass their daily lives (schools, workplaces, government offices and other institutions). We emphasize *next* century because, in the spirit of W. E. B. Dubois's classic study *The Souls of Black Folk* (1905), it is clear to us that, for an oppressed people, emancipation is a multi-generational struggle, and it is likely to remain so for decades, possibly centuries, to come.

Works cited

Acton, T. and Gheorghe, N. (2001) 'Citizens of the World and Nowhere: Minority, Ethnic and Human Rights for Roma'. In: Guy, W. ed. *Between Past and Future: The Roma of Central and Eastern Europe*. Hatfield, University of Hertfordshire Press, pp. 54–70.

Biró, A. (1995) 'The Prince, the Merchant, the Citizen … and the Romany'. *Mágyar Hírlap [Hungarian Daily]*, 30 May.

Bukovská, B. (2006) '*Dignitati Memores*, as *Optima Intenti*…? Some Reflections on the Human Dimension of Human Rights Work'. Proceedings of the Human Rights and Public Interest Law Fellows Retreat (unpublished), Cairo, 26–29 January.

Buti, A. (2004) 'The Removal of Indigenous Children from Their Families – US and Australia Compared'. *University of Western Sydney Law Review*, 6. Available at http://search.austlii. edu.au/au/journals/UWSLRev/2004/6.html (accessed 20 January 2009).

Carnegie Council on Ethics and International Affairs (2000) 'Introduction: Human Rights Litigation: Promise v. Perils'. *Human Rights Dialogue*, 2(2). Available at www.cceia.org/ resources/publications/dialogue/2_02/articles/621.html.

Césaire, A. (2000) *Discourse on Colonialism*. New York, Monthly Review Press.

Chen, T. and Churchill, D. (2005) 'Neoliberal Civilization and the Economic Disciplining of Human Rights: Convergence of Models in the US and China'. *Rhizomes*, 10 (spring). Available at www.rhizomes.net/issue10/chen.htm (accessed 20 January 2009).

Clark, C. (2004) 'Severity Has Often Enraged but Never Subdued a Gipsy: The History and Making of European Romani Stereotypes'. In: Saul, N. D. B. and Tebbutt, S. eds. *The Role of the Romanies: Images and Counter-images of Romanies/'Gypsies' in European Culture*. Liverpool, Liverpool University Press, pp. 226–46.

Cox, R. W. (1999) 'Civil Society at the Turn of the Millennium: Prospects for an Alternative World Order'. *Review of International Studies*, 25(1), p. 7.

Elias, N. (1978) *The Civilizing Process*. Oxford, Blackwell.

Erlanger, S. (2000) 'Czech Gypsies Knock Harder on the Closed Doors'. *New York Times*, 12 May.

Fanon, F. (1965) *The Wretched of the Earth*. London, MacGibbon & Kee.

Gandhi, L. (1998) *Postcolonial Theory: A Critical Introduction*. St Leonards, Allen & Unwin.

Gilroy, P. (2004) *Between Camps: Nations, Cultures, and the Allure of Race*. London, Routledge.

Gowan, P. (1996) 'Eastern Europe, Western Power and Neo-Liberalism'. *New Left Review*, 1, p. 216.

Guilhot, N. (2005) *The Democracy Makers: Human Rights and International Order*. New York, Columbia University Press.

Hall, S. (1999) 'From Scarman to Stephen Lawrence'. *History Workshop Journal*, 48, p. 188.

Hancock, I. (1997) 'The Struggle for the Control of Identity'. *Transitions*, 4(4), p. 4.

—— (2002) *Ame Sam e Rromane Dzene/We are the Romani People*. Hatfield, University of Hertfordshire Press.

Harvey, D. (2005) *A Brief History of Neoliberalism*. Oxford, Oxford University Press.

Heuss, H. (2000) 'Anti-Gypsyism Is Not a New Phenomenon. Anti-Gypsyism Research: The Creation of a New Field of Study'. In: Acton, T. ed. *Scholarship and the Gypsy Struggle*. Hatfield, University of Hertfordshire Press, pp. 52–68.

Kállai, E. and Törzsök, E. eds. (2000) *A Roma's Life in Hungary*. Translated by T. Wilkinson. Budapest, Bureau for European Comparative Minority Research (BECMIR).

Kawczynski, R. (1997) 'The Politics of Romani Politics'. *Transitions*, 4(4), pp. 24–29.

Kemény, I., ed. (2005) *Roma of Hungary*. Translated by A. Gane. New York, Columbia University Press.

Kennedy, D. (2004) *The Dark Sides of Virtue: Reassessing International Humanitarianism*. Oxford, Princeton University Press.

Kóczé, A. (1999) 'Taking Control of Our Identity'. *Roma Rights*, 3, p. 69.

Kohn, M. (1995) *The Race Gallery: The Return of Racial Science*. London, Jonathan Cape.

Kovats, M. (1998) *The Development of Roma Politics in Hungary 1989–1995*. PhD thesis, University of Portsmouth.

—— (2001) 'Problems of Intellectual and Political Accountability in Respect of Emerging European Roma Policy'. *JEMIE*, autumn. Available at www.ecmi.de/jemie/indextitle.html (accessed 20 January 2009).

—— (2003) 'The Politics of Roma Identity: Between Nationalism and Destitution'. Open Democracy. Available at www.opendemocracy.net/people-migrationeurope/article_1399.jsp (accessed 20 January 2009).

Maguire, G. (1995) *Wicked: The Life and Times of the Wicked Witch of the West*. New York, Harper Collins.

McIntosh, P. (1988) 'White Privilege and Male Privilege: A Personal Account of Coming to See Correspondences Through Work in Women's Studies'. Working Paper No. 189. Wellsey, MA, Center for Research on Women, Wellsley College.

Mills, C. W. (1959) *The Power Elite*. Oxford, Oxford University Press.

Nkrumah, K. (1965) *Neo-colonialism, the Last Stage of Imperialism*. London, Nelson & Sons.

Oprea, A. (2005) 'Child Marriage a Cultural Problem, Educational Access as a Race Issue? Deconstructing Uni-dimensional Understanding of Romani Oppression'. *Roma Rights*, (journal of the European Roma Rights Centre), 2. Available at www.errc.org/cikk.php?cikk=2284 (accessed 20 January 2009).

Ost, D. (2005) *The Defeat of Solidarity: Anger and Politics in Postcommunist Europe*. Ithaca, NY, Cornell University Press.

Petrova, D. (1999) *Human Rights in the Aftermath of Kosovo*. Human Rights Dialogue Series. New York, Carnegie Council on Ethics in International Affairs (CCEIA).

—— (2003) 'The Roma: Between a Myth and the Future'. *Social Research*, 70(1), pp. 111–61.

Pinnock, K. (1998) 'Social Exclusion and Strategies of Inclusion: Romani NGOs in Bulgaria'. Seminar on New Directions in Romani Studies, University of Greenwich, 11 June, pp. 7–8.

—— (1999) *Social Exclusion and Resistance: A Study of Gypsies and the Non-governmental Sector in Bulgaria 1989–1997*. PhD thesis, University of Wolverhampton.

Ringold, D., Orenstein, M. A. and Wilkens, E. (2003) *Roma in an Expanding Europe: Breaking the Poverty Cycle*. Washington, DC, International Bank for Reconstruction and Development.

Schmitt, R. (1996) 'Racism and Objectification: Reflections on Themes from Fanon'. In: Gordon, L. and White, R., *et al.* eds. *Frantz Fanon: A Critical Reader*. Oxford, Blackwell.

Simhandl, K. (2006) '"Western Gypsies and Travellers" – "Eastern Roma": The Creation of Political Objects by the European Union'. *Nations and Nationalism*, 12(1), pp. 97–115.

Stubbs, P. (2007) 'Community Development in Contemporary Croatia: Globalisation, Neoliberalisation, and NGO-isation'. In: Dominelli, L., ed. *Revitalising Communities*. Aldershot, Ashgate Press, pp. 161–74.

Todorova, M. (1997) *Imagining the Balkans*. Oxford, Oxford University Press.

Trehan, N. (2001) 'In the Name of the Roma? The Role of Private Foundations and NGOs'. In: Guy, W. ed. *Between Past and Future: The Roma of Central and Eastern Europe*. Hatfield, University of Hertfordshire Press.

—— (2006a) 'Neo-liberal Human Rights Entrepreneurs as a New Power Elite: The (Un)intended Consequences of the "Romani Rights Movement" in Eastern Europe'. Proceedings of the conference on C. Wright Mills and 'The Power Elite' (unpublished), Columbia University, New York, 14 April.

—— (2006b) 'Racialising Hegemony Within the Marketplace of Romani Emancipation in Europe'. Proceedings of the conference White Terror/(Post)Empire (unpublished), London School of Economics, London, 19–20 May.

—— (2009) *Human Rights Entrepreneurship in Post-Socialist Hungary: From 'Gypsy Problem' to 'Romani Rights'*. PhD thesis, London School of Economics.

Vesely, I. (2005) 'Where Are the Romani Organizations?' *Transitions Online*, 3 February. Available at www.tol.cz/look/TOL/home.tpl?IdLanguage=1&IdPublication=4&NrIssue=333 (accessed 20 January 2009).

Wessely, A. (1996) 'The Cognitive Chance of Central European Sociology'. In: Hadas, M. and Vörös, M. eds. *Replika* (Hungarian social science quarterly), special issue, 'Colonisation or Partnership? Eastern Europe and Western Social Sciences'.

Woodiwiss, A. (2006) 'The Law Cannot Be Enough: Human Rights and the Limits of Legalism'. In: Meckled-Garcia, S. and Cali, S. eds. *The Legalisation of Human Rights: Multidisciplinary Perspective on Human Rights and Human Rights Law*. London, Routledge.

Wrench, J. (2006) 'Conference Keynote Address'. Proceedings of the conference Racism, Postcolonialism, Europe (unpublished), University of Leeds, Leeds, UK, June.

Zoltan, F. (2006) 'Citizens or Denizens? The Future of Romani Integration in Europe'. Proceedings of panel presentation, Centre for the Study of Human Rights and Central London Europe Group (CLEG), London School of Economics, London, June.

Part II
Racisms of migration

CHAPTER 5

'A soft touch': racism and asylum-seekers from a visual culture perspective

Alex Rotas

The writer and political activist A. Sivanandan has argued that 'poverty is the new black' (2001). Refugees and asylum-seekers are, he suggests, demonized according to a racist rhetoric whereby they are singled out as a coherent group, then denigrated and reified. This process is xenophobic, since it draws on an implied 'natural' fear of strangers that is not, as he describes it, 'colour-coded', although its underlying racist rhetoric makes it 'xeno-racism': racist in substance but 'xeno' in form. Xeno-racism is, he asserts, a feature of global capitalism. It is meted out by the western nations of Europe, which are seeking to preserve their national identities and their economic prosperity by excluding impoverished strangers, whatever their skin colour or cultural background, whom their own political, social and economic policies have now displaced. That they can do this at all reflects the balance of hegemonic economic power in a postcolonial world, where it is the interests of capital that ultimately dominate and prevail (Young 2001, p. 57). In such a world, discrimination is less between putative 'races' (whether defined by so-called biological means or culturally) and more between the rich and the poor, with poverty thereby becoming the new defining feature that is identified, reified and then discriminated against. The philosopher Michael Dummett, arguing along similar lines to Sivanandan, observes that, in the British situation:

> the racism that still festers amongst the whole British public has been ignited and expanded from a loathing and contempt for coloured people to a loathing and contempt for foreigners in general, including white people – more precisely poor white foreigners. (Dummett 2001, p. 128; see also Fekete 2001; Gibson 2003)

In this chapter, I look at some of the different ways in which professional visual artists among asylum-seeker and refugee populations address issues to do with the new racism within which they are viewed in Europe, and specifically in Britain, and the implications these strategies have for indigenous viewers of their work.[1] In my discussion, which draws on findings from a much larger research project, I take a pragmatic, rather than a legal definition of asylum-seekers and refugees, partly due to difficulties in agreeing on international definitions and partly due to my own personal reluctance to probe individuals about their precise political status.[2] My loose definition of an asylum-seeker relies on the subjective view of the individuals concerned, that they have felt forced to leave the countries of their birth in order to seek their safety, and that of their families, elsewhere, with Europe in general, and Britain in particular, being the 'elsewhere' on which I have focused my attentions here.

As far as Britain is concerned, contemporary attitudes have developed within a historical context of ongoing immigration, with the same arguments being rehearsed and repeated from the end of the nineteenth century, throughout the twentieth and into the beginning of the twenty-first. When Jewish refugees were fleeing to Britain from the pogroms of eastern Europe, for example, it was commented in Parliament that 'the places of our workpeople ... [are] to be taken over by the scum and refuse of foreign nations' (*Hansard*, quoted in Hayes 2002, p. 32). This comment was echoed in the *Dover Express*, with its now infamous headline, 'we want to wash the dross down the drain', on 1 October 1998. Crucially, in terms of building up resentment against them, both then and now, as historian Debra Hayes argues, refugees were connected with the issue of welfare, to the point where these two separate issues are now indelibly linked (Hayes 2002). The result is that the reasons why individuals currently flee from their home countries fade into the background of arguments that instead focus on the threat they pose to the host nation's benefits system and hence economy. Story-lines in popular newspapers repeatedly rephrase the belief that 'they' are all scroungers and 'we' are a soft touch: asylum-seekers and refugees are not seen in terms of their plight or, indeed, their human rights, but as coming wilfully and specifically to milk a generous social service provider. Since the 1905 Aliens Act, in other words, as Hayes demonstrates, 'the

---

1   The author gratefully acknowledges the artists' permission to use the images.
2   Even supposedly unambiguous definitions given by the United Nations (UN) are becoming increasingly contested and the international law these definitions create is ever more problematic in its implementation (Chimni 2000, p. 2; Gemenne 2005; Lavoyer 2000, p. 61; Mecham 2005; Mertus 2003, p. 253; Tuitt 1996, p. 23). Article 3 of the European Convention on Human Rights, for example, makes it illegal to return individuals to their country of origin if the economic and social conditions are inhuman or degrading, and not only if they will be subject to political persecution, as specified in the UN Convention of 1951 (Röhl 2005). I have also adopted a pragmatic definition because this is a time when asylum-seekers and refugees are frequently vilified in the popular press and the term 'asylum-seeker' has even become a highly charged street term of abuse. Interrogating individuals from these populations about their precise political status has therefore seemed either insensitively prurient or inappropriately official. Various artists I have met from these groups, however loosely defined, have also suggested to me that an informal taboo exists among would-be refugees themselves against asking such questions of each other.

long-term construction of the refugee has been as burdensome, needy, socially costly and consequently undesirable' (31).

Many visual artists from refugee populations living in Europe address these issues in their work, and in this chapter I shall examine two ways in which they do so. On the one hand, they may explore issues in their work that are to do with why they left their countries in the first place, reminding the British viewer of the *real* reasons for their presence here now – issues to do with war, imprisonment and torture, for example. On the other hand, they may investigate issues that are to do with being an asylum-seeker in a so-called host country, with such issues relating to the living conditions they now find themselves in or the mistrust with which they are viewed by the media or individuals.

The first image I want to consider is a painting by Naman Hadi, an Iraqi artist living in Paris, which illustrates the existential condition in which many refugees feel they live (Figure 1). This painting is called *Le Déraciné* (*The Uprooted*) and it plays on the metaphor of rupture that many of those who have been through involuntary migration feel is central to their experience. 'The concept was born from the personal suffering of exile', observes Hadi:

In some ways it is a self-portrait. However, the reactions of many people who have undergone the same experience and who recognise themselves in the painting lends the artwork the dimension of a 'collective self-portrait'. (Quoted in Faraj 2001, p. 100)

Figure 1. Naman Hadi, Le Déraciné (Uprooted). *Oil on canvas, 1984, 130 cm × 195 cm, artist's collection. Photograph: Atelier 80.*

Having shown this image to an audience of Palestinians in Ramallah, I can confirm the degree to which so many people there seemed to identify with the particular emotional anguish that it so graphically represents.

The notion of rupture as an event that creates a 'before' and 'after' has elemental and geological undertones (such as volcanic eruptions, for example, or ruptures of a medical nature), suggesting events that lie beyond the possibility of any individual attempt at resistance. Moments of rupture are also the points around which acts of memory proliferate, since they signal the loss of something that henceforth can be perceived only as an absence (Bardenstein 1999, p. 148). Hadi references the natural world in his human figure whose feet have become the roots of an uprooted tree. The image's emotional impact derives from its simplicity: the rupture caused by forced displacement to human lives relies on another metaphor, the notion of the roots that supposedly link us to the land of our birth and the community that lives upon it. Hadi's supine figure lies desolate now that he has been wrenched from the earth that once succoured him, his emotional pain thereby given a physical – and hence visual – dimension. Just as an uprooted tree is a dead (or dying) tree, the implication here is that the individual, exiled from the homeland that once allowed him to flourish and stand tall, exists now in a state of 'living death'.

This image raises a number of important issues, but my present concern is with the notion of suffering that is implicit within it and that is also implicit in so much of the work of visual artists from refugee populations. Without wishing to elevate a reified notion of suffering as the overarching and defining characteristic of displaced individuals or peoples, I have yet to meet anyone who has been through the experience of forced migration who has not felt some degree of emotional pain. That is not to say that their past and present lives were and are blighted with a process of continual suffering, but it seems to be indisputable that the event is inevitably linked to a sense of existential (as well as tangible) loss – even if it also holds the potential for existential enrichment and gain. This suffering may relate to the generalized loneliness of the displaced individual, now a stranger in an unfamiliar country and separated from family and community, or to more specific issues that arise either in the country of birth or in the new host nation. Images of suffering are testimonial in nature, bearing witness to pain that has been endured by the artist and/or his or her community and, as such, they arguably make ethical demands on the viewer, calling for an acknowledgement, a response.

If we look at work that is more specific in the suffering that it represents, such as Saad Hirri's *The Great Party* (Figure 2), this point may become clearer. Saad Hirri is another Iraqi artist, living in Britain, who has documented his experiences at the hands of Saddam Hussein's torturers; *The Great Party* is a still from a DVD that was shown on a small television screen at the 'Sanctuary' exhibition at Glasgow's Museum of Modern Art in 2003. The images on this DVD are akin to diary sketches, implying a need to record and document events as they occur. They make for very uncomfortable viewing, which is at the same time compelling. The exhibition's curator, Sean McGlashan, remarked that every time

Figure 2. Saad Hirri, The Great Party, *still from DVD shown at 'Sanctuary', Glasgow, 2003; image taken from 'Letter to Van Gogh from Hell', Saad Hirri, published by Freight Design on behalf of the Scottish Refugee Council, 2003: 21.*

he visited the upstairs gallery where this piece was showing during the five and a half months of the exhibition, there were clusters of viewers around it.[3] Susan Sontag has investigated the ghoulish attraction that 'the pain of others' can often exert and which, indeed, may well have made *The Great Party* such a popular exhibit as much as, if not more than, the work's formal qualities (Sontag 2003).

As a representation of Hirri's personal experience and suffering, this image places a moral imperative on the viewer to acknowledge the specificity of this suffering. Viewers may not be able to share Hirri's ordeal, but they can bear witness to it by watching and listening to his story and seeing, in the words of Elaine Scarry, civilization being 'undone' through the process of torture (Scarry 1985, pp. 38–45). Torture, as Scarry points out, systematically annihilates the prisoner's world by alienating objects, events and even people from their normal

---

3   Personal communication with author, 19 August 2005.

use and context, so that they are no longer what they once were. Beds and chairs become shackles rather than places of repose; bathtubs, refrigerators and tables become weapons and sources of terror; doctors become torturers rather than relievers of pain; a 'great party' becomes a social gathering of an altogether sinister kind. Hirri's narrative testimony is, however, an act of agency that interprets and organizes the experiences he was forced to endure. Recontextualizing trauma through the process of making art is, among other things, an attempt to remake the world that the torturers have previously torn apart, a mark of control over events that were, at the time, uncontrollable.

The demands such testimonial works make on the viewer situate the suffering represented, moreover, within the nexus of social relationships: the empathic human dyad, negated during the experience of torture, starts to be recreated. Artworks destined for the public domain (unlike those created specifically within the context of art therapy) demand the presence of a viewer, just as Spivak famously demonstrated that the speech act is completed through the process of being heard (Spivak 1998; and more specifically Spivak 1996, p. 292). Hirri's work raises many issues about the nature of pain and the possibility (or not) of its representation, about its potential commodification in the gallery, as well as about voyeurism, over-identification or even what has been termed the 'secondary traumatization' of the viewer (Hartman 2001, p. 119). For the moment, however, my focus is on the different ways in which visual artwork that is testimonial in nature may be received by British audiences, and how this depends on where the suffering occurs.

Other artists from refugee and asylum-seeking populations address issues in their countries of birth that have sometimes caused, sometimes contributed towards, their flight overseas. Kurdish artist Rebwar, who lived for a while in exile in Britain (but who returned to Kurdistan Iraq after the fall of Saddam Hussein), has produced a large body of work about the gassing in March 1988 of Halabja, during the Iran–Iraq War. Some of this work has been developed into an educational project that tells the story 'of the day when birds dropped from the sky like drops of rain – the first victims of the deadly gas'.[4] This project toured France, Belgium and Poland for seven years and after the artist's arrival in Britain in 1992 he continued to use it in schools and community centres. Rebwar was in the mountains close to Halabja when the chemical bombs were dropped and he made a conscious decision to take on the testimonial role: 'that day, I told myself: If I am not like you, a lost story, I promise to tell the moving story of all the Kurdistan birds to all humanity in order that we might understand better the voiceless screams of my grieving country'.[5]

Iranian artist Mohsen Keiany, now living in Birmingham, is still haunted by his experiences as a fourteen-year-old soldier in the Iran–Iraq War in 1983, and has produced graphic paintings of the scenes of devastation he endured on the

---

4   Artist's presentation of his work given to the author in December 2003.
5   *Ibid.*

front line. Iraqi artist Yousif Naser, living in west London, explores the horror of the continuing conflict in Iraq in *Black Rain*. This work consists of a series of large expressionistic canvases on which he struggles to convey a sense of the pain of war as it is felt and experienced by all who get caught up in it. *Black Rain* is neither illustratively representational nor partisan: it is his intention to provide a diatribe against war in general and the suffering it causes, and is neither anti- nor pro-American.[6]

These works can make for difficult viewing but they represent suffering that takes place in the artists' home countries (or in Hadi's case with *Uprooted*, in some unspecified and metaphorical liminal zone). Viewers can safely feel sympathy for the plight of people in distant and very foreign lands within a context of cultural difference or even macabre exoticism. The exotic, after all, is something that is removed from one context and reinstated in another, where it becomes praised and celebrated from a point of view of ignorance. Once an issue or an object is understood, however, its exotic allure disappears (Appadurai 1986, p. 28; Huggan 2001, pp. 13–17; Mason 1998, pp. 3–6; Stewart 1993, p. 149). Either context – cultural difference or exoticism – allows viewers to absolve themselves from feeling any direct responsibility for the suffering they see. (Perhaps it is also worth remembering at this juncture that the process of looking at artwork involves aesthetic pleasure, which makes the viewer's position even more problematic when the subject matter it draws upon is decidedly unpleasurable.) But when artwork addresses suffering endured in Britain, as the country that now hosts those who have been forcibly displaced, British viewers are not so easily let off the hook.

Suzanna Tamamovic, an artist from the former Yugoslavia, has explored, in two installations, the hospitality asylum-seekers receive once they reach Britain. In *(Un)rested* (Figure 3) she demonstrates that the apparent safety Britain offers is literally paper thin. Her carefully crafted, life-size hammock is made of recycled paper (old bills, bank statements and junk mail). Although it appears inviting, it offers no support at all and anyone trying to rest on it would fall rapidly to earth, together with their dreams. *(Un)rested*, shown at the 'Insomnia' exhibition in London during Refugee Week in June 2005, evokes the asylum-seeker's insecurity once he or she reaches the goal of the host country and discovers the tenuousness and fragility of the apparent safety it offers. As a guest, but an unwelcome one, the asylum-seeker finds that refuge is both offered and denied at the same time.

In *People Tell Me to Cheer Up, It Could be Worse* (Figures 4 and 5) Suzanna Tamamovic uses transfer lettering to reproduce the actual phrases of asylum-seekers (of whom she herself once was one) over found household objects in the exhibition space, evoking the bleak and desolate housing conditions in which many asylum-seekers find themselves. The absence of possessions and personal memorabilia speak of the fullness of the life lost; the empty bookshelf reminds

---

6   Personal interview with author, 30 June 2004.

Figure 3. Suzana Tamamovic, (Un)rested, 360 cm × 90 cm, recycled paper (old bills, bank statements, junk mail), wood, fishing wire. 'Insomnia' exhibition, London, 19–26 June 2005. Photograph: author.

the occupant of books left at home, an empty plate speaks of past feasts, empty photo frames and coat pegs reflect missing family members. 'I had a real life once', another message on the bare wall reminds the viewer.

In these works, Tamamovic examines the notion that asylum-seekers are in receipt of a particular form of hospitality from which any notion of generosity has been drained. Labour Home Secretary Charles Clarke made it clear in an interview with David Frost in 2005 that the host–guest relationship was in place when, according to *The Times*, he 'admitted that the British people's sense of fairness and hospitality had been tested by abuse of the asylum system' (Ford 2005), as sociologist Sarah Gibson notes (Gibson 2005; and more specifically Gibson 2006, p. 694). Gibson is not alone in her observations that framing the discussion around notions of hospitality raises the issue of how the normal conventions of hospitality are abandoned when it comes to the treatment and detention of asylum-seekers (Cohen 1994, p. 99; Young 1999, p. 112). It is on this debasement of the concept of hospitality that Tamamovic turns her attention in her work.

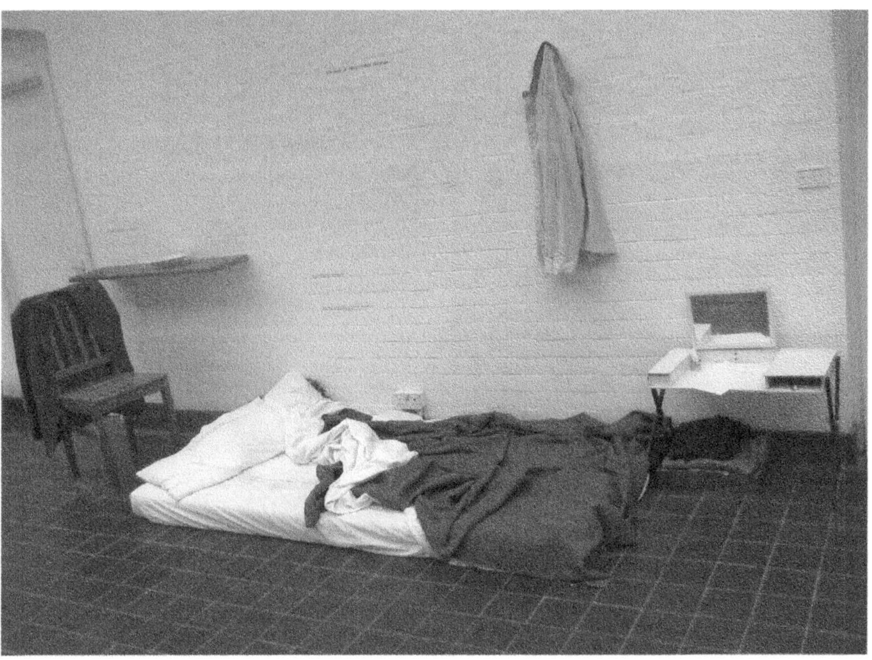

Figure 4. Suzana Tamamovic, People Tell Me To Cheer Up, It Could Be Worse, *2003. 'Leave to Remain' exhibition, Central Space Gallery, London. Photograph: artist.*

Figure 5. Suzana Tamamovic, detail from People Tell Me To Cheer Up, It Could Be Worse, *2003. 'Leave to Remain' exhibition, Central Space Gallery, London. Clothes hooks, transfer lettering. Photograph: artist.*

Figure 6. Gonkar Gyatso, Soft Touch, *2003. 'Leave to Remain' exhibition, Central Space Gallery, London. Fabric, dressmakers' pins, 78 cm × 78 cm. Photograph: Adam Nieman.*

Gonkar Gyatso, an artist who arrived in Britain as an asylum-seeker from Tibet, specifically addresses the notion that this country is an easy target for overseas scroungers in *Soft Touch* (Figure 6). Like Tamamovic's hammock, Gyatso's cushion initially appears soft and inviting, but closer inspection of the terry towelling fabric that covers it, with its Union Jack emblem on the upper surface, shows that there are scores of dressmakers' pins piercing the flag. Britain is actually not very 'soft' at all.

Zory, an artist from Iran, explores the perception that asylum-seekers are considered a threatening presence to the host society in her *Danger! Keep Them Away* series (Figure 7). Popularly objectified as a lumpen group, asylum-seekers are commonly seen as harbingers of disease, as posing risks to law and order, and as being the potential perpetrators of rape as well as determinedly pursuing the benefits of 'soft touch' Britain. Zory's sad resin heads, however, are mounted like trophies on a wall and linked together in long safety-pin chains, staring impassively and mutely at the viewer, their individual features blurred under their muslin masks. Arranged in a grid, this pathetic and sorrowful bunch of individuals has been cowed, corralled and contained; Zory challenges the notion that they are in any position whatsoever to pose a danger to local residents.

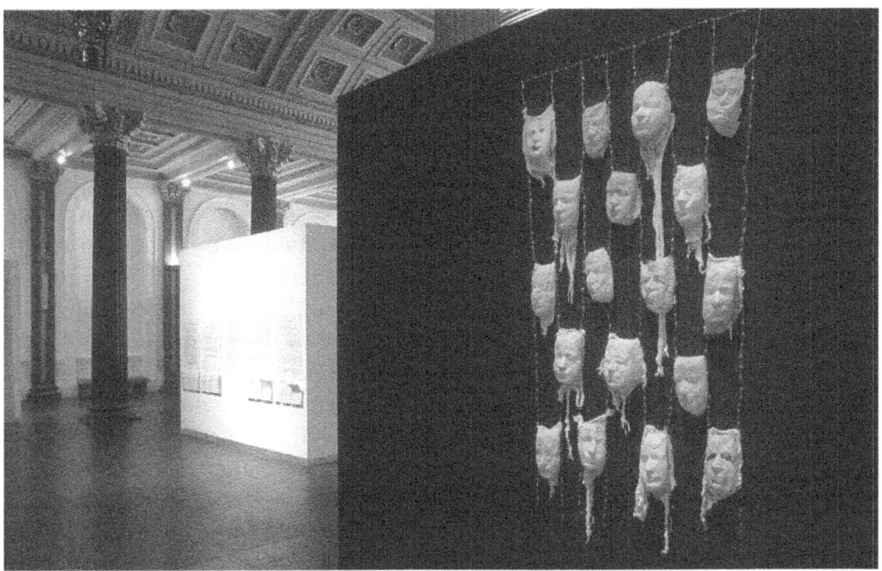

Figure 7. Zory, Danger! Keep Them Away, #10, *2003. Latex and muslin on canvas. 'Sanctuary' exhibition, Glasgow Museum of Art. Photograph reproduced courtesy of artist and Glasgow City Council Museums.*

Untitled (OK, If You Insist, the 'Brit Melt'), by Margareta Kern, like Tamamovic an artist from the former Yugoslavia, suggests the way stereotypes about asylum-seekers are distorted and absorbed by members of the host culture with Lettraset words melting into a waxed canvas. The text was taken from a story in the *Sun* newspaper about asylum-seekers apparently eating the Queen's swans. Kern replaced all references to asylum-seekers with categories commonly used in the equal opportunity sections of official forms and then applied this modified text in Lettraset to a waxed surface. Allowing the surface then to melt, the distorted text – in which each ethnic group takes it in turn to be accused of stealing the royal swans – reveals fragments of what inevitably transpired to be an entirely fictional story.[7]

These are just a few examples of both categories of artwork – work that addresses suffering in the country of origin and work that addresses suffering in the so-called host nation – done by the considerable number of talented professional artists who have arrived in Europe as asylum-seekers or refugees. Significantly, at 'Leave to Remain', an exhibition in London in 2003 which featured work exclusively created by artists from refugee and asylum-seeking

---

7   See www.margaretakern.com/projects/archive/britmelt.htm.

populations, artist/curator Margareta Kern overheard a revealing comment. Looking at work such as that by Tamamovic and Gyatso, which responds to the less than fulsome welcome the European host nation so often extends to asylum-seekers, certain viewers could be heard discussing the 'ingratitude' of the artists who saw fit to produce such work. Perceived quite clearly as guests in the national space, these artists appeared to be criticizing their putative host. They were thereby in transgression of the laws of social behaviour that preclude guests from ever making any criticism of the hospitality – by definition an act of generosity – that might be extended towards them.

Asylum-seekers, however, experience grave difficulties in accessing the national and international rights that are available to them, and thereby securing the protection that these rights notionally offer them as their due. Indeed, the difficulties they encounter in the process reveal these rights as being more hypothetical than real. As a result, individuals end up in the liminal spaces represented by Tamamovic and other artists, 'guests' rather than plaintiffs, in debt now to the host country by virtue of the welcomeless hospitality it offers (rather than grants) them. In her insightful analysis of the trope of British hospitality, Gibson draws on Derrida's opposition between unconditional hospitality (an ethical position that focuses on the 'other' and undermines the self) and hospitality-as-economy (a political position that consolidates the self) (Derrida 2000; Derrida and Dufourmantelle 2000). Like Sivanandan, with whose remarks I opened this chapter, she suggests that this situation has come about through a new type of racism, one no longer based on either biological difference or prejudice about cultural 'others', but rather on poverty. In this new-style reconfiguration of prejudice, it is economic considerations that primarily define unwanted intruders in the national space. Hence the economic underpinnings of notions of the 'host' and 'guest' move into the foreground and Derrida's articulation of the discourse of hospitality, with its emphasis on social actors orienting and respecting standards and limits, rather than interacting with each other on the basis of ethical principles, becomes particularly pertinent (Raffel 2001). Derrida demonstrates that absolute hospitality will always be impossible, as it undermines the condition of ownership and autonomy. The nation state is constituted by the concept of the border, just as the house is by the closed door, which serves to keep out the unexpected arrival of the uninvited guest, on whom the notion of absolute hospitality depends. Visitors tread a thin line between being considered guests and parasites, and it is the self-limiting laws of reciprocity and mutual obligations between guest and host that govern the relationship and maintain its legitimacy (Derrida and Dufourmantelle 2000, pp. 59–61). Ultimately, the generosity of the host is based on a power dynamic: he or she gives while at the same time remaining in control. Being in a position to offer hospitality affirms ownership: I can only welcome you to my house by stressing that it is mine (Derrida 2000, p. 14; see also Gibson 2003, p. 376; Gibson 2006, p. 695, for an excellent treatment of these issues).

In her discussion of the French situation, Mireille Rosello observes that the link between immigration and hospitality has become so accepted that by now it seems to need no explanation. 'The vision of the immigrant as guest is a metaphor that has forgotten it is a metaphor', she asserts (Rosello 2001, p. 2). Even when the word itself is not explicitly used, she argues, notions of hospitality underpin any discussion of immigration issues and the policies that may result from such discussions. For the shift in racist ideology away from biology and culture and towards economic status to occur seamlessly, it is important that this myth of national hospitality is maintained. The welcome that has been, and continues to be, given to some 'others' must be stressed in order to underline the reasonable rejection of other 'others', allowing, for example, the binary notion of the bogus and the genuine asylum-seeker to develop in public and political discourse (Ahmed 2001, pp. 363–65). Right-wing politicians have therefore shown no reluctance in invoking mythic ideas of past warm welcomes, skidding over memories of the hostile response that was extended towards previous generations of black immigrants. Attempts have even been made to corral 'blacks and Asians' to the cause of the present wave of economically based racism, where, as Sivanandan observes, it is now poverty, epitomized by the destitute asylum-seeker, that marks individuals as objects of hate (Figure 8).

That this new xeno-racism has not passed unnoticed by those towards whom it is directed is hardly surprising. Popular rhetoric, now vilifying asylum-seekers, just as it has always singled out vulnerable minority groups to blame for all manner of broader social ills, inevitably has an insidious and powerful impact on those whom it targets. 'We all internalise the discourse of the master, the coloniser, the aggressor', as Lisa Appignanesi observes. 'Jews, blacks, immigrants – all carry within them that little nugget of self-hatred, the gift of the

Blacks must help stem tide of asylum seekers, says Tory aide

THE Tory Party was at the centre of a race controversy yesterday after a senior aide urged immigrants to lead a campaign to curb asylum seekers.

Conservative adviser Laurance Wedderburn said blacks and Asians had most to lose from the rising number of refugees because many would live on their doorstep, putting pressure on local schools and hospitals. They had a duty to speak out because they could not be accused of racism.

The comments by Mr Wedderburn, an adviser to

Shadow Home Secretary Oliver Letwin, contrast with attempts by some Tories to soften the party's hard-line stance on immigration.

Conservatives had to ignore 'siren voices that accuse us of racism every time we mention the asylum debate', said Mr Wedderburn, a prospective Tory Party candidate for the next General Election.

Blacks and Asians needed to 'grasp the asylum issue' – or see their standard of living suffer.

'School and hospital provision in some poor, ethnic areas in London

is already sub-standard,' said Mr Wedderburn, whose parents came to Britain from the West Indies. 'If more asylum seekers are allowed in, it will get worse.'

He said the ethnic community had to 'commit' to being Britons. 'People of all backgrounds must rally round the Union Flag. We like our multi-cultural society. But we cannot cope with the demographic changes now taking place.'

Mr Letwin said he supported the call for 'controlled immigration and an orderly asylum system in a small and crowded island'.

Figure 8. Article that appeared in the Mail on Sunday, *17 August 2003, reproduced in 'What's the Story?', Buchanan* et al., *research project monitoring media coverage of refugees and asylum-seekers over a 12-week period from October to December 2002, kindly supplied by Professor Terry Threadgold, Cardiff School of Journalism, co-author.*

dominant culture to its "lesser" mortals' (Appignanesi 2000, p. 34). This particular master discourse, one whose rhetoric focuses on impoverished asylum-seekers, is finding oblique resistance in the varied practice of different artists from refugee populations. Their individual and collective voices not only signal their agency, but also offer opportunities that help indigenous Britons examine their prejudices: prejudices largely centred around the commonplace that 'we' are a soft touch and that 'they' are scroungers. These voices also encourage reflection about the nature of hospitality itself and the complex relationship that always exists between hosts and guests.

Works cited

Ahmed, S. (2001) 'The Organisation of Hate'. *Law and Critique*, 12, pp. 345–65.

Appadurai, A. (1986) 'Introduction: Commodities and the Politics of Value'. In: Appadurai, A. ed. *The Social Life of Things: Commodities in Cultural Perspective*. Cambridge, Cambridge University Press, pp. 3–63.

Appignanesi, L. (2000) *Losing the Dead: A Family Memoir*. London, Vintage Press.

Bardenstein, C. B. (1999) 'Trees, Forests and the Shaping of Palestinian and Israeli Collective Memory'. In: Bal, M., *et al.* eds. *Acts of Memory: Cultural Recall in the Present*. London, Dartmouth College University Press, pp. 148–68.

Buchanan, S., *et al.* (2003) *What's the Story? Results from Research into Media Coverage of Refugees and Asylum Seekers in the UK*. London, Article 19.

Chimni, B. S., ed. (2000) *International Refugee Law: A Reader*. London, Sage.

Cohen, R. (1994) *Frontiers of Identity: The British and the Others*. London, Longman.

Derrida, J. (2000) 'Hostipality'. *Angelaki*, 5 (3), pp. 3–18.

Derrida, J. and Dufourmantelle, A. (2000) *Of Hospitality*. Stanford, CA, Stanford University Press.

Dummett, M. (2001) *On Immigration and Refugees*. London, Routledge.

Faraj, M. (2001) *Strokes of Genius: Contemporary Iraqi Art*. London, Saqi Books.

Fekete, L. (2001) 'The Emergence of Xeno-racism'. *Race and Class*, 43(2), pp. 23–40.

Ford, R. (2005) 'Clarke Plans to Curb Rights for Dependants'. *The Times*, 7 February. Available at www.timesonline.co.uk/article/0,,2-1473799,00.html (accessed 21 January 2009).

Gemenne, F. (2005) 'A Legal Status for Environmental "Refugees"? Issues at Stake'. Proceedings of the conference Seeking Refuge, Seeking Rights, Seeking a Future (unpublished), Oxford Brookes University, 13–14 May. Abstract available at www.brookes.ac.uk/schools/planning/dfm/FMSC/abstracts.htm (accessed 21 January 2009).

Gibson, S. (2003) 'Accommodating Strangers: British Hospitality and the Asylum Hotel Debate'. *Journal for Cultural Research*, 17(4), pp. 367–86.

—— (2005) 'British Hospitality: The Strange(r) Figures of the Tourist and the Asylum Seeker'. Proceedings of the conference Fortress Europe and Its 'Others': Cultural Representations in Film, Media and the Arts (unpublished), School of Advanced Study, University of London, 4–6 April.

—— (2006) '"The Hotel Business Is About Strangers". Border Politics and Hospitable Spaces in Stephen Frear's Dirty Pretty Things'. *Third Text*, 20(6), pp. 693–702.

Hartman, G. (2001) 'Tele-suffering and Testimony in the Dot Com Era'. In: Zelizer, B. ed. *Visual Culture and the Holocaust*. London, Athlone Press, pp. 111–26.

Hayes, D. (2002) 'From Aliens to Asylum Seekers: A History of Immigration Controls and Welfare in Britain'. In: Cohen, S., *et al.* eds. *From Immigration Control to Welfare Controls*. London, Routledge, pp. 30–46.

Huggan, G. (2001) *The Postcolonial Exotic: Marketing the Margins*. London, Routledge.

Lavoyer, J. (2000) 'Forced Displacement: The Relevance of International Humanitarian Law'. In: Bayefsky, A. F. and Fitzpatrick, J. eds. *Human Rights and Forced Displacement*. The Hague, Martinus Nijhoff, pp. 50–65.

Mason, P. (1998) *Infelicities: Representations of the Exotic*. London, Johns Hopkins University Press.

Mecham, M. (2005) 'At the Margins: The Politics of International Law and the Situation in Western Sahara'. Proceedings of the conference Seeking Refuge, Seeking Rights, Seeking a Future (unpublished), Oxford Brookes University, 13–14 May. Paper available at www.brookes.ac.uk/schools/planning/dfm/FMSC/P&A/mecham.pdf (accessed 21 January 2009).

Mertus, J. (2003) 'Sovereignty, Gender and Displacement'. In: Newman, E. and van Selm, J. eds. *Refugees and Forced Displacement: International Security, Human Vulnerability and the State*. Tokyo, United Nations University, pp. 250–73.

Raffel, S. (2001) 'On Generosity'. *History of the Human Sciences*, 14, pp. 111–28.

Röhl, K. (2005) 'Fleeing Violence and Poverty: Non-refoulement Obligations Under the European Convention of Human Rights', Working Paper No. 111. UN Refugee Agency. Available at www.unhcr.org/41f8ef4f2.pdf (accessed 21 January 2009).

Rosello, M. (2001) *Postcolonial Hospitality: The Immigrant as Guest*. Stanford, CA, Stanford University Press.

Scarry, E. (1985) *The Body in Pain: The Making and Unmaking of the World*. Oxford, Oxford University Press.

Sivanandan, A. (2001) 'Poverty Is the New Black'. *Race and Class*, 43(2), pp. 1–5.

Sontag, S. (2003) *Regarding the Pain of Others*. London, Hamish Hamilton.

Spivak, G. C. (1996) 'Subaltern Talk: Interview with the Editors, 1993–4'. In: Landry, D. and Maclean, G. eds. *The Spivak Reader*. London, Routledge, pp. 287–308.

—— (1998) 'Can the Subaltern Speak?' In: Nelson, C. and Grossberg, L. eds. *Marxism and the Interpretation of Culture*. Urbana, IL, University of Illinois Press, pp. 271–313.

Stewart, S. (1993) *On Longing: Narratives of the Miniature, the Gigantic, the Souvenir, the Collection*. Durham, NC, Duke University Press.

Tuitt, P. (1996) *False Images: Law's Construction of the Refugee*. London, Pluto Press.

Young, J. (1999) *The Exclusive Society*. London, Sage.

Young, R. J. C. (2001) *Postcolonialism: An Introduction*. Oxford, Blackwell.

CHAPTER 6

Migration, racism and postcolonial studies in Spain

Landry-Wilfrid Miampika and Maya García de Vinuesa

Introduction: global worlds and hybrid identities

The present globalized world is developing in a context of variable, multiple and, in many cases, multicultural identities, helping to produce a single space of different cultural modalities with their own specific value systems, their own founding myths, their own strategies to assert themselves in the public arena, and their own practices linked to particular histories and to their own sense of what is politically necessary, economically viable and morally or ethically good.

Cultural differences in our time urgently demand an intercultural consciousness which has, as its basic mode of operation, the concept of a reinvigorated multicultural society – a creative society that is capable of integration, one that allows for the possibility of a concrete utopia. The different modalities of hybridity and diaspora, in particular, not only modify such traditional concepts as 'identity', 'culture', 'difference/diversity' and 'human equality', but also require new ways of understanding politics and its ambiguous relation to social and cultural knowledge and the workings of the state. Hybridity – understood by the Argentinian theorist Néstor García Canclini in terms of those 'socio-cultural processes in which discrete structures or practices, which [previously] existed in a separate form, [now] combine to generate new structures ... and practices' (García Canclini 2001, p. 45) – is the key vector for all cultural processes, transcending fixed notions of cultural origin, purity and authenticity, and casting these aside in favour of new, transnational or transcontinental understandings of the fraught relations between different human beings and different social/cultural groups (Appadurai 1996).

This transnational or transcontinental dimension of culture and its local/global transformations is often seen as resulting from a new condition of voluntary and involuntary displacements (mass migrations, global diasporas and so on) that indicate a world that is increasingly connected by technological advances, but that is not necessarily unified or interdependent in terms of economics, culture and media. Some new cultural agents in Europe, for example, come from regions in Africa, Asia and Latin America where the lack of a sustainable economy, and of legitimate cultural and political institutions, seriously undermines the possibility of human emancipation on both the global and the local scale. In this context, the recognition of human *diversity* – the play of differences at work within larger categories of cultural diversity (see Bhabha 2004) – is indispensable as a tool both to anticipate new (and not so new) forms of cultural racism and to counteract their multiple social and historical effects.

Cultural pluralism, multiculturalism and cross-cultural interaction (sometimes called 'interculturalism') all present problems that urgently require collective solutions. They also require new understandings of identity as a dynamic, continually renegotiable process linked to discontinuous realities – realities confronted by the Martinican poet and theorist Édouard Glissant with his capacious notion of *la Relation*: 'a latent, open poetics [that] intends to be multilingual and … is legitimized by means of a recognition of … differences [that] flow, adjust [and] oppose one another'; by means of a recognition, in other words, of the diverse (Glissant 1995, p. 98). Glissant's poetics, however, poses numerous problems of its own, not least in relation to changing notions of 'the other'. How is 'the other' to be thought of in the context of multiple, fragmented identities? Do new, postcolonial societies offer alternative understandings of 'the other'? Can the poetics of *la Relation* help to broaden the horizon beyond exotic and/ or colonial representations of 'the other' as an immiserated subject? And what of 'the other' in the context of a rapidly expanding, nominally 'postcolonial' *Europe*? How is this 'other' to be articulated, and how are the new, apparently divisive but also potentially emancipatory social relations it brings into being to be explained?

Migrations and cultural mutations in Spain

In 2004, the then Secretary-General of the United Nations, Kofi Annan, wrote:

> Managing migration is not only a matter of opening doors and joining hands internationally. It also requires each country to do more to integrate new arrivals. Immigrants must adjust to their new societies – and societies need to adjust too. Only with an imaginative strategy for integrating immigrants can countries ensure that they enrich the host country more than they unsettle it. (Annan 2004, p. 2)

One of the most appropriate fields within which to formulate proposals for the productive coexistence of immigrants and the host society is *education*. In working to improve intercultural relations in the context of a postcolonial society, education must confront several crucial issues. What educational projects can be developed, for example, that will balance the idea of integration against that of multiple, diverse cultures? And can education help to produce new human subjects in the face of mass migrations and the inevitable social/cultural disturbances they cause?

These questions are central in Spain, particularly in view of a 2006 newspaper survey of the problems that the Spanish population was interested in: unemployment (49 per cent); immigration (29 per cent); and terrorism by ETA (28 per cent) (*El País*, 27 January 2006). Other statistics are equally telling:

- Spain has 3.7 million people of foreign origin, or immigrants. It was the member state of the European Union (EU) with the most immigrants in 2005, with the largest numbers coming from Morocco (511,294), Ecuador (497,799) and Romania (317,366).
- The population of Madrid, the capital of Spain, comprises 16 per cent (and rising) immigrants. In January 2001, the number of immigrants was 194,297; by January 2006 this number had risen to 596,824 (Ecuador was the country of origin of 26 per cent of this immigrant population; Colombia 9 per cent; Romania 7 per cent; Peru 6 per cent; Morocco 5 per cent).
- Immigrants from sub-Saharan Africa are a growing group, many of them still *ilegales*, constituting around 4.5 per cent of the estimated illegal immigrant population. These immigrants are subject to a greater degree of racism, both direct and indirect, than their Latin American and east European counterparts, these latter being seen as culturally and 'racially' closer to the mainstream group. The African immigrant group is frequently perceived to be homogeneous, and to be devoid of either history or culture: a jaundiced view that was bolstered until quite recently by the almost exclusively Eurocentric education most Spaniards received at school.
- Presently over 2 million Spanish people live outside Spain. However, this number is lower than the number of immigrants (3.7 million: see above) currently living in Spain. Surveys undertaken by the Organisation for Economic Co-operation and Development (OECD) clearly show that Europe needs immigration to boost its economy and to offset its demographic decline. Projections suggest that within the next twenty years at least 15 per cent of the total Spanish population will be immigrants.

In Spain there is no consensus on whether integration and intercultural mutation should be managed according to a French model (assimilation), a British one (communitarianism), or some combination of both (Naïr 2005a, 2005b, 2005c). Similarly contested is the question of whether 'non-western'/'non-European' citizens should be given the right to vote. These debates are obviously relevant not just to Spain, but to the whole of a 'postcolonial' Europe seeking to balance the principles of integration, inclusion and citizenship in the embattled context of continuing, sometimes exacerbated, social inequalities and uneven global cultural/economic flows (Gilroy 2004). Certainly, integration in Spain needs to be thought of in *global* terms; it belongs to the general debate on permeable cultural boundaries and identities in an increasingly globalized world. It also needs to be thought of in *European* terms, as part of a regional initiative to counteract institutionalized racism and social exclusion – fuelled by the 'moral panics' of the media – widespread prejudice and inflexibility in the labour market, and the frequently discriminatory management of public funds, public projects and public space.

The monitoring of racist practices in Spain started recently with the creation of various institutions, the impact of which it is not yet possible to evaluate. It is difficult to compare the effectiveness of these institutions with other European monitoring centres, such as the Institute of Race Relations in Britain, founded in 1958, which has a history of intervention in law and policy-making and of denouncing racist practices. That Institute should ideally act as a beacon for Spain and other southern European countries, where new migrants find themselves in societies in which debates on multiculturalism are just opening up and rampant discrimination is taking place at all levels. As for the wave of non-EU migration over the last decades of the twentieth century, Britain is fundamentally different from Spain because there are 'second' and 'third generations' of citizens ('black and minority ethnic' citizens, a label with implications that would need to be the subject of another essay), who have achieved full political participation and who have created mechanisms for the control of discriminatory practices.

One of the areas requiring urgent intervention is that of discrimination in the labour market; here, the transfer into Spanish law of the main European anti-discrimination directives of 2000 and 2002 was implemented only in 2004. These measures promote: (1) the application of the principle of equality among people regardless of their racial or ethnic origin, and the establishment of a general framework for equality of opportunity in employment; and (2) the application of the principle of equality for men and women in access to employment, training and promotion at work. One of the consequences of these Spanish laws has been the creation of specific organizations at a regional level (in the 17 *comunidades autónomas* or 'autonomous communities') and within a number of councils. These organizations are tasked with investigating the living conditions and socio-economic realities of the immigrant population and their level of integration, as well as campaigning for and defending their right to vote in local elections.

To give an example, the Comunidad de Madrid has created 35 organizations; prominent among these is the Observatorio de las Migraciones y de la Convivencia Intercultural de la Ciudad de Madrid (the Monitoring Centre for Migration and Intercultural Exchange of the City of Madrid – discussed in the next section, p. 96). The choice of the term 'intercultural' emphasizes the aspect of 'dialogue' among cultures, as opposed to the mere juxtaposition of cultures in isolation, which has been identified as one of the main reasons for the failures of the 'multicultural' model in northern Europe. The 2006 survey published by the Observatorio de las Migraciones contributed to the dissemination of knowledge and the creation of bridges between associations of immigrants, state institutions and research centres in universities.

The serious cases of discrimination and exploitation in the Spanish labour market affect all resident and 'illegal' non-EU men and women, mainly of Latin

American, African and eastern European origin. These people are hit disproportionately by unemployment in comparison with the indigenous population, and they tend to occupy the so-called 'secondary' sectors of the labour market: domestic service, agriculture, the hotel and catering trade, the building sector and retail. New migrants are concentrated within the first two sectors. Furthermore, domestic service is almost wholly feminized (80 per cent of the workforce are women), while agriculture and the building sector are masculinized to an even greater degree (with a 93 per cent male workforce). A sectoral analysis reveals a close relation between 'specialization' and the geographic (and racial) origin of immigrants: the agricultural sector is composed of 95 per cent foreigners, of whom 75 per cent are of Moroccan origin; and the building sector is composed of 78 per cent foreigners, of whom 70 per cent are also Moroccan (Cachón 2005, p. 12). In this sense, the state serves to ratify what the market has already selected, legalizing those migrants who have already been contracted within this range of activities. The disproportionate concentration of migrants in this range is undoubtedly because these sectors have the worst working conditions in the Spanish labour market.

The lack of correspondence between the characteristics of the jobs occupied by immigrants with their professional qualifications and educational level reveals the sharp ethno-stratification of the occupational pyramid, the peak of which consists of EU and North American foreigners, while its base comprises non-EU foreigners and migrants from Central and South America and Africa. Some surveys have highlighted recruitment by companies as the critical stage at which most of the labour discrimination takes place: semi-qualified Moroccan young men suffer more discrimination than indigenous young people or those belonging to other 'particular ethnic groups' who are considered 'less prone to generate conflict' or 'more obedient', such as Ecuadorians. Thus, 'culture', or the lack of adaptation 'due to culture', emerges as the new racism. On the other hand, surveys on salary differentials between indigenous and immigrant workers reveal the existence of a hierarchy of wages depending on nationality and on the type of job, with frequent cases of exploitation in the sectors of domestic service, agriculture and building. Finally, it is imperative to investigate and denounce those extreme situations of discrimination, characterized by the media and the police as situations of 'semi-slavery', which are managed by criminal networks that control illegal workers, particularly in agriculture and in the large underground or 'black' economy (Cachón 2005, pp. 11–18).

Racism and intercultural exchange in Madrid

The capital of Spain, Madrid, is the city with the most immigrants in the whole country. The Monitoring Centre for Migration and Intercultural Exchange, founded in 2005 by a research group at the Autónoma University (Madrid), had the remit of preventing overt or covert demonstrations of racism and discrimination in the social, economic and educational sectors of Madrid; it aimed to study integration policies and to observe the presence of immigrants and their interaction with the indigenous population (in 2008 the Centre's management was passed to a private company and its remit changed). One of the responsibilities that this Monitoring Centre took up was to try to reflect precisely on the problems which may arise, or indeed on existing conflicts, in the course of interaction between immigrants and their immediate environment: the perceptions that one group (the Spanish) have of others (immigrants) and vice versa at the level of integration; the sense of belonging, or not, within the indigenous community; and the analysis of concerns over unemployment, housing, education, and so on.

The *Annual Record of Intercultural Exchange*, published by the Monitoring Centre, provided diverse data and analyses on discrimination and racism. The 2006 survey dealt with the coexistence of different groups on the basis of four questions: 'attitudes towards immigration; the likes and dislikes displayed towards different national groups; the assessment of diversity in different aspects; and opinions on the possibility for non-EU immigrants to vote in local elections' (Observatorio de las Migraciones 2006, p. 219). According to data provided by the survey, a greater openness towards diversity was registered from different groups and towards each other, although 11 per cent of *madrileños* evaluate diversity negatively. As for likes and dislikes, the indigenous population was the one favoured by most, while Moroccans appeared to generate the most dislike among the foreign communities living in Madrid. The diversity of food and artistic expression was highly valued by all communities. But negative attitudes emerged with respect to different religions, other languages and non-western clothing.

With regard to discrimination and racism on the grounds of gender, race, ethnicity, religion or country of origin, 90 per cent of the population of Madrid did not feel discriminated against. But some areas in which the population had felt discrimination were related to nationality (11 per cent), culture (6 per cent) and religion (4 per cent). It is important to highlight that both rejection and acceptance may be subjective, and thus more reliable methods of evaluation of racism and discrimination are required.

The cultural diversification of Madrid is progressing in a way accepted by a wide variety of communities, although stigmatization of at least some of these communities can readily be found. This requires, as a problem of daily life and interaction, a particular type of monitoring. Continuing stigmatization obviously impedes diversification and can result in confrontation between communities and a general failure in the design of integration policies (with inequalities leading to the further social, economic and political marginalization of ethnic minority groups).

In light of this situation, it is still too early to present precise perceptions of racism and discrimination beyond the stridently negative representations that often appear in the media. But it is imperative to design strategies and policies focusing on the living conditions of immigrants in Spanish society. These should be conceived by means of intercultural mediation, which has the aim of harmonizing integration, citizenship and political rights.

A more positive view of immigration also needs to include (without romanticizing) the advantages that can be offered by the productive co-habitation of different peoples in the European region, and the creative synergies – social, cultural, political – that can be produced within the dynamic 'contact zones' of intercultural encounter in the world today (Gilroy 2004; Pratt 1992).

Schools and institutions of higher education could play a key role in working towards consensus on an immigration policy aimed at redressing social and political marginalization and at making immigrants more aware of both their civic responsibilities and their civil rights. One of the particular challenges facing Spanish higher education is how to incorporate alternative 'non-western' areas of knowledge – those highly differentiated areas of knowledge that derive, for instance, from the vast African continent. One goal here might be to create a new space of 'conviviality' that promotes the vision of a multicultural society capable of transcending racialist ideologies and fundamentalist particularisms in the greater service of human cooperation and goodwill (Gilroy 2004). The 'alliance of civilizations' currently being promoted by the Spanish government belongs to this project, insofar as it aims to found a new human contract, disseminated widely across the region, which combats xenophobia and racism in all social spheres.

Challenges and cultural practices in a transcultural society

It is in Shakespeare's *The Tempest* that we find the creation of two figures – two divided image-metaphors, one accorded to the arrogant colonizer (Prospero), the other to his disaffected subaltern (Caliban) – who have apparent connections to the equally dichotomous, 'civilizationist' view of world culture sometimes articulated today. As this chapter has been suggesting, a different view of the Prospero–Caliban relationship is now needed: one based on Deleuze and Guattari's concept of 'rhizomatic' as opposed to 'single-root' identities, and on the idea of 'culture' as a volatile space within which disparate elements – including people – alternately collide and converge (Deleuze and Guattari 1997). The term 'transculturation', derived from cultural anthropology, is helpful in showing how cultures are not implacably locked in a struggle of irreconcilable differences, but rather combined in ways that suggest that these differences are not necessarily tethered to European cultural norms (Pratt 1992).

'Postcolonial' is another term under which these alternative readings of cultural difference may shelter, for example by gesturing towards possibilities of intercultural reconciliation or by positing indefinite 'third spaces' (Bhabha 2004) that move beyond traditional ideas of 'culture' as a homogenizing force. Postcolonial literatures, for example, bring with them other visions and versions of 'the other' that create bridges between the same and the diverse. As narratives of emancipation, postcolonial literatures mediate a dialectical relationship between history and geography, showing what (ex-)colonizers and (ex-)colonized have in common, but do not necessarily share. In this sense, their resistance foreshadows a new intellectual and political consciousness, a new framework of human understanding which, in addressing the colonial situation, simultaneously looks forward to the time when that situation will be eventually overcome.

Postcolonial (literary) study in Spain is arguably in the ascendancy, although, as the following thumbnail sketch will illustrate, it still has a long way to go before it can consider itself an institutionalized field. Literary study in Spanish universities is currently divided into discrete language areas, so that some of the literatures of Spain's former colonies – Latin American and Moroccan literatures, for instance – may be studied as part of a Spanish or an Arabic degree. The Spanish-language literature of Equatorial Guinea, Spain's other former African colony, is not officially on any programme of Spanish or Spanish studies, although it occasionally makes a cameo appearance in a postgraduate course.

Thus, while undergraduate and postgraduate programmes of Spanish or Spanish studies offer a restricted range of subjects related to, say, Latin American literatures, there are currently no specific departments of Latin American literature in Spain. Latin American literature is offered regularly as both compulsory and optional elements within a Spanish degree (which operates, like all degrees in Spain, on a cumulative credit system); but it is usually taught by individual specialists who have not yet been able to develop their specializations into an area of study in its own right. 'Latin American' or, sometimes, 'Hispanic American' prevail here as generalizing labels; regional subdivisions (Central or South America, Caribbean, etc.) are nowhere to be found. Some state funding is provided for the visit of Latin American academics, but – in a move that is frustratingly symptomatic – these academics are enjoined to carry out research not on the emergent literatures of their own countries, but, typically, on the eternal wisdoms of Cervantes' *El Quijote* (*Don Quixote*).

Afro-Hispanic studies, similarly, are institutionally marginalized; interest in this particular literary/cultural area has developed seriously only outside Spain. Thus, excellent writers like Donato Ndongo, Maria Nsue Angüe and Francisco Zamora Loboch, among the first wave of African writers living in Spain and writing in Spanish, constitute something of a 'lost generation', like their 1960s black British counterparts (although far more attention is given to black British writing than to black Spanish writing, which is also a reflection of relative demographics in Britain and Spain).

While Francophone literatures are similarly peripheral to humanities study at Spanish universities, the situation is slightly better for Anglophone literatures, sometimes also called 'postcolonial literatures in English', even though postcolonial (literary) studies can hardly be considered central to any European language and literature degree. In fact, current evidence suggests a state of marginalization across the board (Latin American literatures, around 4 per cent of compulsory credits in Spanish degrees; Anglophone or postcolonial literatures in English, up to 6 per cent of optional credits in English degrees as a whole). However, the gravitation in Spanish higher education towards more specialized postgraduate programmes may yet allow postcolonial literatures, and particular postcolonial literatures in English, to evolve into fields in their own right.

Conclusion: global utopia and transcultural identities

In *Culture and Imperialism* (1993), Edward Said was right to insist on valuing the contributions of 'non-European' artists and intellectuals to the culture of Europe, as well as their contributions to the necessary project of 'provincializing' Europe (Chakrabarty 1992), claiming common ground both within and outside the region for whites and non-whites alike. Taking its cue from Said, this chapter ends with some unashamedly utopian thoughts on the emancipatory potential of the 'transnational imaginary' (Wilson and Dissanayake 1996) and on the possibilities it might offer for a re-imagined Europe:

- Culture is not just a creative inventory of the past and present of a community; it is also a space for a renegotiation of identities and the projection of hybrid identities, both at present and for future times.
- The grounds and principles for conviviality need to be established through a dialogue that takes into account equal rights and social opportunities, political and religious freedoms, and opportunities for economic (self-)realization in the context of a society in which the pursuit of competition should never allow for the sacrifice of care.
- In terms of the relations between a globalized world, solidarity and interculturality, we must ask, with Jose Monleón, whether globalization does not also include international solidarity. Does not globalization, after all, 'entail the awareness of a new relation among the social realities and interests of different countries' (García Selgás and Monleón 1999, p. 12)?
- Multiculturalism is a possible, even a desirable, goal. It is a common space, without fundamentalism or essentialism, in a society in permanent dialogue, a society that enriches all those who live in it and that does not discriminate on the basis of gender, ethnicity, racial origin or religious belief.
- The subversive hybridity of cultures, histories and identities revitalizes a utopia, the envisioning of which is both possible and necessary. Such a utopian vision includes, foregrounds, those previously excluded or considered marginal; develops new modes and models of cross-cultural communication; and projects specific forms of human utopia based on the transcultural, ecumenical view of Glissant's *tout-monde* (Glissant 1995). 'Postcolonial Europe' belongs to this project, not just in the sense of provincializing Europe, but of joining Europe to a plural world and propagating the ideal of common belonging that a properly transcultural vision of the world brings, and that all people living in it deserve.

Works cited

Annan, K. (2004) 'Why Europe Needs an Immigration Strategy', 29 January. Available at www.un.org/News/ossg/sg/stories/sg-29jan2004.htm (accessed 26 January 2009).

Appadurai, A. (1996) *Modernity at Large: Cultural Dimensions of Globalization*. Minneapolis, MN, University of Minnesota Press.

Bhabha, H. (2004) *The Location of Culture*. London, Routledge.

Cachón, L. (2005) 'Discriminación étnica en el mercado laboral'. *Puntos de Vista*, 5, pp. 7–24.

Chakrabarty, D. (1992) 'Postcoloniality and the Artifice of History: Who Speaks for "Indian" Pasts?' *Representations*, 37, pp. 1–26.

Deleuze, G. and Guattari, F. (1997) *Milles Plateaux: Capitalism and Schizophrenia*. Minneapolis, MN, University of Minnesota Press.

García Canclini, N. (2001) *Culturas híbridas. Estrategias para entrar y salir de la modernidad*. Buenos Aires, Paidos.

García Selgás, F. J. and Monleón, J. B. (1999) *Retos de la postmodernidad*. Madrid, Editorial Trotta.

Gilroy, P. (2004) *After Empire: Melancholia or Convivial Culture?* London, Routledge.

Glissant, E. (1995) *Introduction a une poetique du divers*. Paris, Gallimard.

Naïr, S. (2005a) 'Guerra de identidades en Londres'. *El Pais*, 21 July, p. 13.

—— (2005b) 'Lo que ocurre allí'. *El Pais*, 8 October, p. 15.

—— (2005c) 'Las llamas francesas'. *El Pais*, 12 November, p. 17.

Observatorio de las Migraciones y de la Convivencia Intercultural de la Ciudad de Madrid (2006) *Anuario de la convivencia intercultural*. Madrid, Publicaciones del Observatorio de las Migraciones y de la Convivencia Intercultural de la Ciudad de Madrid.

Pratt, M. L. (1992) *Imperial Eyes: Travel Writing and Transculturation*. New York, Routledge.

Said, E. W. (1993) *Culture and Imperialism*. New York, Knopf.

Wilson, R. and Dissanayake, W. eds. (1996) *Global/Local: Cultural Production and the Transnational Imaginary*. Durham, NC, Duke University Press.

CHAPTER 7

The 'sick man' beyond Europe: the orientalization of Turkey and Turkish immigrants in European Union accession discourses in Germany

Christoph Ramm

'Turkey in Europe has come to an end, she must get out, and the less trouble she makes the better.'[1] This statement by Kaiser Wilhelm II expressed his disappointment that the Ottoman army, though trained by German military instructors and equipped with German weapons, had performed poorly against Serbian, Greek and Bulgarian troops during the Balkan War in 1912, and that the Ottoman Empire had lost all its remaining provinces in the Balkans and Macedonia, with even its capital Istanbul under threat. It seemed only a matter of time until the Anatolian and Asian parts of a weak and declining Empire would be divided between the European powers as well, and Germany expected to get its fair share (Adanır 1991, pp. 202–3).

Centuries earlier, after the Ottomans had conquered Constantinople in 1453 and later extended their Empire to the gates of Vienna, 'the Turks' – as the Ottomans were mostly referred to – were perceived as powerful rivals and as a constant threat to European states. With increasing cultural encounters, particularly in the sixteenth and seventeenth centuries, ambivalent impressions of curiosity, amazement and admiration were added to the popular image of the Turks as barbarians, infidels and the cruel enemy (Çırakman 2002, p. 35). Increasing Ottoman defeats in the eighteenth century, however, and the resultant shift in the balance of power between western Europe and the Empire gradually altered European perceptions of its Turkish counterpart (Çırakman 2002, p. 28). Emerging civilization theories, particularly about 'oriental despotism' (see Adanır and Schneiderheinze 2001), contributed to an increasingly reductive view of Ottoman society, which was portrayed as 'a static and slavish

---

1   Telegraphic order to the German Imperial Chancellor, 15 November 1912 (No. 10, A. 20263, Politisches Archiv des Auswärtigen Amtes, Bonn, Türkei 203, Bd. 8). Quoted in Adanır (1991, pp. 202–3). If not further stated, all original German quotes were translated by the author.

society, a backward and corrupt polity, with arbitrary and ferocious rulers governing servile and timid subjects' (Çırakman 2002, p. 216).

In the nineteenth century, the military weakness of the Ottomans encouraged the imperial ambitions of the European powers and competing Balkan national-isms, thereby strengthening the belief that the destruction of a 'decaying' empire was inevitable. It was Russian Tsar Nicholas I who is said to have described the Ottoman state as the 'sick man of Europe' when he proposed (to the British) a division of the Empire in 1853 (Kedourie 1999, p. 237). This plan failed due to rivalries between the imperial powers, leading to the Crimean War of 1853–56, but the expression ascribed to the Tsar embarked on a successful career that has endured to the present day. The 'sick man of Europe'[2] has become such a powerful metaphor for 'Turkey' (and beyond) that even such a dedicated critic of orientalist thought as Edward Said used metaphorical illness when, in his best-known book, *Orientalism* (1978), he referred to British and French interests in 'the territory of the now terminally ill Ottoman Empire' (Said 1978, p. 220).

After the Crimean War, however, the 'sick man' was still alive and well in Europe, and in order to balance the conflicting interests of the European powers the Ottoman Empire gained membership of the Concert of Europe, the state system of the continent (Adanır 2005, p. 408). The image of the 'sick man', on the other hand, does not take into account that the 'patient's' rulers were fully aware of the shortcomings of their state. They duly instigated a simultaneously ambitious and ambiguous modernization process after western models, intensified with the reforms of the *Tanzimat* after 1839 and continued under the rule of the Young Turks after 1908 – with an increasingly Turkish nationalist orientation. But all these efforts did not prevent continuing claims on Ottoman territory. Particularly in the German Empire, colonial aspirations were projected onto the 'Orient', with strategies ranging from cooperation to economic influence, to colonization projects and territorial occupation, some or all of which would be necessary if the Ottoman state were to be divided at last (Adanır 1991, pp. 196–206).

Kaiser Wilhelm's angry order to oust 'Turkey' from 'Europe' did not material-ize. At the end of the Balkan Wars in 1913, the Ottoman Empire kept Thrace and Istanbul, a situation that remained unchanged throughout the First World War and the Turkish War of Independence that followed it. During the inter-war period, Turkey seemed to have lost its special place in European experience and thought. Apart from a certain admiration for the Kemalist transforma-tion process following the establishment of the Turkish Republic in 1923, the country was regarded as being on the European periphery (Adanır 1991, pp. 206–11). During the Cold War, Turkey secured the 'south-eastern flank' for the North Atlantic Treaty Organization (NATO), and the country's status as part of the west was not in question, since it was a member of all of the important western organizations and alliances: NATO, the Organization for Security and

---

2　Other popular versions are 'the sick man on the Bosphorus' or 'the sick man of the east'.

Co-operation in Europe (OSCE) and the Council of Europe (Lossau 2002, p. 136). This perception radically changed, however, when Turkey's accession to the European Union (EU) came on the agenda and, ninety years after the German Kaiser's notorious remarks, 'the Turks' started to trouble Europe again. In many EU countries, particularly Germany, the prospect of the Ottomans' successors joining the common European house triggered a heated debate, one effect of which was to make the 'sick man' rise and walk from the depths of Europe's colonial imagination once again.

Turkey under debate

The question as to whether Turkey should become a member of the EU is not a new one. When the European Economic Community (EEC) and the Republic of Turkey signed an association agreement in 1963, the text referred explicitly to the possibility of Turkey's accession to the Community in future. Until the 1990s, however, the agreement proved difficult to implement (Carnevale *et al.* 2005, p. 32). After the military coup in 1980, the EEC suspended its relations with Turkey, so it was not until 1987 that the Turkish Prime Minister, Turgut Özal, submitted an application for membership. Astonishingly, this was not followed by any significant public discussion, with the fervent debate in Germany in the 1980s and 1990s being focused more on human rights abuses and Turkey's Kurdish policy than on the accession issue (Kramer 2003, p. 7).

The Luxemburg EU summit in 1997, with its decision to exclude Turkey from the new candidate states, and later the Helsinki summit in 1999, which granted Turkey official candidate status, caused rather short-lived debates among the German public. The controversy heated up again though in 2002, when the Turkish government – probably faster than was expected in EU circles – made significant progress in meeting the candidacy criteria and demanded the start of accession negotiations (Kramer 2003, p. 8).

The ensuing debate in Germany was part of a wider European discussion about Turkey's application, since this was a controversial issue in many other EU countries as well.[3] In contrast to Britain, where all major political parties and opinion leaders took a supportive stance on Turkish membership[4] – the

---

3 For a comparative analysis of media discourses on Turkey's accession in different EU countries, see Carnevale *et al.* (2005) and Giannakopoulos and Maras (2005). Both studies emphasize that the debate could hardly be regarded as a common 'European' one, since the issue was predominantly discussed within the various national contexts (Carnevale *et al.* 2005, p. 109; Giannakopoulos and Maras 2005, p. 217).

4 Regarding their anti-Turkish position, even Conservative-leaning publications in Britain (such as the *Spectator* and the *Daily Telegraph*) depicted European conservatives, and especially German Christian Democrats, as 'Islamophobic', 'essentialist' and 'racist' (Oktem 2005, p. 10). The question arises, however, as to how the changing debate on migration in Britain might affect such an anti-essentialist approach to Turkey's EU prospects in future. See for example the following contribution from *The Times*, in which Melanie McDonagh appraises critically

support of the Conservatives often being accompanied by a rejection of further European integration or of the EU itself (Oktem 2005, pp. 3–4) – the German public were deeply split over the issue. In Germany, the opponents of Turkey's accession were mostly conservatives or Christian Democrats, while the majority of supporters were liberal, Social Democrat or Green, but the positions crossed political and party affiliations nevertheless. Unlike in countries such as France and the Netherlands, the German debate on Turkey's bid for EU membership overshadowed other important issues, like the draft European constitution or the call for common European social standards. Indeed, it developed into the most significant EU-related controversy in Germany in recent years.

It was the influential German historian Hans-Ulrich Wehler, a renowned expert in social history and long-time supporter of the Social Democratic Party, who gave a particular boost to the cultural, religious and historical dimension in the growing debate in Germany over Turkey's candidacy. In an article entitled 'Das Türkenproblem' ('The Turkish Problem') and published in the German liberal weekly *Die Zeit* in September 2002, Wehler demanded that 'this Muslim country should never join the EU', because 'as a Muslim state a deep cultural boundary separates this country from Europe'. 'Regarding its geographical location, historical past, religion, culture, and mentality, Turkey is not a part of Europe', Wehler argued, adding that 'the incorporation of 90 million or more Turks would destroy the historical character of the [European] Union'. According to Wehler, 'multiculturalists' were undermining the cherished idea that 'Europe is a club of states imbued with Christian principles':

> The Muslim Ottoman Empire was almost incessantly at war with Christian Europe for about 450 years; once its armies even stood at the gates of Vienna. These events have been deeply inscribed into the collective memory of the peoples of Europe, but also of Turkey. Therefore there is no reason why this incarnation of an antagonism should be admitted to the EU.[5]

In the course of the debate, Wehler's theses were picked up on by several opponents of Turkish membership, although not always in as explicit a manner as his. Similar ideas were embraced not only by the conservative media or Christian Democrat politicians, but also gained support among liberal and Social Democrat politicians, journalists and academics. Even a former Social Democrat Chancellor, Helmut Schmidt, joined the ranks of those fervently attacking the idea of Turkey ever becoming a member of the EU.

The controversy reached its height before the EU summit in Copenhagen in December 2002, where a decision for accession negotiations was made. But it

---

the arrival of Polish immigrants in Britain after the EU enlargement in 2004 and warns of massive immigration from Turkey after its accession: 'Trouble is, Turkey is a country with 80 million people now, and growing fast. And it's barely European. A mere 3 per cent of Turkey, geographically, is in Europe; the rest is in Asia. It's Islamic, with a potential for Muslim extremism which is not true of the C of E-style European Muslims of Bosnia and Albania' (Melanie McDonagh, 'Poles Aplenty? Wait Till the Turks Arrive', *The Times*, 23 August 2006).

5   Hans-Ulrich Wehler, 'Das Türkenproblem' ['The Turkish Problem'], *Die Zeit*, 38, 2002.

flared again in the weeks preceding the summit in Brussels in December 2004, where Turkey got a date for accession talks, and – to a lesser extent – before the decision to start negotiations in October 2005. The arguments rejecting or supporting Turkish EU membership, however, did not change substantially during this period.

Turkey exclusive – the demarcation of Europe

Though in Turco-sceptic discourses an openly culturalist perspective like Wehler's is often disguised behind more 'rational' political or economic arguments, these discourses clearly reveal a tendency to identify Turkey as a non-European place attributed with 'Islamic', 'oriental' and – to a lesser degree – 'Asian' connotations. In these perceptions, a fundamentally different character of Turkey and its population is expressed by a set of representations, or lines of demarcation, that usually appear in various easily identifiable combinations.

The strictest and sharpest imagined line of demarcation is religion, as is the case, for example, in an interview with Wehler in which he describes Islam as a 'militant monotheism whose origin in the world of belligerent Arab nomadic tribes is obvious', thereby connecting Turkey's EU bid with a 'religion which is conspicuously expanding in a rapid way and will pass Christianity soon'.[6] The perceived threat of Islam also lurks behind the more cautious statements of Wehler's colleague Heinrich August Winkler – a well known historian with Social Democrat affiliations – to the effect that, compared with 'the finally successful separation of religious and secular power' in Europe, 'Turkey put through a kind of forced secularization guaranteed by the military until now' and thus 'has not become a Western democracy'.[7] In addition, the widespread and repeated use of certain images in media illustrations of the Turkey debate serve as more subtle forms of religious demarcation. In these illustrations, minarets or women wearing head-scarves often appear as markers of religious difference. Other contributions similarly try to strengthen the religious argument by linking the EU accession of an 'Islamic' country with the dangers posed by Islamism and terrorism: a Christian Democrat motion of December 2004, for instance, declared that, as a result of Turkey's EU prospects, Germany may be confronted with 'a rise in the activities of criminal gangs' and 'an increasing Islamist threat and terrorist danger'.[8]

One apparently more moderate way of demarcating Turkey as non-European is to insist on monolithic civilizations and identities. As in the following editorial taken from a German centre-right economic magazine, European identity is constructed as western identity, while Turkey is located in an imagined 'Islamic civilization':

---

6 *Die Tageszeitung*, 10 September 2002.
7 *Focus*, 16 December 2002.
8 *Die Welt*, 14 December 2004.

> Europe, if it has a meaning, is unconceivable without its civilization, its cultural identity, and that is western identity. Turkey, however, is part of a different civilization, that is to say Islamic civilization. The supporters of Mustafa Kemal Atatürk have been trying to transform the country into a western civilization for decades, but such a transformation has never been accomplished in the history of the human race.... Europe's continued existence requires the defence of western civilization. Peace on earth requires civilizations living together with an equal status.[9]

The stressing of the equal status of supposedly unalterable civilizations covers an underlying essentialism with a gloss of modernity.

The religious/cultural argument is often wrapped in historical narratives that exclude Turkey from European history. These mostly impassioned narratives reclaim a set of 'progressive forces' (e.g. classical Greek–Roman antiquity, Judaeo-Christian culture, the Protestant reformation, the Renaissance, secularization, the Enlightenment, or the scientific revolution) as Europe's unique historical experience. In this sense, the German conservative daily *Die Welt* claims that the 'heritage of classical antiquity, Jewish-Christian ethics, the Renaissance and the Enlightenment left [Turkey] as untouched as we were untouched by the culture of the Harem'.[10] Instead, this heritage is exclusively ascribed to 'European identity' and 'European values', as in the following statement by Edmund Stoiber, head of the Christian Social Union (CSU) and former Prime Minister of the German state of Bavaria: 'Turkey did not participate in the Enlightenment and in the struggle the peoples of Europe fought for liberty, emancipation and solidarity. These, however, are the foundations of European values and identity.'[11]

The supposedly unchangeable nature of geography serves as another objection against Turkish candidacy, when, for instance, the leading Christian Democrat politician Wolfgang Schäuble – who became Federal Minister of the Interior in 2005 – states that 'Turkey ends at the Iraq border' and 'as a whole ... is not a part of Europe'.[12] However, considering the arbitrary drawing of Europe's boundaries, the rejection of Turkey's Europeanness simply for geographical reasons appears even to some critics of Turkish EU membership as too crude an argument, and one that might end up casting doubt on the European character of French, British or Dutch overseas territories as well. These critics prefer instead to emphasize the dubious and dangerous character of neighbouring states, a strategy which is employed in the following question in an editorial from the conservative daily *Hamburger Abendblatt*: 'Why should the EU agree to get charming neighbours like Iraq, the Syrian dictatorship, the Iranian theocracy and eroding states like Georgia or Armenia?'[13] Others

---

9 'Selbstmord Europas' ('European Suicide'), *Wirtschaftswoche*, 12 December 2002.

10 'Zehn Gründe gegen den EU-Beitritt der Türkei' ('Ten Arguments against Turkey's EU Accession'), *Die Welt*, 24 September 2004.

11 *Süddeutsche Zeitung*, 11 December 2002.

12 *Süddeutsche Zeitung*, 19 December 2002.

13 'Fass ohne Boden' ('An Endless Drain'), *Hamburger Abendblatt*, 17 December 2004.

warn about the possible dangers awaiting Europe if its 'boundaries are moved towards regions which have been a comfortable place for gangs of smugglers, traffickers and criminals for centuries'.[14]

In contrast to essentialist categories like religion, culture, history or geography, other objections against Turkey's EU application seem more 'rational' or 'realistic'. However, political and economic arguments focusing on the EU's structural problems and Turkey's unstable economic condition often play with underlying fears, in particular when warnings against an 'overstretching' of the Union are combined with demographic references to the size of the Turkish population. The following statement of former Bavarian Prime Minister Edmund Stoiber, for instance, conveys this perceived threat of 'Turkish domination':

> At the moment of accession Turkey with its now 69 million inhabitants would be the member state with the largest population. It would occupy most seats in the European Parliament and would gain most votes in the EU Council of Ministers. This would mean again tremendous changes in the EU structures.[15]

One of the most popular arguments against Turkey, especially among Turco-sceptics with a liberal or left background, is a persistent emphasis on human rights violations and insufficient democratization. These shortcomings are not regarded as something that might be changed during the EU accession process, as the proponents of Turkish membership claim, but are more or less explicitly attributed to certain deep-rooted 'national' or 'Islamic' traditions. The following editorial from the liberal *Süddeutsche Zeitung* illustrates this attribution: 'For Europe, supposedly a "community of shared values", it is a constant danger to its survival to open the door to Turkey, where the blood of torture victims is still coagulating on the prison walls'.[16]

A popular variation on this theme is the depiction of patriarchal violence, such as forced marriages or so-called 'honour killings', as traditional elements of 'Turkish' or 'Islamic' culture. Elke Heidenreich, for instance, a popular German author and literary critic, asks why a 'country whose fathers still force daughters into marriage and whose women, even if they have been raped, are still killed because of so-called family honour … should join the EU?'[17] Christian Democrat leader and, later, Germany's first female Chancellor, Angela Merkel, put it more cautiously, suggesting Germany and Turkey have different ideas regarding women's rights.[18]

This category of demarcation also includes the efforts of some opponents of Turkish membership to create a link between the EU accession process and

---

14 'Unbehagen an der Europäischen Union' ('Unease about the European Union'), *Die Welt*, 16 December 2004.
15 *Süddeutsche Zeitung*, 11 December 2002.
16 Christian Wernicke, 'Die Mega-Union' ['The Mega Union'], *Süddeutsche Zeitung*, 16 December 2002.
17 *Stern*, 8 June 2004.
18 *Süddeutsche Zeitung*, 12 December 2004.

the refusal of the Turkish government and official Turkish historiography to recognize the genocide of the Ottoman Armenians in 1915. The genocide, which has become increasingly the subject of a controversial debate in Turkey as well, is levelled against modern Turkish society as a whole, sometimes even invoking hoary colonial stereotypes of 'Turkish barbarism'. At the same time, the issue may also be used to create a positive vision of Europe, in which EU countries have fully come to terms with their past, as can be seen in a parliamentary motion put forward by the German Christian Democrats on the ninetieth anniversary of the Armenian genocide in April 2005:

> This negative stance [on recognition of the Armenian genocide] contradicts the idea of reconciliation which is a guiding principle of the European Union, a community of shared values, membership of which Turkey aspires to…. The states of the European Union are distinguished by their willingness to recognize their colonial past and the dark sides of their national history.[19]

In the specific German context, though, one of the most important lines of demarcation against Turkey and Turkish people is the migration issue. Many critics directly link the situation of the three million plus immigrants of Turkish origin currently living in Germany to Turkey's EU candidacy. This move must be seen within the framework of a changing debate on immigration, with the spread of a German integrationism characterized by assertions about 'failed multiculturalism', demands for more pressure to intensify the immigrants' 'integration', and calls for a German *Leitkultur*.[20] The course of the debate reflects a significant shift in the perception of immigrants in general and the large Turkish community in particular. Older images of Turkish immigrants emphasized their ethnic and cultural 'otherness' as *Ausländer* (foreigners); more recently, the notion was advanced of a second generation 'caught between two cultures' (see Ramm 2006). Now, however, the increasingly heterogeneous German-Turkish community is being reduced to the vision of a Muslim collective living in 'parallel societies' and 'resisting integration'. The public 'Islamization' of German Turks is thus able to attribute social exclusion, educational shortcomings and forms of patriarchal violence to the immigrants' Islamic origin. Opponents of Turkey's EU membership such as Wehler repeatedly use the notion of 'failed integration' as a key element of their argument against the country's accession:

> Overall in Europe Muslim minorities defy assimilation and retreat to their subcultures. It is well known that the Federal Republic [of Germany] does not have a problem with foreigners, it has a problem with the Turks alone.[21]

---

19 CDU/CSU parliamentary motion, 19 April 2005.

20 The German term *Leitkultur* includes connotations of both 'guiding cultural values' and 'leading culture'. While the adherents of *Leitkultur* insist on its meaning as 'guiding values', they deny the hegemonic overtone.

21 Hans-Ulrich Wehler, 'Das Türkenproblem' ['The Turkish Problem'], *Die Zeit*, 38, 2002.

A central part of this narrative is the apocalyptic scenario of millions of poor Anatolians queuing up to pour into the EU, and particularly into Germany, once freedom of movement has been granted to Turkish citizens:

> The freedom would get many Anatolian peasants moving. Experts fear that up to 3 million people could migrate towards the north-west. About 15 million Muslims live in the EU, 2.5 million Turks in Germany alone. With some exceptions their integration has failed.[22]

Accordingly, the former Social Democrat German Chancellor Helmut Schmidt – a strong adversary of Turkey's candidacy – has said that 'it is vital to restrict immigration from different cultural spheres conjointly'.[23]

Turkey half inclusive – enriching Europe and its geopolitical ambitions

In the various discourses against Turkey's EU accession analysed above, culturalist representations and racist stereotypes are relatively obvious and can be traced rather easily. On the other hand, neither are the mainstream discourses in favour of Turkish membership free of the notion of unchangeably separate cultures and persistent images of the Orient and the Occident. In this respect, a diplomatic-political argument focusing on the long history of relations between Turkey and the European Community/European Union appears to be least influenced by cultural demarcations, emphasizing the obligations deriving from earlier treaties and the promises made by European governments in the past.

Since the media debate is dominated by controversy about Turkey's geographical/historical/cultural 'location', some supporters of Turkish membership try to 'prove' Turkey's 'Europeanness' through alternative historical accounts, often affirming the Kemalist modernization project in the first half of the twentieth century and praising the Republican state model. The German-Turkish author Zafer Şenocak argues in the left daily *Die Tageszeitung* accordingly: 'Since the establishment of the Turkish Republic in 1923 it has no longer been the question of whether Turkey is a part of Europe. Today Turkey is a member of all European organizations.'[24]

This view is less common, however, than the argument that it is precisely the country's 'otherness' or 'in-betweenness' that may enrich European culture (Carnevale *et al.* 2005, p. 81). In this narrative, Turkey is frequently imagined as a place somehow 'in-between Europe and the Orient', a 'bridge between the civilizations', as the following editorial from the *Süddeutsche Zeitung* illustrates:

---

22 'Zehn Gründe gegen den EU-Beitritt der Türkei' ('Ten Arguments Against Turkey's EU Accession'). *Die Welt*, 24 September 2004.
23 *Die Zeit*, 25 November 2004.
24 Zafer Şenocak, 'Auf ewig anders?' ['Forever Different?'], *Die Tageszeitung*, 25 November 2002.

> Turkey is a country between the civilizations, a country which will open new geopolitical horizons to Europe.... Turkey is a bridge, a country between the continents, a synthesis of European Christian and Middle Eastern Islamic culture.[25]

This argument is usually combined with references to Turkey's prospective contribution in the field of geopolitics and global strategy. The EU candidate is presented as a country that is not fully European, but still a necessary safeguard for Europe's security and its strategic interests in the Middle East. Its membership might thus upgrade the global strategic role of the EU; in this sense, the former Social Democrat German Chancellor Gerhard Schröder states that Turkish EU membership 'would mean a large gain in security for Europe and for Germany',[26] and a committee of the Social Democratic Party (SPD) sees 'Turkey's geostrategic importance' in 'its geographical location between the Orient and the Occident': 'Turkey will play an increasingly important role as a transit country for oil and gas from the Caucasus and Central Asia, and also in the field of migration control and the fight against terror, drug trafficking and organized crime'.[27]

A complementary narrative is centred on the idea that a 'modernized' Turkey as a member of the EU might help avoid a conflict between 'Islam' and 'the west' and thus increase global security. In this perspective, democratization, human rights or gender equality are reduced to elements of a modernization process modelled on 'European' or 'western' standards, as is the case in the following statement by the Social Democrat politician Gernot Erler, who regards Turkey's EU accession as 'the crucial force for this unique modernization in an Islamic country':

> I see, above all, security gains. If Turkey becomes the case of a successful modernization on the European model and thus sets an example to other Islamic states, this would contribute to the prevention of the clash of civilizations.[28]

A similarly functionalist view of the country can be traced in some statements praising the economic opportunities EU membership might create for German and European business, although contributions in this field normally prefer to emphasize 'mutual gains' deriving from Turkey's economic integration into the Union. In addition, many proponents of Turkey's candidacy also address the controversial migration issue but, in sharp contrast to their opponents, they claim that Turkish accession to the EU would send inclusive signals to the German-Turkish community. This approach, however, does not go much beyond the predominant integrationist discourse: the leading Green politician Claudia Roth, for example, stresses that the accession process 'will have positive effects on the integration of Turkish migrants'.[29]

---

25 Heribert Prantl, 'Der Mond unter den Füßen' ['Moon Under the Feet'], *Süddeutsche Zeitung*, 18 November 2002.
26 *Die Welt*, 13 October 2004.
27 Paper of the SPD Turkey Coordination Committee, 17 December 2002.
28 *Die Welt*, 9 November 2004.
29 *Die Welt*, 16 December 2004.

Making Turkey 'sick' – the obsession with European identity

'Where Does Europe End?' This headline in the German magazine *Der Spiegel* (9 December 2002) illustrates the limitations of the debate on Turkey's EU accession in Germany, and in many other member states of the EU. The controversy proves to be a rather self-centred search for 'European identity', and says more about Europe's 'longing for its limits' than about Turkey's desire to join the EU. Most contributions to the debate provide very little information, if any, about politics, the social situation, the economy or daily life in the candidate country. The controversial discussion within Turkish society itself – where an odd coalition of Turkish nationalists, traditional Kemalist elites, factions of the army and bureaucracy, dogmatic leftist groups and radical Islamists is conducting a vehement campaign against EU membership – is neglected altogether.[30]

Thus, the accession debate in Germany and other EU countries shows a tendency to reduce the various, complex and ambivalent realities in which people in Turkey live to visions of a society characterized as purely 'non-European' or as 'in-between Europe and the Orient'. While the first qualification has a clearly demarcating function, the construction of an in-between status seems more blurred, but according to Julia Lossau this form of 'a negative, precarious hybridity' is equally exclusionary (Lossau 2002, p. 145). In both narratives, the country and its population are 'orientalized' and 'Islamized' in order to exclude them, fully or partly, from the respective imaginations of Europe.

In this respect, Turco-sceptic discourses prove particularly susceptible to culturalist representations, above all demarcations focusing on religious difference. Angelos Giannakopoulos and Konstadinos Maras, who have conducted a comparative analysis of the accession debate in different EU countries, conclude that the arguments used by opponents of Turkey's membership, but also media representations aimed at a wider public, tend to display an image of Islam 'whose constituent elements are terrorism, Islamist fundamentalism, a restriction of women's rights, poverty, illiteracy, incomplete modernization and a proneness to dictatorial regimes' (Giannakopoulos and Maras 2005, p. 226). Historical events, colonialist myths and racist stereotypes are thus reformulated together with images of 'western' modernization (enlightenment, democratization, human rights, the emancipation of women) in order to construct Europe and European identity against 'oriental' Turkey and 'Muslim' Turks. Seen through a soft-focus lens against its Turkish and Muslim 'other', Europe appears as a continent with a homogeneous culture and civilization, a democratic, peaceful and tolerant society which has come to terms with its colonial past and the 'dark side' of its history.

For Mehmet Mihri Özdoğan, such attempts to find 'retrograde, essentialist definitions for a so-called European identity' are not antidotes to nationalism; on the contrary, they help create a new form of collective 'Euro-nationalism'

---

30   For a survey of the debate on EU accession in Turkey, see, for example, Insel (2005).

(Özdoğan 2004, p. 99). Roberta Carnevale, Stefan Ihrig and Christian Weiß, who have analysed accession discourses in British, German, French and Italian newspapers, argue in a similar manner, suggesting that 'the idea of producing a European identity by constructing a common history and culture' is likely only to 'raise the exclusionary mechanisms of the nation state to the European level' (Carnevale *et al.* 2005, pp. 113–14).

The effort to create a European identity, however, not only includes elements of national identity formation, but also reaches beyond the traditional features of nationalism. Its significant transnational dimension is shaped by the heritage of Europe's colonialist expansion, just as it is influenced by the EU's attempts to position itself in a globalizing world. Classic Eurocentrism or, in Edward Said's words, 'the idea of European identity as a superior one in comparison with all the non-European peoples and cultures' (Said 1978, p. 7) – an ideology inextricably linked with the processes of colonization, the 'civilizing mission' and European empire formation – is only one version of it. A more recent form of the European self-image is less expansive and more introverted, a 'form of introspection' that Philomena Essed calls 'Europism' (Essed 1996, p. 138; see also Chapter 9 of this volume). This is the self-contradictory discourse of old borders and new boundaries: 'On a cultural level Europism is manifest in the nostalgia for the past, which people tend to think of as culturally homogenous, although in fact that is a myth' (Essed 1996, p. 138). Referring to Essed, Helma Lutz defines Europism as 'the defensive discourse of constructing a "pure Europe" as a symbolic continent whose territory is cleansed of foreign and "uncivilized elements"' (Lutz 1997, p. 95).

Investigating European attitudes towards Turkey in the 1990s, Kevin Robins describes the relationship to Turkey 'in terms of closure': 'Europe … can only see the Turks in terms of a "negative identity"' (Robins 1996, p. 80). Thus, in its cultural development 'Europe came to see itself as self-identical and self-sufficient', drawing back to a 'restricted and particular identity' (80–81). It is this defensive discourse on European identity, together with the projection of a unified Europe onto negative images of Turkey, which culminated in the accession debate, in particular in the violent reactions in Germany and elsewhere against Turkey's prospective EU membership. When Turkey dares to enter the European house, the obsession with European identity seems to rouse nineteenth-century civilizationist reflexes that strive to make the country imaginatively unwell again, recreating a 'sick man' *beyond* Europe.

Compared with the restricted, introverted conception of the anti-Turkish narratives, the vision of Europe presented in the pro-Turkish approaches initially appears more open and less essentialist: a heterogeneous EU based on universal, political and secular values, spreading democratization, human rights and the rule of law on the continent. This 'humanitarian mission', however, proves to be problematic when modernization, as is often the case, is reclaimed as a process of 'westernization' or 'Europeanization', thereby reintroducing cultural criteria through the back door. In addition, elements of both Eurocentrism and Europism can be traced in pro-Turkish statements insisting on Turkey's intermediate status between 'developed' Europe and a 'less developed' Orient. Such visions are often combined with neo-imperial scenarios in which the country is functionalized as Europe's geopolitical outpost on the Middle Eastern 'frontline'. In this rather paternalistic view, Turkey continues to be a 'sick man' *between* the Orient and the Occident, a patient that can be cured only by its integration into the EU.

In their perspectives on Turkish immigrants in Germany, anti-Turkish and mainstream pro-Turkish discourses both operate within the dominant German paradigm of integrationism. Despite opposite conclusions concerning EU accession, the Turkey controversy addresses more or less openly Islamophobic notions regarding German Turks. The debate on migration in Germany persistently emphasizes religious difference, cultural in-betweenness, patriarchal violence and social degradation, all of which are collectively attributed to this particular immigrant group. The integrationist view thus contributes to a reshaping of public perception, turning 'the Turks' increasingly into a collective Muslim 'other' while constructing a kind of 'sick man' *within* Germany itself.

Works cited

Adanır, F. (1991) 'Wandlungen des deutschen Türkeibildes in der ersten Hälfte des 20. Jahrhunderts'. *Zeitschrift für Türkeistudien*, 2, pp. 195–211.

—— (2005) 'Turkey's Entry into the Concert of Europe'. *European Review*, 13(3), pp. 395–417.

Adanır, F. and Schneiderheinze, K. (2001) 'Das Osmanische Reich als orientalische Despotie in der Wahrnehmung des Westens'. In: Kürşat-Ahlers, E., Tan, D. and Waldhoff, H. P. eds. *Türkei und Europa*. Frankfurt am Main, IKO – Verlag für Interkulturelle Kommunikation, pp. 83–121.

Carnevale, R., Ihrig, S. and Weiß, C. (2005) *Europa am Bosporus (er-)finden? Die Diskussion um den Beitritt der Türkei zur Europäischen Union in den britischen, deutschen, französischen und italienischen Zeitungen*. Frankfurt a.M., Peter Lang.

Çırakman, A. (2002) *From the 'Terror of the World' to the 'Sick Man of Europe': European Images of Ottoman Empire and Society from the Sixteenth Century to the Nineteenth*. New York, Peter Lang.

Essed, P. (1996) *Diversity, Gender, Color, and Culture*. Amherst, MA, University of Massachusetts Press.

Giannakopoulos, A. and Maras, K. (2005) 'Der Europäische Türkei-Diskurs: Eine Vergleichsanalyse'. In: Giannakopoulos, A. and Maras, K. eds. *Die Türkei-Debatte in Europa*. Wiesbaden, VS Verlag für Sozialwissenschaften, pp. 213–29.

Insel, A. (2005) 'Europäisierung der Türkei: Eine historische Reifeprüfung der nationalen Würde?' In: Giannakopoulos, A. and Maras, K. eds. *Die Türkei-Debatte in Europa*. Wiesbaden, VS Verlag für Sozialwissenschaften, pp. 197–212.

Kedourie, S. ed. (1999) *Seventy-Five Years of the Turkish Republic*. London, Routledge.

Kramer, H. (2003) *EU-kompatibel oder nicht? Zur Debatte um die Mitgliedschaft der Türkei in der Europäischen Union*, SWP-Studie 2003/S34, Berlin, SWP.

Lossau, J. (2002) *Die Politik der Verortung. Eine postkoloniale Reise zu einer 'ANDEREN' Geographie der Welt*. Bielefeld, transcript.

Lutz, H. (1997) 'The Limits of European-ness: Immigrant Women in Fortress Europe'. *Feminist Review*, 57, pp. 93–111.

Oktem, K. (2005) 'British Perceptions on Turkey's EU Accession Prospects: Euroscepticism and Turcophilia?' Proceedings of the South East European Studies at Oxford (SEESOX) European Studies Centre Occasional Paper Series (unpublished), Oxford, UK, June.

Özdoğan, M. M. (2004) 'Zum EU-Beitritt der Türkei. Grenze der Erweiterung oder Grenze der Vernunft?' *WerkstattGeschichte*, 37, pp. 95–99.

Ramm, C. (2006) 'Head On – Hybridity as Fascination and Irritation in Constructing the Turkish Community in Germany'. In: Heidemann, F. and de Toro, A. eds. *New Hybridities: Societies and Cultures in Transition*. Hildesheim, Georg Olms Verlag, pp. 172–81.

Robins, K. (1996) 'Interrupting Identities: Turkey/Europe'. In: Hall, S. and du Gay, P. eds. *Questions of Cultural Identity*. London, Sage Publications, pp. 61–86.

Said, E. W. (1978) *Orientalism*. New York, Vintage Books.

Part III
Multiculturalism and its discontents

CHAPTER 8

Postcolonial racism: white paranoia and the terrors of multiculturalism

Ashwani Sharma

It is not without political significance that the discourse of multiculturalism has become increasingly interrogated in Britain since '9/11', and in particular after the July 2005 London bombings. The sheer frequency of essays, talks, journalistic articles and debates in the print, broadcast and online media directly discussing multiculturalism suggests that the term has become a key locus of public anxiety.[1] It now seems as if everyone has suddenly become an expert on the subject. This intense scrutiny raises a number of questions: Why has the 'multiculturalism debate' been so central to the nation and its concerns about 'terrorism' and 'security'? How has the connection between multiculturalism and the 'war on terror' been articulated? What is the relationship between multiculturalism and racism now? What sort of 'political work' has the term 'multiculturalism' been doing, and for whose benefit? This chapter develops the notion of 'postcolonial racism' through an engagement with the politics of multiculturalism as a key modality in which race and racist paranoia have been delineated in recent times, especially in its mobilization in relation to the 'war on terror'.

In Britain, multiculturalism has effectively acted as the cultural front in the 'war on terror', where identity and difference have been identified (again) as the troubling antagonism to national belonging and social harmony. Tellingly, the positions taken on multiculturalism have been multiple and divergent – there has been no clear political alignment of what it means and whether it is a good thing or not. Multiculturalism has simultaneously been presented as the 'problem' and the 'solution' to the contemporary crisis. For example, after the London bombings, the 'resilient spirit' of the capital city and the nation was

---

1 See OpenDemocracy, 'Multiculturalism: Translating Difference', at www.opendemocracy. net/arts-multiculturalism/issue.jsp for a good snapshot of the multicultural debate.

invoked by recourse to the cultural diversity of the metropolis – the mayor of London, Ken Livingstone, began a campaign celebrating London's multiculturalism. Given that the bombings occurred immediately after London had been awarded the 2012 Olympic Games, it was revealing how the juxtaposition of these two events enabled a direct connection to be drawn between London's apparent cosmopolitanism and the 'war on terror'. The Olympic bid's images of joyful, multiracial East London schoolchildren were presented as symbolic of a 'new Britain', a postcolonial nation comfortable with its harmonious diversity, confronting the alien ideologies of 'Islamic extremism'.

Whereas this celebratory multiculturalism – especially in the arts, education and public services – had become hegemonic for 'New Labour' (and increasingly as well in neo-liberal corporate culture), influential figures close to the political regime, such as Trevor Phillips, former chair of the Commission for Racial Equality (CRE), warned that multiculturalism was leading to cultural segregation and the creation of 'ethnic ghettos'.[2] This view has converged, perhaps unwittingly, with the views of many commentators on the political right, such as David Goodhart, editor of *Prospect* magazine, who, in a well publicized article, had previously denounced the increasing cultural diversity of Britain (Goodhart 2004).[3] Meanwhile, from a different political and theoretical persuasion, noted writer and anti-racist Kenan Malik has made a number of scathing attacks on the ideologies of multiculturalism and diversity, arguing, with many other figures on the left, that it is the source of the problem itself.[4]

Floating signifier

This recent proliferation of variable and at times contradictory uses of multiculturalism reconfirms the argument made by the postcolonial theorist Homi Bhabha:

> Multiculturalism – a portmanteau term for anything from minority discourse to postcolonial critique, from gay and lesbian studies to chicano/a fiction – has become the most charged sign for describing the scattered social contingencies that characterise contemporary *Kulturkritik*. The multicultural has itself become a 'floating signifier' whose enigma lies less in itself than in the discursive uses of it to mark social processes where differentiation and condensation seem to happen almost synchronically. (Bhabha 1998, p. 31)

---

2 Trevor Phillips presented his views on multiculturalism and Britishness on a number of occasions in public lectures and speeches. In 2007 Phillips became chair of the new Equality and Human Rights Commission, which took over the work of the CRE. Its Website (www.equalityhumanrights.com) includes examples of his talks and speeches.
3 It is interesting to note that Trevor Phillips (2004) was critical of Goodhart's piece. This illustrates well the complexity and contradictions in the multicultural debate.
4 See www.kenanmalik.com for an archive of Kenan Malik's articles.

As a floating signifier, multiculturalism has been mobilized to support, contest or stand in for a range of political and ideological arguments. At this conjuncture it is increasingly difficult (if it were desirable) to present the different conceptualizations and uses of multiculturalism that are currently in circulation, which would just add another view to an increasingly intellectually and politically fraught debate. It is not my intention here to proliferate the meanings that the concept may have, or to evaluate competing interpretations, but rather to attempt to consider briefly how multiculturalism as a problematic has been ideologically framed. What are the underlying conditions and assumptions that inform the debate in relation to postcolonial racism?

I do not wish to argue that the concept of multiculturalism is a problem in itself, a position of anti-multiculturalism that has become increasingly frequent. I do think, however, that the expansion of the debate signals a heightened state of national anxiety about racial and cultural difference and otherness. I also think that 'multiculture' is an important contested site of politics in the current globalized conjuncture, even if 'culture' itself often continues to be understood in a problematic or reductive way. What it is important to recognize here is that the notion of multiculturalism has opened up, albeit in a limited manner, the possibility of addressing more directly questions of race and ethnicity. In Britain, and even more so in the rest of Europe, discussions of race and racism continue to be repressed in public discourse, as if they were still too traumatic to confront directly. Race continues to manifest itself in coded and/or spectacular forms, usually at moments of social or national crisis.[5]

Similarly, academic work on multiculturalism and race has proliferated in recent years. In contrast to the more publicly visible anti-multiculturalism, critical studies, especially in disciplines such as sociology, political science and cultural studies, have tended to consider more sympathetically the theoretical and political conceptualizations of multiculturalism in relation to notions such as diaspora, racialization, globalization and the state.[6]

While, as I have indicated, there appear to be as many multiculturalisms as there are commentators, the key argument here is that hegemonic discourses have articulated this floating signifier with the master (if empty) signifier of contemporary politics – 'terrorism' – and have thereby exposed the mutating forms of a postcolonial racism. The processes of decolonialization and globalization have made the borders of European nations increasingly porous to people and

---

5 There have been some significant moments of 'racial crisis' that have generated media panic and official government reports. In recent times, other than 9/11 and the London bombings, these have included: the civil disturbances in major British cities of 1981 and 1985, as well as in the northern cities in 2001; and the Macpherson inquiry in 1998 into the death of the black teenager Stephen Lawrence.

6 Goldberg (1994) and Hesse (2000) are two good edited collections exemplifying the range of work on multiculturalism in the academic field over the last twenty years. While the majority of academic study of multiculturalism has been in the United States, in Britain it has remained a concern rather marginalized to 'race' scholars. However, the situation is now beginning to change.

cultures from the formerly colonized worlds, in spite of continual and violent attempts to police and militarize entry into Europe. Territorial colonialism was sustained by the binary logic of 'west' and 'rest', where racist discourse, especially in the form of orientalism, sustained an imperial governmentality, and where the boundary between the racialized white Occident and its 'others' was clearly marked and secured. This binarism, however, has been increasingly difficult to sustain over the last century, with postcolonial Europe being increasingly populated by a multiplicity of migrant peoples and cultures. The demands and movements of capital and labour have brought into crisis the historical colonial divisions. The (European) modern state has had to deal continuously with questions of inclusion and exclusion. In fact, 'race' has been constitutive of the modern state from its beginnings (Goldberg 2002). The challenge for nation states has been not just to exclude but also to monitor, control and subjugate the increasing presence of racial and cultural others inside the west. Western nations have used different strategies to meet this challenge – in this context, multiculturalism, in its many variants and modalities, can be understood as a specific political model of managing cultural heterogeneity in times of postcolonial 'hyper-globalization'.

Multicultural empire

As Michael Hardt and Antonio Negri in their 2000 book *Empire* argue:

> Empire establishes no territorial centre of power and does not rely on fixed boundaries or barriers. It is a *decentred* and *deterritorializing* apparatus of rule that progressively incorporates the entire global realm within its open, expanding frontiers. Empire manages hybrid identities, flexible hierarchies, and plural exchanges through modulating networks of command. (Hardt and Negri 2000, p. xiii, original emphasis)

For these authors, this new 'empire' has shifted from the exclusionist, racial logic of colonialism; it now works through cultural difference and inclusion in the reproduction of global power. This is an argument that Sanjay Sharma and I have considered and developed in more theoretical detail in our essay 'White Paranoia: Orientalism in the Age of *Empire*' (Sharma and Sharma 2003). To summarize our argument: Hardt and Negri suggest that the racism of empire is a cultural neo-racism of segregation, which primarily *integrates* others (differences are ordered and controlled). This is distinguished from the colonial racism of division and hierarchy, which takes place across the racial boundary of self–other (differences are excluded and negated). Hardt and Negri contend that cultural racism needs to be conceived of as a 'strategy of differential inclusion', as opposed to the absolute exclusion, of the other:

> White supremacy functions … through engaging alterity and then subordinating differences according to degrees of deviance from whiteness. This has nothing to do with the hatred and fear of the strange, unknown Other. It is a hatred born in proximity and elaborated through degrees of difference of

the neighbour.… Subordination is enacted in regimes of everyday practices that are more mobile and flexible but that create racial hierarchies that are nonetheless stable and brutal. (Hardt and Negri 2000, p. 194)

Cultural racism, as Hardt and Negri have stated, is one of *proximity* to a normalizing whiteness. While the deterritorializing global capitalism of empire furiously traverses national, cultural and racial borders, paying little heed to place, its multicultural ideology seemingly appreciates, or actively requires, the difference/distance of the other. As Slavoj Žižek has argued:

> multiculturalism is a disavowed, inverted, self-referential form of racism, a 'racism with a distance' – it 'respects' the Other's identity, conceiving the Other as a self-enclosed 'authentic' community towards which he, the multiculturalist, *maintains a distance* rendered possible by his privileged universal position. (Žižek 1997, p. 44, emphasis added)

It is precisely the 'empty point of universality' of multiculturalism that enables it to respect the specificity of the other by maintaining proper distance and by asserting its own superiority. If we accept that global capitalism articulates a contemporary orientalism – that is, cultural racism – we need to resist merely exposing the (false) universality of multiculturalism as harbouring Eurocentricism masking its own particularity (Žižek 1993, p. 44). Instead, as Žižek argues, the 'particular cultural background or roots which always support the universal multiculturalist position … conceals the fact that the subject is already thoroughly "rootless", that his true position is the void of universality' (44). Žižek contends that rather than pointing out the particular characteristics of the universal subject (white, male, heterosexual, etc.), which inevitably represses and subordinates differences, 'identifying universality with its empty point of exclusion' (51) is more likely to challenge capitalist hegemony. However, if contemporary orientalism as cultural racism operates by an inclusive hegemony (which has no outside), we need to interrogate further *what* exactly occupies the void of universality.

In his analysis of multiculturalism, Žižek crucially falls short of marking the empty place of the universal as the positionality of whiteness. This contention is not an attempt to identify the particularities of whiteness, because its own inscription has no content. Rather, whiteness as 'absent presence' seeks to stand for and be a measure of all humanity. It operates as a universal point of identification that strives to structure all social identities.[7] In this respect, whiteness functions as an 'empty signifier' that needs to fill or hegemonize the empty place of the multicultural universal in order to uphold its own authority.

---

7   In Sharma and Sharma (2003), we further argue: 'We should not therefore confuse or conflate Whiteness with particular white identities. In discussions of Whiteness … there is often an immediate action to identify the specific characteristics of white identities, to highlight their gendered, ethnic or class location, for example. However, the effect of such a move results in only further securing the hegemony of Whiteness' (pp. 306–7).

Integrating Muslims

It is the 'empty place' of whiteness around which the contemporary debate on multiculturalism is structured. While the vitriol against 'asylum-seekers' and 'refugees' can generally be explained with reference to notions of racial exclusion, it also needs to be recognized that it is their racially coded, differentially marked otherness that confirms their *relative* alien status. It is not insignificant that multiculturalism has emerged as an anxious discourse principally in relation to Muslims and Asians – cultures constructed through 'postcolonial orientalism' as a culturally distant relative to the norms of whiteness. Trevor Phillips's problematic calls for greater 'integration' and the consolidation of 'Britishness' have been addressed implicitly to working-class Muslims and South Asians more generally, the implicit argument being that the mere concentration of Muslims and Asians in an area constitutes a threat to the nation and 'social cohesion'. This version of multiculturalism makes the questionable but commonly held assumption that the formation of 'spatial' ethnic communities separates them from mainstream (i.e. white) British life. In fact, there is no real evidence to suggest that these 'imagined ethnic ghettos' actually exist or that in segregated communities there is a rabid anti-Britishness present which is fuelling the creation of terrorists. As has become evident, Islamic militants are as likely to be from the leafy green white suburbs of the southern Home Counties as from the racially marked inner cities of Bradford or Birmingham. Phillips's neo-orientalism is entirely consistent with the integrative logic of postcolonial empire. Integration and racial exclusion have been central tenets of post-war race relations ideology in Britain, but crucially not assimilation, with its potential erasure of difference and loss of identity. Cultural integration is now the 'stratification of difference', where degrees of difference are positioned in relation to a presumed universal (white) norm. Citizenship is defined by adherence to sets of cultural values that demarcate the field of integration and a 'new multicultural Britishness', as codified for example in the recently established citizen tests.

The strategy of integration to a racialized British norm is a faltering attempt to demarcate and police diversity. This is evident in the continual, well established practice of racial stereotyping, which identifies and divides the other into 'good' and 'bad'. At present, the splitting of the other into the 'moderate' and 'extremist' Muslim is necessary to differential racism. The problem, and hence the source of anxiety, is that it is impossible to know who is who. It is not only that whoever is defined as moderate or extremist is not fixed within a neo-orientalist framework, but also that Islamist discourse does not legitimate or support these categories within theological or political doctrine. So the argument that is constantly being circulated in the west since 9/11, that it is not Islam we are fighting but rather extremists and terrorists who have nothing to do with Islam, is unsustainable: it is a politically futile attempt at racial and cultural differentiation. (What seems impossible to countenance for the 'narcissistic' white, western world is that what we are seeing are politically different and competing readings *within* Islamist discourse.) This fetishistic and anxious repetition of the

124

moralistic Manichaeism of 'good' and 'evil' – 'good' and 'bad' Muslims – has informed and delimited the debate on multiculturalism, especially after the London bombings. For example, immediately in the wake of the bombings we saw the media image of one of the suspected male suicide bombers juxtaposed with one of the victims, a young Muslim woman. The intended impact of this comparison was dependent on a set of racial and cultural ideologies already circulating at least since 9/11, if not since the 'Rushdie affair' in the late 1980s: the alienated, male Pakistani suicide bomber from the north of England with no job and few prospects being contrasted with the identifiably 'integrated' young British-Bangladeshi woman from East London who was a student with a potentially bright future. The gendering of racial discourse has remained central in the attempt to differentiate and integrate Muslims. While men have largely been seen as the problem, women have been represented as mere victims of Islamic patriarchy. The difficulty is that this construction has been unsustainable even in the dominant media sphere. For example, Mohammad Sidique Khan, one of the 7 July London bombers, seems to have been considered by local whites and Asians to be a 'respectable member of the community', a learning mentor at a primary school in Dewsbury, who worked with children of all ethnicities. A series of vox-pop interviews with mainly white parents in the news media in the wake of the bombings exclaimed that 'he was a lovely man', 'he was good with *our* children', 'he was *normal*'. What has been particularly disconcerting, both ideologically and culturally, has been the realization that the London bombers were British, speaking English with colloquial regional accents. Attempts to locate them as connected to, or at least indoctrinated by, the alien ideologies of al-Qaeda have largely failed.[8] White racialized anxiety is produced by the inability to tell terrorists from the presumed norm; what is really troubling is that 'Muslim terrorists' act and behave just like *us*.[9]

Anxious times

The shooting of the Brazilian-born Jean Charles de Menezes, who had no connection to Islamist militancy, by security forces after the second attempted wave of London bombings, on 21 July 2005, is symptomatic of this racial anxiety, which is marked by the increasing paranoia of being unable to discriminate politically or ethnically between Muslims, Asian or black people. The situation is even more fraught when we are faced with 'white Muslims' – in such instances the ideological construction of whiteness has totally imploded, causing great

---

8   An official governmental report published in April 2006 stated that the 7 July bombers had no links with al-Qaeda.

9   This 'sleeper cell theory of Islamic terrorism' is based on the assumption that we are unable to tell the difference between 'us' and 'them'. Although this is a source of 'racial anxiety', it is also unsurprising to see that this fear been made into a mainstream US television series – *Sleeper Cell* (2005) – a case, perhaps, of 'enjoying your symptom'?

disturbance to allegedly 'stable' processes of cultural and racial identification and differentiation.

This anxiety over white identification with Islam was well captured in the striking film documentary *The Last White Kids* (Channel 4, November 2003). The programme title itself presents a sense of the impending racial tragedy that underpins contemporary racial paranoia. The documentary was about the last few working-class white families left in now a principally Asian Muslim area in Manningham, Bradford. Essentially, the film presented a melancholic vision of the fate and difficulties of the white families, mainly through the sympathetic portrayal of a young white girl, Amy. What the film suggested was particularly disturbing was that Amy was interested in Islam and Muslim culture. Throughout the film we see Amy playfully wearing Islamic dress and presenting the virtues of Muslim culture in the local area. In a memorable scene, she fluently quoted verses from the Quran in Arabic to surprised and impressed Asian male youths in a pizza café. She followed this up with a further demonstration of her extensive knowledge of Islam by identifying the particular form of Islam that was being practised by her mosque. In both its formal and its ideological organization, the film was structured around an absolute binary division between whites and Islam. The liberal anxiety evident in the film was signified through the marginalization of the white working-class community by the apparent Islamization of the area. In the film, the lack of social and economic opportunities for the white families was tied to the loss of their (white) cultural milieu. A particular source and symptom of this anxiety was how Amy (along with some of the other white girls) was positively engaging with Islam. In particular, Amy's taking on of elements of Islamic religious rituals and cultural forms, especially her adoption of culturally coded female dress, was presented as a monstrous aberration. As a young girl, she was positioned as the hapless victim of an alien cultural and religious orthodoxy.

For the film, Islam is outside 'normality', and remains so in spite of the high level of cultural and political dialogue and ethnic mixing in cities like Bradford. Muslims, it seems, continue to be marked by their apparently despotic patriarchal culture and by their unfathomable ethical codes. However, Amy calls into question this ruling binarism. Her reciting of Quranic verse 'undoes' the security of whiteness, produced through the exclusion of Muslims. In effect, Amy's active embracing of Islam is coded as a loss of the universality of white identity through her self-designation as 'ethnic'. For the film, this form of 'cultural mimicry' and 'racial passing' is a sign of the crisis of whiteness itself: Amy's liminal position deconstructs the structures of racialized white hierarchy through her transgressive identification with an everyday working-class multiculture. Her Muslim performativity destabilizes and reconfigures the territorializing regime of cultural demarcation and the claims of white superiority.

The Last White Kids is a symptomatic example of white subjectivity unravelling in the face of cultural heterogeneity, where characteristically in liberal discourse the figure of the white working class is represented as a collective victim of multicultural belonging. It is by such class displacement that 'white liberal multiculturalism' has sustained the advantages of white privilege and unmarked positionality by distancing itself from ethnic and class particularity. Clearly, this task of monitoring and marking particular others, thereby sustaining the universality of whiteness, is impossible. It presumes that one can map, make visible and fix cultural, religious and political identities within the porous borders of European nation states, and in the constantly shifting, culturally hybrid demography of urban spaces. This impossibility has led to a generalized state of fear, and to a culture of racial anxiety and paranoia. Where is the Muslim? Is he one of 'us' or one of 'them'? A sort of cultural hysteria ensues: What does the Muslim want from me? What have we done to them? This mode of paranoid 'multicultural governmentality' is driven by the production of a white norm, and by the 'symbolic' and 'material' invisibility of those who cannot be mapped within its hegemonic formation. Exclusion, incarceration and death now become a state of normality; what was once limited to outside Europe now exists inside it, as part of a general attempt to sustain the regime of liberal white life as the norm in Europe, as well as across the wider world. Whiteness is a form of biopower and, to use Achille Mbembe's evocative phrase, it is informed by a 'necropolitics' – both beyond and within a west that is finding it increasingly difficult to sustain its hegemony (Mbembe 2003). Anxiety, paranoia and violence – both lawful and not – under the empty signifier of the 'war on terror' are the signs of the west's geopolitical unravelling.

Another postcolonial multiculturalism?

This racialized anxiety and narcissism points to the extreme limitations of the present debate about multiculturalism in these times of global conflict and turmoil. Radicalized Muslim militants – suicide bombers or not – and a multitude of global sympathizers are challenging the hegemony of western subjectivity and its attendant racial and cultural erasures, exclusions and violence. What this 'decentring' of the west – this direct challenge to the west's claims to universality – brings in its wake is the questioning of the presumed ethical norms of how we live, of belonging, of being a subject, of being human. A British Muslim woman who decides to wear a *hijab* questions the very idea of freedom and individuality that is so cherished by Eurocentric white liberalism – it seems paradoxically to be a choice for 'unfreedom', at least within a certain frame of European modernity. In the western post-ideological world of apolitical consumerism and flexible identities, the ideas of community, belonging and collectivity – the very idea of cultures of 'passionate attachment' – posit a challenge to the notion of a 'rootless' universal subjectivity. For example, although we have witnessed differing responses to the demand by Muslim girls to wear religious dress in school in France and Britain, what the two responses – exclusionist and assimilationist in universalist France and 'differentially integrative' in multicultural Britain – have in common is the norm of white universality at their (invisible) centre. The different models of managing diversity are alike in reproducing the ideological fantasy of the cultural other as essentialized and fixed. However, Muslim, Asian and African diasporic cultures are constantly mutating, hybridizing and changing; marked by divisions, contradictions and class, they exemplify the antagonisms of a disavowed 'vernacular multicultural-ism'. A form of postcolonial utopian political imaginary attempting to counter the violence and exclusions of contemporary globalization.

This 'subaltern multiculturalism' is one that is already being practised in the alternative public spaces of urban existence, where in many respects a culture of conviviality is transforming the norms of everyday working-class living, in which racism is just one 'ordinary' aspect of the multitude of social antagonisms (Gilroy 2004). The social shift is reconfiguring whiteness as it transforms and decentres itself. For example, figures like Amy in *The Last White Kids*, white hip-hoppers or black British converts to Islam present diverse forms of cultural integration that diverge from the one presented by the doyens of liberal multiculturalism. The emergence of this imagined vernacular multiculturalism is being constituted in urban culture, and increasingly in local grass-roots class politics, making visible the 'absent presence' of whiteness.

This is not the place to address the complexity of this anti-racist class politics, but suffice to say that this vernacular multiculturalism – maybe better under-stood as 'anti-anti-multiculturalism' – is in dialectical opposition to the discourse of white anxiety and paranoia that is presenting itself as being unable to work through its 'postcolonial melancholia' – an interminable mourning for empire and whiteness at its core (Gilroy 2004). Anti-anti-multiculturalism could be the concept we use 'under erasure' – inadequate but necessary – to interrogate the new complex conjuncture of globalization, nation and decolonization. Instead, multiculturalist discourses are effectively being blamed for the end of empire, the decline of the nation and the loss of white identity. For example, in a 2006 study, the authors of *The New East End* effectively reproduce the idea that the white working class are the victims of the welfare state and local governmental politics, underpinned by social multiculturalism, and that this ill judged wel-farism explains the white racism towards East London Bangladeshis (Dench *et al.* 2006). While this is now a well versed and rather predictable neo-liberal critique of 'rights and needs' state welfare, its significance for the argument presented here lies in how Asian Britons, as represented by East End Bangladeshis, are constructed as the cause of the social problem. It is the migrants' arrival and their transformation of the locality through claims to social housing and welfare benefits that are seen as the problematic result of a multiculturalist ideology. The study's nostalgia for white working-class family life before the arrival of the Bangladeshis is matched only by the similar idealization of closely knit contem-porary working-class Asian families. In spite of the quite sympathetic portrayal of diasporic Bangladeshis, *The New East End* remains locked into an analysis that assumes and reproduces whiteness as the defining norm (and victim) of this historical transformation. The understanding of Asian British life is clearly marked by its absolute difference to white culture. This is evident in the way the study conceptually reduces Tower Hamlets into two separate communities that are inherently antagonistic to each other. (Other migrant groups, from North Africans to eastern Europeans, with the potential to undermine this binary difference are hardly mentioned.) While everyday racist discourse is rationalized as a reaction to official welfare policies, little is critically developed about the everyday multicultural friendships and coexistence that even many of the white racist contributors to the study also mention.

What is missing from the analysis in *The New East End* is how neo-liberal capitalism, as well as everyday cultures, are producing the new spaces of post-colonial heterogeneity, where racism *and* conviviality constitute social relations. What we are witnessing in many urban localities in Britain, and increasingly in parts of metropolitan Europe, are certain forms of putative and distinctive multicultures that are being produced through a set of new economic forces that are redefining the contours of diasporic locality and transnational belonging. It is principally white anxiety, racism and geographical flight that are fuelling the paranoid calls for cultural integration and the end of multiculturalism. It is this form of postcolonial racism – a spatial racism – that is trying to locate and contain cultural otherness in conditions where this is increasingly impossible.

Whiteness is anxiously attempting to determine the boundaries of multi-culturalism, when the very possibility of singular, clearly defined cultures is increasingly difficult. The 'post' in postcolonial racism also marks the (utopian) (im)possibility of moving beyond this reactionary form of racial superiority and ethnic exceptionalism. The continual references to the Second World War and the Blitz in many white narrations of Britishness are tellingly anxious signs of a national history that has not come to terms with its multicultural futures, where the fantasies of whiteness are unravelling. Against this, small signs of an albeit unruly and contradictory cultural politics of vernacular multiculture continue to reconfigure the nation. For example, a minor but significant symptom of the future that counters the imaginings of cultural ghettoization is the ubiquitous waving of the historically regressive sign of insular English nationalism – the St George's flag – by Bangladeshi, white and black youths during international football tournaments in places such as Brick Lane in Tower Hamlets, which offers further evidence that 'popular integration' comes in many complex forms, as notions of multiculturalism and Britishness strain under the weight of ideo-logical conflict. Given the continuing contested modalities of racialized logics overdetermining the present conjuncture, one needs to delineate further the social anxieties and ideological fantasies that are being condensed into this postcolonial 'floating signifier'. The 'war' over the meaning of multiculturalism is one site in the new politics of transnational (anti-)racism.

Works cited

Bhabha, H. (1998) 'Culture's in Between'. In: Bennett, D. ed. *Multicultural States – Rethinking Difference and Identity*. London, Routledge, pp. 29–36.
Dench, G., Gavron, K. and Young, M. (2006) *The New East End: Kinship, Race and Conflict*. London, Profile Books.

Gilroy, P. (2004) *After Empire: Melancholia or Convivial Culture?* London, Routledge.

Goldberg, D. T., ed. (1994) *Multiculturalism*. London, Blackwell.

—— (2002) *The Racial State*. London, Blackwell.

Goodhart, D. (2004) 'Discomfort of Strangers'. *Guardian*, 4 February. Available at www.guardian.co.uk/race/story/0,11374,1154684,00.html (accessed 26 January 2009).

Hardt, M. and Negri, A. (2000) *Empire*. Cambridge, MA, Harvard University Press.

Hesse, B. ed. (2000) *Un/settled Multiculturalisms: Diasporas, Entanglements, Transruptions*. London, Zed Books.

Mbembe, A. (2003) 'Necropolitics'. *Public Culture*, 15(1), pp. 11–40.

Phillips, T. (2004) 'Genteel Xenophobia Is As Bad As Any Other Kind'. *Guardian*, 16 February. Available at www.guardian.co.uk/comment/story/0,3604,1148847,00.html (accessed 26 January 2009).

Sharma, S. and Sharma, A. (2003) 'White Paranoia: Orientalism in the Age of *Empire*'. *Fashion Theory*, 7(3/4), pp. 301–18.

Žižek, S. (1993) *Tarrying with the Negative*. Durham, NC, Duke University Press.

—— (1997) 'Multiculturalism, or, the Cultural Logic of Multinational Capitalism'. *New Left Review*, 225, pp. 28–51.

Intolerable humiliations

Philomena Essed

In a PhD workshop on 'discourse and racism', two students – opposite genders, both black – get into an argument. Words fly across the empty space between the two arms of the U-shaped table setting. Total disagreement. The female student shrugs her shoulders – hopeless guy, this is useless – stating: 'I am sorry that you are so *backward* that you do not even have the *information* to know that … [she rephrases her point of view]'. The male student leans forward, agitated facial expression promising an explosive response. As the facilitator of the discussion my spontaneously quick intervention directed at the young woman is with humour, suggesting that she can say *almost* the same in different words. How about: 'I am sorry we do not seem to have the same information about this; what I know is …'. The room is silent when she looks at me, hesitating, a touch of scepticism in her eyes. But then with a twinkle and a broad smile, she signals 'okay, fair enough'. The young man relaxes with a 'she got it' look on his face, fellow students chuckle and the conversation continues constructively.

The workshop took place in Durban, South Africa, in a gender and racially mixed class. I responded to the unacceptability of calling anyone 'backward', let alone a black student, given past and present racist representations of black Africans lagging behind in progress and development (Goldberg 2002). But equally problematic is ridiculing a fellow student in South Africa for lack of access to information, an issue charged with economic and racial privilege.

Some readers may think: 'What nonsense! Students should be able to handle a bit of abuse.' Not an uncommon point of view, but I do not quite agree. Why would 'toughening up' be such a good thing? Would students really need any encouragement from us, teachers, to get 'heavy-handed'? Is it not already easy, often *too easy*, to resort to epithets, words that hurt? This introduces the topic of this chapter: damage caused by offensive language, whether subtle innuendos or grossly humiliating labels, in ethnically tense situations (Essed 1997).

Humiliation is 'the catalyst that turns grievances into nuclear bombs of emotion', says Evelin Lindner (2006, p. 169), prolific researcher in the emerging area of humiliation studies. The hurt of humiliation 'instigates extremism' and 'hampers moderate reactions and solutions'. To be humiliated is 'to be placed, mostly against one's will and often in a deeply hurtful way, in a situation that is greatly inferior to what one feels one should expect' (172). A less dramatic definition identifies humiliation as particular acts or conditions that give a person or group sound reason to consider their self-respect injured (Margalit 1996). Obviously, a point of contestation is what constitutes 'sound reason' and according to whose point of view, questions too complex to address here (Margalit 1996). On all accounts, humiliation involves emotional pain inflicted upon the target, whether or not intentionally (Ahmed 2004). The degree of hurt depends on a number of factors, including the issue at stake, how it is embedded in the social, historical and cultural experiences of both parties, and how the offended perceives the humiliator. Because all human beings desire respect and recognition of their intrinsic worth, put-downs and demeaning actions involve violations of the target's full and legitimate belonging to humanity (Margalit 1996, p. 135).

Humiliation is more than feeling or emotion. It influences *how* conflict is expressed and experienced. As a form of aggression, it involves the infliction of harm, pain or injury, which can be verbal, physical or symbolic (Fry 2006, p. 11). Humiliation 'should be seen within a wider context as a central aspect of the interaction between human beings and their social and natural environment' (Lindner 2001, p. 51). For the purpose of this chapter, I am mostly interested in humiliation as a cultural phenomenon, the function of which is to discourage or to punish resistance against oppression or, the other way round, to take revenge for infliction done. Not only the relatively powerless can feel humiliated: those in power can also experience humiliation, from the very groups they despise. It seems increasingly difficult to turn the tide once denigration, resentment and counter-humiliation are the mode through which conflicts of interest are fought over. This is often the case in the arena of race and ethnic relations.

I pursue the theme of social risks and costs of humiliation[1] as applied to the Netherlands (and western Europe more generally), where ethnic minorities, and lately Muslims in particular, are routinely exposed to public scorn (European Monitoring Centre on Racism and Xenophobia 2006). At the same time, western Europe is often considered the vanguard of tolerance. Tolerance has been addressed in many studies. Rather than adding another version of tolerance critique, I focus mostly on one characteristic that has been relatively overlooked: its ambiguous relation to the phenomenon of racism. On the surface, the ideal

---

1   I am grateful to Achille Mbembe for our conversation about the senselessness of humiliating. He also reminded me that the South African Bill of Rights includes the right to be respected as a human being. This right overrules the right of freedom of expression, as a result of which the South African government made it illegal to show 'the Danish cartoons' that many Muslims and non-Muslims around the world took offence at. For an analysis of these cartoons, see the following chapter.

of tolerance suggests that racism is absent or that it occurs only as an aberration from normal practice. In order to sustain the western image of non-racism, the definition of racism is often limited, to include only the most obvious and blunt expressions, where racist motives are explicit in the very act. Thus racism becomes an exception, a deviance from 'normal' practice. Because the function of tolerance is to allow for aberrations to be tolerated, tolerance comes to include the tolerance of racism.

The ideal of tolerance also suggests openness and space for individual difference and cultural diversity. In the Netherlands, tolerance counts as a national characteristic, a sign of civilization, of enlightenment, generated by those seen as 'genuinely' Dutch. In this view, immigrants, in particular Muslims, are considered intolerant about religion, women's emancipation and homosexuality. Thus, the Netherlands and the 'genuinely Dutch' claim cultural superiority and the moral obligation to serve as normative models, symbolically speaking not much different from the historical 'white man's burden'. It is true that over the past century the Netherlands has advanced in honouring civil rights and freedoms. It is questionable, however, to overlook or to mitigate lingering gender, racial, ethnic and other forms of structural discrimination prevalent in the Netherlands while calling others backward.

The Netherlands is an interesting case, because the degree of *muslimophobia* is high compared with that in other European countries (Boog 2006). The Dutch obsession with Islamic immigrants had reached an earlier peak when the Netherlands held the highest European number of anti-Islam attacks in the period immediately after 11 September 2001. According to a 2004 survey, over 50 per cent of western Europeans felt that Muslims in Europe are viewed with suspicion. The Netherlands and Sweden scored highest (72 per cent and 75 per cent, respectively). One year later, 51 per cent of the Dutch had negative views about Muslims, the highest figure for western Europe. Next highest was Germany, with 47 per cent. Britain scored lowest, with 14 per cent (European Monitoring Centre 2006, pp. 36–37). The Netherlands has also been the stage for extreme responses against advocates of absolute freedom of speech: kill the speakers. In the new millennium, Pim Fortuyn, outspoken politician and aspiring candidate for the position of Dutch Prime Minister, was assassinated in 2002 by a white Dutch animal rights extremist. But Fortuyn will most likely enter the Dutch history books for provoking, if not insulting, 'hypocrites of the establishment' and Muslims – the latter for abusing women. Two years later, in 2004, Theo van Gogh, a filmmaker, paid with his life for opinions taken to be anti-Islamic. The assassin, a Moroccan-Dutch man, claimed to have acted in defence of his religion.

Both assassinations can be placed in the larger context of Dutch in/tolerance. In the course of the 1990s, anti-immigrant public discourse, once the sole privilege of politicians at the extreme right of the spectrum, became *salonfähig* (respectable). The frequency with which mainstream politicians and public advocates of free speech verbally denigrate ethnic groups has made 'ethnic bashing' appear normal and acceptable in European societies (Law 2001). This does not mean that many people always agree with the content of anti-immigrant views, but there does seem to be broad agreement that it is acceptable to use offensive language in the name of freedom of speech. Why? What is the purpose? Why resort to demeaning statements when (self-)humour, gentle but firm objections, or sharp but polite disagreements can also work to address concerns majorities may feel about ethnic groups?

Inflicting cultural pain

Whereas durable social inequality is largely the result of exploitation and marginalization of the relatively powerless (Tilly 1999), its sustainability is sealed by humiliation, the infliction of physical or emotional pain. However, when there is a strong sense of righteousness and legitimacy among the excluded, torture, insults and symbolic mud thrown at them may fuel their belief in their own moral superiority over the offenders. In addition, the hurt of humiliation may also become a fertile ground for violent response. In situations of ethnic conflict, the pain of humiliation is shared pain, what I call *cultural pain*, because it is pain experienced as a result of the denigration of the culture, religion or ethnicity the targets of humiliation identify with. Once set in, cultural pain can be difficult to heal, broken trust a mountain of resistance to overcome (Ahmed 2004; Cockburn 1998; Lindner 2001).

On an abstract level, humiliation presupposes the humanity of the person who is humiliated (Margalit 1996). In practice, humiliation entails infliction, a breach of social contract, whereby the humiliator contests or denies the dignity and human worth of the other. A number of remarkable books, including *On Apology* (Lazare 2004), *The Decent Society* (Margalit 1996), *Rock My Soul* (hooks 2003), *The Six Pillars of Self-Esteem* (Branden 1994) and *A Human Being Died That Night* (Gobodo-Madikizela 2003), have reinforced my belief that respect for the dignity of being human is an enormous challenge for individuals and societies to live up to. Extraordinary human rights leaders – Aung San Suu Kyi, Desmond Tutu, Nawal El Saadawi, Wangari Maathai, to name but a few – have been able to give constructive meaning to the political, racial and gender degradations they have been exposed to throughout their lives and careers (Allen 2006; Maathai 2006; Parameshwar 2005). Many other members of marginalized groups, less exceptional and maybe disposed differently, may suffer loss of trust in self, or in the potential goodness of people, due to sustained humiliations.

How do humiliations affect people's lives and behaviours? In my earlier studies on everyday racism, I found that denigrating and abusive words, and being patronizing and other violations of the integrity of a person's self-esteem, tend to undermine the self-confidence needed to resist oppression (Essed 1990, 1991). I felt hesitant about pursuing the theme of damaged racial self-esteem for fear of pathologizing the very 'victims'. Today, other authors confirm the central role of self-esteem in determining whether individuals or groups succeed. They point to the social crises emerging from sustained societal humiliations (hooks 2003).

Self-esteem is a fundamental human need (Branden 1994). It allows us not only to feel better but also to live better, to respond in constructive ways to challenges in life. The undermining of self-esteem can damage the flexibility and resilience people need to bounce back, to take adverse situations as opportunities for growth rather than as excuses to resort to aggression and violence. Against this background, I address how the norm of tolerance has come to license public humiliation – in particular, the symbolic humiliation of Muslims and Islam – in the name of freedom of the word. In the course of this process, one response to severe public denigration of Islam and the prophet Mohammed has been extreme physical humiliation – the assassination of a radical advocate of 'freedom of the word', Theo van Gogh. At this stage I am certainly not reducing the cause of radical violence to injured self-esteem, only very cautiously suggesting that the two forms of radicalism – the claim of absolute freedom to humiliate and the annihilation of the humiliator – might be related. In other words, it amounts to *cultural character murder* – that is, the symbolic murder of the culture or religion of an ethnic group – in contrast to *physical murder*. I cannot fully explore this theme in this chapter, but I try to shed some light on one part of the matter, the increasingly open and socially sanctioned public humiliation of (those perceived as) Muslims in Dutch society.

Public humiliations

Public humiliations of ethnic groups are a form of everyday racism often reproduced discursively and through media representations (Essed 1991; van Dijk 1997). For the purpose of illustration, I have selected from news stories reported on one Dutch Website (www.kranten.nl) for one random day: 29 October 2006. Any other day could have worked just as well.

I find a report about Prime Minister Jan Peter Balkenende, who nostalgically calls for a return of the VOC[2] mentality. This is a historically and culturally indexed reference to the mentality of the Dutch traders who, during the Dutch golden (seventeenth) century proved to be so successful for the Dutch economy – conveniently forgetting that the same mentality also produced the African slave trade. A group of immigrants from the former Dutch colony of Suriname, including descendants of African enslaved peoples, rises in protest.

Another news item has national politician Geert Wilders call for a five-year immigration stop for 'non-western' people and for an immediate prohibition on the building of mosques. He warns of a 'tsunami'[3] of non-western people, obviously appealing to images of non-whites and non-Christians ready to invade, to 'swamp' the Netherlands. To compare non-western people to a natural disaster evokes memories of Enoch Powell's and Margaret Thatcher's populism.

---

2   VOC is Verenigde Oost-indische Companie, the very profitable trading company that operated between the Netherlands and the East Indian colonies.

3   Geert Wilders is quoted in Pechtold (2006), who calls these views disgusting.

Balkenende, Wilders, Powell and Thatcher speak from a similar 'we whites' against 'them tainted' perspective. They speak *for* non-immigrants, no doubt defining themselves as *real* Europeans in defence of their national culture. How different from Californian Governor Arnold Schwarzenegger, who in an interview leading up to the November 2006 mid-term elections commented that, as an immigrant, he felt gratitude and wanted to give back to the country that had given him so many opportunities. He felt recognized as an immigrant with potential and worth. What he did not say, but could have added, is that his whiteness, his masculinity and his western European Christian background probably helped along the way – for his talents to be seen rather than overlooked or retaliated against (Roediger 2002).

The impact of anti-immigrant public discourse can hardly be underestimated. Prime Minister Balkenende apologized, with the explanation that he did not mean to mitigate slavery, but only wanted to celebrate the mentality of 'risk and courage' the Netherlands seems to have lost. And again he missed the point. The image of the Dutch historical adventurer taking risks while sailing into the unknown is not a neutral symbol. In its assumption of the whiteness and masculinity of the adventurer, risk culture naturalizes racial and gender inequalities. It 'reminds us we deserve our situation in life. In its encounters with nature, it teaches us again that races have their proper places' (Braun 2003, p. 200). And for other than whites, the proper place is not the Netherlands, Wilders could have added. His populism was rewarded during the national elections of November 2006 with a jump from zero, as a new political party, to nine (out of 150) parliamentary seats. In the meantime, the expression 'VOC mentality' has been added officially to the Dutch dictionary.[4]

Public humiliations of ethnic groups are by their very nature anonymous, not addressed against any one particular person. Rather, all members of the particular racial/ethnic group(s) are targeted generically. It may well be the case that public humiliations, because of their public nature, are particularly inviting of a public response. Of course, this does not preclude *reactions* in the private sphere, as a way of processing the hurt of cultural pain, whether destructively (for instance, domestic violence) or constructively (for example, investing in a better future for the next generation). The anonymity of public denigrations might make it difficult to respond without taking into consideration the impact one wants to make on all those other eyes and ears that have witnessed and hence been exposed to the humiliating words as well. Once discursive 'ethnic bashings' are tolerated, if not condoned, by society at large as a legitimate public habit, all members of those ethnic groups are expected to tolerate exposure to public humiliation.

---

4 This was announced during the last week of 2006 in the publication of the end-of-the-year list of 'new words' to enrich the Dutch language.

Ethnic reductionism, humiliating tolerance

The construction of otherness, that is, the view that ethnic groups are culturally *completely* different, if not deviant, is a necessary condition for sustaining the self-image of an enlightened Europe, tolerant of difference. Ethnic reductionism is like the glue upholding a sense of homogeneous whiteness, a tolerant Europeanness. Without 'others' there would not be any need for tolerance either. At the same time, ethnic groups, Muslims and immigrants of colour in particular, are seen as a cultural threat, as an inconvenience, as essentially non-European. This paradox of needing difference but rejecting it at the same time becomes insufferable. The need to create mutually exclusive difference on the basis of colour, ethnicity and culture in order to validate the claim of tolerance, a code for European cultural superiority, becomes intolerable to live up to when dominant groups feel victimized by their own tolerance, as if thinking: 'We let you in, and this is what we get, no gratitude, only problems'. In the words of Jan Peter Balkenende, stated in 2002, just before he became Prime Minister: 'For me the multicultural society is not something to pursue ... over-tolerance and qualifying one's own culture have led to the acceptance of deviant behaviour'.[5]

Cultural diversity is not a question of being for or against, but a social condition. It is more common to the history of humankind than the modernity myths of racial or cultural homogeneity (Goldberg 2002). Some 10–15 per cent of the Dutch population are first-, second- or third-generation immigrants. The largest groups are from the former colonies of Indonesia and Suriname, from the Dutch Antilles, from the countries of labour recruitment in the 1960s – Morocco and Turkey – and first-generation refugees from Ethiopia and Eritrea, Iran, Iraq, Somalia and Rwanda. Then there are other communities: Ghanaians, Pakistanis, Cape Verdeans, to mention just a few. The Surinamese used to be the largest minority group, but now probably rank second after the Turks. The percentage of people of colour in the largest cities varies between 20 and 40 per cent, but in Amsterdam over 50 per cent of children in schools are children of colour.

It has been documented that throughout Dutch history the notion and practice of tolerance implied the perception of a range of 'deviances' to be dealt with, including deviant religions (heathens, Catholics, Jews) and beliefs (magic); sexualities (sodomy, same-sex); sense of property (theft, slavery); heritage and looks (ethnic minorities, Roma and Sinti, Jews); and so on (Gijswijt-Hofstra 1989). One way to deal with the ambivalence towards tolerance is by humiliating the (perceived) other. This is where I would speak of *humiliating tolerance*:

> We (dominant group) tolerate you (racial/ethnic groups) among us but we will let you know that you are not really worthy of being here – your culture does not deserve that much respect. You are not worthy of our tolerance, because you, your religion, your culture are not tolerant either.

---

5 Jan Peter Balkenende, 2002, quoted in one of the largest Dutch daily newspapers, *De Telegraaf* (see McNally-Schoonen 2005, p. 9).

This attitude is clearly visible in the Dutch immigration debates, where ethnic groups (from Islamic countries) are accused repeatedly of fundamentalism, backwardness and culturally lagging behind (Essed and Nimako 2006).

In spite of generations of immigration, western Europe is not a welcoming place for people of colour (Puwar 2004). Moreover, like a number of other European countries, the Netherlands seems obsessed with real or assumed cultural/ethnic differences (Evens Foundation 2002). Ethnicity is treated as if it were a fixed, inherent characteristic, as if it concerned a second skin, a biological characteristic. In Dutch public discourse, ethnic groups are invariably called *allochtonen*, which means 'from the outside, non-native'. The lumping together of all non-native Dutch contributes to the sensibility that they represent another type of people, whose traditions are construed foremost in negative terms, as completely different from Dutch culture and as an obstacle to their integration. The 'others', people of colour, people of non-Christian religions, in particular Muslims, have become more and more stigmatized, perceived as a threat to European culture.

The humiliation of ethnic groups is symbolically captured in categorical thinking and the reduction of complex human beings and cultures to their ethnic identities or features. Without suggesting that ethnicity is only a projection, and not also a claim by its bearers, it should be seen that ethnic or racial reductionism implies that human beings with unique life stories and multiple layers of identity are boxed in terms of only one trait or perceived identity: race-ethnicity. *The act of ethnic reductionism implies the temporary denial of the wholeness of self, of the fullness of being.* That is in itself a form of humiliation.

Humiliation is a central feature of modern society (Lindner 2006). The formation of unequal racial, gender, culture and class structures in our societies has been sustained and these structures are being reinforced by the systemic humiliation of individuals and groups in order to keep them in subordinate places and spaces (Goldberg 2002). Historically, dehumanizing representations of the other served the construction of the European identity as the bearer of civilization. As Edward Said has pointed out in his seminal writings on orientalism, Islam was seen through Eurocentric if not racist eyes and arrogantly judged to be a fake, or degenerated, form of Christianity. Today, there is still the mix of arrogance, hate and fear. It has become *bon ton* in western European circles to call Islam inherently dangerous and incompatible with European identity. In this light must be seen also the reluctance among the majority of European member states to include Turkey in the European Union (see Chapter 7). The search for and defence of European identity is not a new phenomenon, but the particular constellation of global forces in which this process takes place is specific.

In *Diversity: Gender, Color and Culture*, I drew a distinction between feelings of Eurocentrism and what I call 'Europism', both of which are part of European identity (Essed 1996, pp. 137–38).

> Eurocentrism was a product of the history of conquest and colonization, of the 'age of Europe' (Amin 1989; West 1993). Ideologies of European superiority,

and in particular the idea that Europe is the cradle and the norm for human civilization, typify an extroverted mode of European assertion. Today, a more introverted process of Eurocentrism is taking place, *Europism*, a form of introspection. Whereas Eurocentrism emerged from the victory of conquest and the 'civilizing mission', Europism is based in the defeat of Europe, first by the United States, now gradually being followed by the Far East. Five centuries after Columbus gave effect to the idea that country borders should be extended limitlessly in order to include more and more territories, European countries today close their borders in order to exclude the 'other'. The 'fortress Europe' ideology, and the bureaucratic machinery operating to create legal, economic and political boundaries to protect Europe against the rest of the world, in particular the south, can be considered part of the phenomenon of Europism. Economic decline and internal discomposure are giving way to identity crises and the construction of new enemies: enemies within, first-, second- and third-generation racial and ethnic minorities; and enemies on the doorsteps, refugees who are supposedly pouring in by the millions in order to take advantage of western European welfare.

Tolerance and belonging

One must never underestimate the degree of hatred that Dutch people feel for Moroccan and Turkish immigrants. My political success is based on the fact that I was prepared to listen to such people. (Frits Bolkestein[6])

No matter how culturally assimilated you are, colour, ethnicity and religion remain markers to identify individuals as not (really) belonging in the Netherlands, or in Europe. There is a long history of religious tolerance in the Netherlands, meaning that different brands of Christianity came to accept as a fact of life that people have different beliefs within Christianity. Dutch tolerance has meant in history that different directions in Christianity, notably Catholicism and Protestantism, were given the opportunity to emancipate separately: among themselves, on their own terms (Voorsluis 2003): you did not have to mingle with dissident believers; you could even avoid them. Thus, the principle of 'we' versus 'them' and the endorsement of *segregated institutionalized spaces* are at the core of Dutch tolerance.

Tolerance is no longer about dissident Christian religious ideas in the Netherlands. Today, Catholics and Protestants have largely joined in mixed Christian political parties, schools and other institutional settings. New neighbourhood and school segregations have emerged: black and white schools, related to black and white neighbourhoods. Tolerance serves as a measure of civilization, as a 'civil' norm to regulate ethnic differences, the effects of

---

6 Quoted in Mair (2006, p. 11). Frits Bolkestein was a former leader of the Volkspartij voor Vrijheid en Democratie (VVD, People's Party for Freedom and Democracy) and a recent European Commissioner.

which maintain structural inequalities. This can be explained by highlighting the following related characteristics of tolerance underlying the reproduction of racial/ethnic inequality:

(1) Tolerance tacitly assigns conditions to the privilege of belonging

People who belong, *tolerators*, by definition cannot be in the position of being merely tolerated. Inversely, you can hold the position of *toleratee*, of being 'tolerated', only if you are otherwise defined as a party that does not (really) belong. This is expressed in the idea of the 'threshold of tolerance', first introduced in France and then adopted in the Netherlands and other European countries. As such, there is nothing wrong with the idea that societal openness to other cultural influences can be conditional. After all, all cultures have dimensions that do not sufficiently honour the dignity of being human. The threshold paradigm is different, in that it is arrogantly assumed that white or (western) European dominant groups do not need to change anymore: they are done with democratization. The Dutch 'becoming a citizen legislation' (*inburgeringswetgeving*) is an example where Dutch culture, as a whole, gets to be elevated to the level of 'better than thou'. Consistent media and parliamentary opinions accusing immigrants of failure, if not unwillingness, to adapt to the superiority model of western democracy breathe contempt.

(2) Exclusion from access to belonging as a form of discrimination

One explicit manifestation of this characteristic of tolerance comes from the Netherlands and Belgium, where the word *allochtoon* (alien, non-native) has been added to the Dutch language in order to distinguish between 'them' (outsiders) and 'us' (insiders). Criteria for qualifying as belonging to 'us' are a mixture of closeness in terms of *colour* (white is better than non-white), *religion* (Christianity is better than Islamic, Jewish, Hindu or other religions), *nationality* (western countries score higher than non-western ones) and *language* (national language is best, then English, other western European languages rank third, fourth, and so on, while further down the list still are non-European languages). Since the desire to belong to a larger cultural context is a fundamental part of being human, the contestation of belonging may violate a fundamental human need.

(3) Discrimination as violation of the right to live with dignity

Access to work and decent working conditions is one route to recognizing the worthiness of people. But the exclusion of people of colour and other ethnic minorities from the labour market is up to three and four times the white Dutch average (European Monitoring Centre 2006; Wrench 1996). This applies as well to those with higher education. Ethnic minority identities, in particular those perceived as Muslim, have become the target of ridicule, humiliations, rejections, exclusions, dehumanizations, and what amounts to ethnic-religious character murder. Discrimination is rampant: in the labour market, in schools and housing, and in the media (European Monitoring Centre 2006).

(4) Society's tolerance of racism as a form of humiliation

Ethnic groups are seen as 'having' problems, because they 'are' disadvantaged, and as 'creating' problems, because they 'are' a strain on societal resources and because their presence 'leads to' racism. Those who protest against racism ruin the positive dominant self-image of the tolerant. Reactions can become aggressive: how dare you accuse 'us' of racism (Essed and Nimako 2006)? In the name of tolerance, ethnic groups have to be able to take a racist joke, have to be able to take blunt critique, have to be able to tolerate even the most deeply hurting forms of symbolic humiliation. A case in point is the short film *Submission* (2004, by Ayaan Hirsi Ali). As neither subtle, artful nor comprehensive in its representation of women under Islam, it leaves little space for a nuanced appreciation of critical work (Moors 2005). This short film has often solicited extreme reactions: either anger and disgust or admiration. There is hardly an in-between position. The medium chosen is one predicated on free speech and images, including nudity and disrespectful references to the Koran. Where Islamic cultures would cover the female body, the film is suggesting that it will show you what is underneath those covers.[7]

Insufferable humiliations

As a cultural product, *Submission* fits very well with the ideology of tolerance: representatives of the dominant culture claim the right to express themselves in any way they wish about Islam, a religion perceived as tolerated only because it does not belong to the Netherlands. In critiquing Islam in this way, little consideration, if any at all, is given to the possibly humiliating impact on the sense of self-respect among Muslims; after all, this only adds to the range of other, everyday negative representations. Probably more than anything, *Submission* reflects a quintessentially Dutch cultural trait, a quality ranking high in the Dutch value system: to speak your mind, whatever it takes. Some would even push the point further, saying that in the Netherlands 'sacrifice for one's beliefs evokes more admiration than whatever those beliefs stand for' (Voorsluis 2003, p. 4).

The makers of the film, Theo van Gogh (director) and Ayaan Hirsi Ali (writer), qualified the video as a critical product, taboo breaking, meant to provoke. But

---

7   With thanks to Mieke Gelley for the long telephone conversation we had about this issue.

others see it as highly offensive, demeaning and pornographic. The video-clip pictures quotes from the Koran written on the body of a battered woman, as a way of protesting about violence against women in Islamic communities. Carefully managed camera shots of the scene seem to highlight the aesthetics of handwritten text decorating the nakedness of the skin. The actress's body posture adds to the effect of eroticizing the abused body. One could say: this amounts to objectification, if not abuse, of the Muslim female body in order to protest against the abuse of the very same Muslim female body. Moreover, if the movie is intended to teach Muslims tolerance, the question is whether it can be successful in achieving this goal. The documentary speaks more generously to a white, non-Muslim (Dutch) audience than to Muslims. As a Muslim you will first have to swallow religious humiliation and the embarrassment of stereotyped Muslim behaviour before you might be able to appreciate the critique of the abuse of the female body. There is also the double meaning in the title of the movie: one layer is a critique of the submission of women to Muslim (male) culture; at the same time, the hidden agenda is that if Muslims submit to Dutch (western) civilization, they will be cured of (what is perceived as) their backwardness.[8]

Theo van Gogh used to address Muslims by the epithet of 'goat f***ers'. He made it a point to ridicule (Islamic devotion to) Allah. He already had a record of insulting Christians and Jews: he was not shy to crack racist and anti-Semitic jokes of the lowest level thinkable.[9] Muslims were his latest targets. This is not meant to suggest that non-Muslims cannot be critical of Islamic practices. Quite the contrary: critical perceptions, self-reflections and dialogue are all crucial for improving the quality of human relations in a diverse society. I disagree with the *humiliation* of individuals and people in the name of critique, whether that critique is well founded or not. Critique can hurt, but does not have to leave a scar. Humiliations create wounds and some wounds do not heal properly, if they heal at all. It is easier to wound than to deal with wounded souls and with the necessary healing. The damage of public ethnic humiliations increases, or deepens, when the audience, the public, remains largely a silent majority tolerant of the idea that 'anything can go'. In the course of the 1990s and into the new millennium, just about any insult could be thrown at Muslims (often generically referred to by the code word 'Moroccans', the third largest immigrant community in the Netherlands).

Who would have thought that reverse violence, counter-humiliation, would take place in the Netherlands in the name of Islam: the assassination of arguably the most radical Dutch representative of free speech, a value at the heart of western interpretations of democracy? Here is T. G. Ash's summary in the *New York Review of Books*:

---

8   Conversation with David Theo Goldberg.

9   "'Je bent voor of je bent tegen" – bij de dood van Van Gogh', 6 November 2004, on the Website Grenzeloos, www.grenzeloos.org/artikel/viewartikel.php/id/675.html (accessed 28 January 2009).

2 November 2004: Dutch society is thoroughly shaken when a Dutch film-maker, Theo van Gogh is found dead in the streets of Amsterdam, the victim of a ritual assassination. The assassin, Moroccan-Dutch Muslim fundamentalist, mutilated van Gogh's body, thereby also symbolically mutilating what van Gogh, according to many, symbolically represented: freedom of the word. Van Gogh had to pay with his life for insulting Allah, for claiming the legal right to speak out, even when offensive. Stabbed into his lifeless body was an alarming note proclaiming the downfall of the US, Europe and the Netherlands, and that Ayaan Hirsi Ali would be the next one to go. (Ash 2006, n.p.)

Hirsi Ali, an immigrant from Somalia and former member of the Dutch parliament for the VVD, is a vehement critic and crusader against Islam. Some have referred to her zeal as a *liberal jihad*. The Koran, she insists, approves of men abusing women, if not encourages it. Her most important mission is fighting Islam and the abuse of Muslim women by any (legal) means possible. In a 2006 speech, when she was still a member of the Dutch parliament, she insisted on *the right to offend*.[10]

Both the radical nature of *Submission* and the extremism of the assassination disrupted the taken-for-granted national self-definition of the Netherlands as the epitome of moderation and of tolerance. Many Dutch Muslims, as well as a substantial minority among the non-Muslim Dutch, felt that *Submission* was deeply offensive. When there are surely other ways to criticize the abuse of women in Muslim communities, why stigmatize all and only Muslims for oppressing women? Whatever the opinion about van Gogh, most if not all in the Netherlands – Muslims and non-Muslims alike – felt deeply shaken by the gruesome murder.

As a short film, *Submission* was a public intervention: seen, discussed, commented upon throughout Dutch society and globally. The assassination of van Gogh was a public response as well, humiliating, wounding Dutch society as a whole while causing global shock and consternation. In July 2005, the assassin was sentenced to life imprisonment.

In the name of Muslim women

A lot has been said about the assassination, but few have questioned the gender dimensions of the events that led to the liquidation. Van Gogh claimed to speak for Muslim women, that is, in protest against what he called the backward position of Muslim women and the violence of Muslim men against Muslim women. His rejection of the abuse of women and of women's social subordination echoes feminist critiques across the globe, including critical voices of Muslim women themselves (Karam 1998; Pektas-Weber 2006; Yuval-Davis 1997). But van Gogh was

---

10   See www.nettime.org/Lists-Archives/nettime-l-0602/msg00059.html (accessed 19 August 2009).

never otherwise known to be an advocate of feminism. Nor has he been quoted for displaying any respect for the female body either. He used to enjoy his freedom of speech, among other things, with misogynist statements. Both van Gogh and Hirsi Ali deploy a universal model of women's emancipation, as necessarily including secularization, without any nuance of how gender is shaped historically, nationally, religiously, culturally or ethnically. In so doing, they reinforce the stereotype of ethnic minority women as passive victims of their cultures, thereby denying agency and the realities of everyday resistance among women in ethnic communities (Bhavnani 2001; Botman *et al.* 2001). Stigmatizing representations, in particular, when coming from opinion leaders, can have profoundly damaging effects. The majority of Muslim women experience discrimination from Dutch employers who refuse to hire a woman with a head-scarf – because they are considered too oppressed.[11] The everyday humiliation of Muslim women in the Netherlands draws from many sources, linking ethnic patriarchies, religious (mis)interpretations, Dutch paternalisms and European racisms.

The scarf has become the symbol of women's oppression, with those using it to cover their heads being routinely exposed to aggressive and pitying gazes (Afshar 2008). Some wearers have been spat at. Intolerable contempt. The scarf seems to irritate, to touch a raw nerve. Why? Fashionable or just plain, scarves attach to young and old faces, educated and non-schooled heads, restless and penetrating eyes, shy and wilful chins, sunken and cheerful cheeks, obedient and self-minded facial expressions, pious and not-really-that-religious souls, women conforming and women resisting. Such diversity. Why this fairly uniform response of rejection? One explanation may have to do with the thinness of gender progress in the Netherlands (and Europe generally, for that matter). Problems newcomers face point to the already existing weaknesses, vulnerabilities and unresolved problems of society. Insufficient respect for women and the integrity of the female body are not ethnic problems only. Western societies, too, are suffering from the condition called *the incomplete emancipation of women.* Pornographic abuse and other despising images of the female body, in particular through the Internet, have taken epidemic forms. The phenomenon of 'seeking coverage against the male gaze' is nothing new. The protection of the rights and dignity of all women in Europe requires the courage to acknowledge that gender inequality is not simply about clashing cultures, but also about different manifestations of a common problem across cultures. One response against the male gaze is to cover up the body (often the *religious* response). Another response is to challenge the gaze with minimal body coverage (often the *secular* response). Neither overdressing nor undressing has proven to be sufficiently effective against sexual abuse.

Yet, in the view of dominant ideology in the Netherlands, women's emancipation has been more or less completed. Non-Islamic feminists fear that Muslims

---

11   See the fact sheet 'Discriminatie en beeldvorming op de arbeidsmarkt' (June 2005), available at www.e-quality.nl/assets/e-quality/publicaties/2005/Factsheets/Discriminatieenbeeld vormingopdearbeidsmarkt.doc (accessed 28 January 2009).

will negatively influence the emancipation of all women in the Netherlands. These and related views have been voiced in *Opzij*, the most popular feminist monthly magazine. Moreover, Cisca Dresselhuys, long-time editor-in-chief, has publicly announced that she would never hire a woman with a head-scarf because the head-scarf is incompatible with feminism. This extreme position, some might say a form of policing, is hardly constructive, and is comparable to the early years of second-wave feminism, when 'real' feminists were supposed not to wear high heels and make-up and not to sleep with men either. More than anything, *the myth that only bareheaded women can have true voice and choice violates the dignity of too many other women.*

Infringements of self-respect can be resisted by insisting on taking back one's dignity (Hodson 2001). Arguably, a head-scarf might have been less crucial to Dutch female Muslim identity if Muslim women in the Netherlands had otherwise experienced appreciation and respect in society at large. The fact of the matter is that an increasing number of *moslimas* in the Netherlands opt to wear the scarf, whether for religious reasons or not. The same holds true for other countries, including Britain (Afshar 2008). Belligerent choice for 'the scarf' goes hand in hand with the increasingly assertive voice of young Dutch Muslim women and men who claim their rightful place and space in the Netherlands (Meulenbelt 2004; Smahane 2006). In this light must also be seen the November 2006 Islamic Women's Manifesto in defence of justice, human respect and equal rights for Islamic women within their cultural communities and in Dutch society at large (Pektas-Weber 2007). The exposure and public rejection of violence against women in non-dominant communities is a necessary step in the process of ethnic and gender emancipation and integration. Public critique is most constructive when formulated in ways that are not stigmatizing, criminalizing or otherwise humiliating for the whole ethnic group (Parekh 2000). Leaders, irrespective of gender and ethnicity, can provide a different, positive example. Words spoken by the Dutch queen at the occasion of the 2006 Christmas speech are a case in point. While contending that freedom of expression and opinion is at the very core of democratic societies, she then qualified the statement:

> Apart from the general limits defined by the law, there are also norms of morality and civilization. These are the fundaments of a society based on respect for fellow human beings. Hence, there is no such thing as the right to offend. By the same token, freedom of religion does not license anyone to cause hurt or to call for hate.[12]

This brings us back to the beginning of this chapter, the importance of leadership interventions against offensive words, whether these consist of small remarks or intolerable humiliations.

---

12 Kersttoespraak Koningin 2006. Het Koninklijk Huis. Available at www.koninklijkhuis. nl/content.jsp?objectid=17228 (accessed 28 January 2009). Translation from the Dutch by Philomena Essed.

Works cited

Afshar, H. (2008) 'Can I See Your Hair? Choice, Agency and Attitudes: The Dilemma of Faith and Feminism for Muslim Women Who Cover'. *Ethnic and Racial Studies*, 47(2), pp. 411–27.

Ahmed, S. (2004) *The Cultural Politics of Emotion*. New York, Routledge.

Allen, J. (2006) *Rabble-Rouser for Peace: The Authorized Biography of Desmond Tutu*. New York, Free Press.

Amin, S. (1989) *Eurocentrism*. New York, Monthly Review Press.

Ash, T. G. (2006) 'Islam in Europe'. *New York Review of Books*, 53 (15). Available at www.nybooks. com/articles/19371 (accessed 28 January 2009).

Bhavnani, K. (2001) *Feminism and 'Race'*. Oxford, Oxford University Press.

Boog, I. ed. (2006) *Monitor Rassendiscriminatie 2005*. Leiden, Anne Frank Stichting and Leiden Universiteit.

Botman, M., Jouwe, N. and Wekker, G. (2001) *Caleidoscopische Visies, de zwarte, migranten- en vluchtelingenvrouwen beweging in Nederland*. Amsterdam, KIT Publishers with Expertise-centrum GEM and E-Quality.

Branden, N. (1994) *The Six Pillars of Self-Esteem*. New York, Bantam.

Braun, B. (2003) '"On the Raggedy Edge of Risk": Articulatons of Race and Nature After Biology'. In: Moore, D., Kosek, J. and Pandian, A. eds. *Race, Nature and the Politics of Difference*. Durham, NC, Duke University Press, pp. 175–203.

Cockburn, C. (1998) *The Space Between Us: Negotiating Gender and National Identities in Conflict*. London, Zed Books.

Essed, P. (1990) *Everyday Racism: Reports from Women of Two Cultures*. Claremont, CA, Hunter House.

—— (1991) *Understanding Everyday Racism: An Interdisciplinary Theory*. London, Sage.

—— (1996) *Diversity: Gender, Color and Culture*. Amherst, MA, University of Massachusetts Press.

—— (1997) 'Racial Intimidation: Socio-political Implications of the Usage of Racist Slur'. In: Riggins, S. H. ed. *The Language and Politics of Exclusion: Others in Discourse*. London, Sage, pp. 131–52.

Essed, P. and Nimako, K. (2006) 'Designs and (Co)incidents. Cultures of Scholarship and Public Policy on Immigrants/Minorities in the Netherlands'. *International Journal of Comparative Sociology*, 47(3/4), pp. 281–312.

European Monitoring Centre on Racism and Xenophobia (2006) *Muslims in the European Union. Discrimination and Islamophobia*. Available at http://fra.europa.eu/fraWebsite/attachments/ Manifestations_EN.pdf (accessed 28 January 2009).

Evens Foundation (2002) *Europe's New Racism: Causes, Manifestations and Solutions*. Oxford, Berghahn Books.

Fry, D. P. (2006) *The Human Potential for Peace: An Anthropological Challenge to Assumptions About War and Violence*. New York, Oxford University Press.

Gijswijt-Hofstra, M. ed. (1989) *Een schijn van verdraagzaamheid: Afwijking en tolerantie in Nederland van de zestiende eeuw tot heden*. Hilversum, Verloren.

Gobodo-Madikizela, P. (2003) *A Human Being Died That Night: A South African Story of Forgiveness*. New York, Houghton Mifflin.

Goldberg, D. T. (2002) *The Racial State*. Malden, MA, Blackwell.

Hodson, R. (2001) *Dignity at Work*. Cambridge, Cambridge University Press.

hooks, b. (2003) *Rock My Soul: Black People and Self-Esteem*. New York, Atria Books.

Karam, A. M. (1998) *Women in Parliament: Beyond Numbers*. Stockholm, International IDEA.

Law, I. (2001) *Race in the News*. Basingstoke, Palgrave.

Lazare, A. (2004) *On Apology*. Oxford, Oxford University Press.

Lindner, E. G. (2001) 'Humiliation and Human Rights: Mapping a Minefield'. *Human Rights Review*, January–March, pp. 46–63.

—— (2006) *Making Enemies: Humiliation and International Conflict*. Westport, CN, Praeger Security International.

Maathai, W. (2006) *Unbowed: A Memoir*. New York, Alfred Knopf.

Mair, P. (2006) 'What's Going On? Murder in Amsterdam: The Death of Theo van Gogh and the Limits of Tolerance'. *London Review of Books*, 14 December, pp. 11–13.

Margalit, A. (1996) *The Decent Society*. Cambridge, MA, Harvard University Press.

McNally-Schoonen, T. (2005) *White Western Foreigners in the Netherlands – Just Another Migrant Group?* MA thesis, Faculty of Law, University of Southampton.

Meulenbelt, A. (2004) 'Cisca en de hoofddoekjes'. *Anja Meulenbelt*, 15 October. Available at http://anjameulenbelt.sp.nl/weblog/2004/10/15/cisca-en-de-hoofddoekjes/ (accessed 28 January 2009).

Moors, A. (2005) 'Submission'. *ISIM Review*, 15.

Parameshwar, S. (2005) 'Spiritual Leadership Through Ego-Transcendence: Exceptional Responses to Challenging Circumstances'. *Leadership Quarterly*, 16, pp. 689–722.

Parekh, B. (2000) *Rethinking Multiculturalism: Cultural Diversity and Political Theory*. London, Macmillan.

Pechtold, A. (2006) 'Uitspraak Wilders te walgelijk'. *Algemeen Dagblad*, 29 October. Available at www.ad.nl/verkiezingen/article753104.ece (accessed 28 January 2009).

Pektas-Weber, C. (2006) *Moslima's: Emancipatie achter de dijken*. Amsterdam, Bulaaq.

—— (2007) 'Feminisme in de Moslimwereld'. *Al Nisa*, March.

Puwar, N. (2004) *Space Invaders: Race, Gender and Bodies Out of Place*. Oxford, Berg.

Roediger, D. (2002) 'Whiteness and Ethnicity in the History of "White Ethnics" in the United States'. In: Essed, P. and Goldberg, D. eds. *Race Critical Theories: Text and Context*. Oxford, Blackwell, pp. 325–43.

Smahane (2006) 'Terecht of onterecht?'. *Wij blijven hier!*, 18 December. Available at www.wijblijvenhier.nl/index.php?/archives/876-Terecht-of-onterecht.html (accessed 28 January 2009).

Tilly, C. (1999) *Durable Inequality*. Berkeley, CA, University of California Press.

van Dijk, T. A. (1997) *Elite Discourse and Racism*. Thousand Oaks, CA, Sage.

Voorsluis, B. (2003) 'Onze basiswaarden, historisch beschouwd' ['Our Basic Values, Historically Seen']. *In de Marge*, 1, pp. 2–8.

West, C. (1993) *Race Matters*. Boston, MA, Beacon Press.

Wrench, J. (1996) *Preventing Racism at the Workplace: A Report on 16 European Countries*. Dublin, European Foundation for the Improvement of Living and Working Conditions.

Yuval-Davis, N. (1997) *Gender and Nation*. London, Sage.

CHAPTER 10

The *Jyllands-Posten* Muhammad cartoons controversy: racism and 'cartoon work' in the age of the World Wide Web

Katarzyna Murawska-Muthesius

From late January well into March 2006, media outlets from all over the world, whether right, left or centre, whether print, broadcast or virtual, from CNN News to the *Fiji Daily Post*, and from radical journals to personal blogs of various persuasions, were inundated with reports, interviews, opinions, photographs, reproductions and maps, as well as cartoons, on the subject of the 'Danish cartoon war'. The conflict, which came also to be known under a variety of other names, like the 'Muhammad cartoon controversy', the 'cartoon jihad' or the 'cartoon intifada', was sparked in September 2005 by the publication of twelve images mocking the Prophet Muhammad in the *Jyllands-Posten*, a Danish tabloid well known for its anti-immigrant stance (Nederveen Pieterse 2006). The cartoons had been commissioned by the newspaper's cultural editor, Flemming Rose, as a calculated measure against the growing reluctance of Danish artists, who were fearful of breaking the taboo against idolatry, to represent the Prophet or to criticize Islam in any way. Twelve cartoonists responded and their works were inserted into Rose's short article, which reprimanded Muslims' demands for respect for their religious sensitivities as 'incompatible with contemporary democracy and freedom of speech, where you must be ready to put up with insults, mockery and ridicule' (Rose 2005, n.p.). The text on its own might have passed unnoticed, but the cartoons, which were meant to teach the Muslims a lesson – especially one by Kurt Westergaard, identifying the Prophet with a suicide bomber – hit the mark, and were received as deeply offensive by the local Danish Muslim community.

It took a good few months, however, and a sequence of diplomatic blunders as well as further provocations from all sides involved before the cartoon affair was amplified on an unprecedented scale. Among the most significant moves was Danish Prime Minister Fogg Rasmussen's refusal, citing freedom of speech as his official excuse, to meet eleven Islamic ambassadors and to face the demand for a public apology. Subsequently, the massive re-publication of the cartoons by newspapers all over the world in manifest support of the same freedom-of-the-press principle inflamed Muslim anger. From the Islamic side, in turn, death threats against the cartoonists and the fabrication of a doctored dossier on the conflict alerted public opinion, but also, as intended, pushed religious fundamentalists and thousands of ordinary Muslims out onto the streets, rallying against religious blasphemy and free speech, and proclaiming Europe to be the enemy of Islam. By the first week of February, the crisis had gone global, culminating in ritual desecrations of Danish flags, the setting on fire of the Danish and Norwegian embassies in Syria and Lebanon, and violent demonstrations in Somalia, India, Pakistan and Afghanistan. The conflict claimed hundreds of dead and injured, and left a trail of physical destruction, despair, resentment, humiliation and anger. It affected the 'west' too, but in a much milder manner. For a while, to be sure, the boycott of Danish products in the Middle East upset Denmark's economy, death threats against the cartoonists were declared but not implemented, and a number of politicians and editors in the west were forced out of their jobs, but, all in all, the 'war' seems to have buttressed rather than subverted the notion of western supremacy, as guaranteed by modernity and its freedoms, and as demonstrated by the repeated revival of Samuel Huntington's metaphor of the 'clash of civilizations' as a ready-made explanation of what had 'really' happened (Huntington 1996).[1]

A global debate began as soon as the conflict erupted, both in the media and in academic circles, around the legal, cultural and ethical boundaries of freedom of speech, around the parameters of discourses of Muslim exceptionality (Hansen 2006a, 2006b), and around the racist dimensions of Islamophobia and its instrumental role in the construction of western identity (Bleich 2006; Bronner 2006; Henkel 2006; Modood 2006a, 2006b; Nederveen Pieterse 2006; Ramadan 2006; Soyinka 2006). Well after the affair has ended, the Muhammad cartoons case continues to be invoked repeatedly in discussions about Muslim minorities in the west, multiculturalism, immigration and xenophobia in Denmark, and has become a *cause célèbre* in any number of subsequent debates that draw directly or indirectly on the 'clash of civilizations' thesis. Several sensational books devoted entirely to the 'cartoon war' have been written (Bech Thomsen 2006; Ghazi 2006; Sifaoui 2006), while many academic publications issued in 2006 and early 2007 refer insistently to the cartoon controversy in hastily adjusted introductions and epilogues (see, for example, Giddens 2006, pp. 132–33).[2]

---

1   There have been many contradictory reports of what happened and in what order; my task here is not to establish a precise chronology but to examine the role of the cartoons in the conflict and I have chosen largely to follow the account on Wikipedia, '*Jyllands-Posten* Muhammad cartoons controversy' (http://en.wikipedia.org/wiki/Jyllands-Posten_Muhammad_cartoons_controversy).

2   The sheer volume of publications, from newspapers to university newsletters, special issues of professional journals in diverse fields from economics and politics to philosophy, religion, anthropology and law, makes it virtually impossible to compile a comprehensive bibliography of the debates about the Danish cartoon war. Wikipedia provides long lists of

Cartoon work and racism

Paradoxically, given what they have caused, the significance of the cartoons themselves has been either de-emphasized or expressly denied by a number of different commentators. Widely perceived as 'mere' symptoms or triggers, or discarded as 'clumsy' and 'banal' and as not meriting serious interest, the cartoons have also been blamed for taking the world's attention away from the real atrocities committed by the west in the Middle East. As Tariq Ali has remarked:

> What I find interesting is that these demonstrations and embassy-burnings are a response to a tasteless cartoon. Did the Danish imam who travelled round the Muslim world pleading for this show the same anger at Danish troops being sent to Iraq? (Ali 2006)

In other words, while the anger of the Muslim community would have been justified had it been targeted against real crimes against humanity in the Middle East, to shed blood over cartoons somehow seems wrong-headed. It is not my intention here to ascribe excessive value or gravity to the cartoons, to elevate them (as some have done) to the status of murder weapons, but I do believe that the anger about the war in Iraq is impossible to tell apart from anger about the cartoons. I also believe that ignoring the significance of the cartoons implies compliance with the western argument that absolutizes freedom of speech while turning a blind eye to demeaning strategies of representation and cultural racism. Further, as the incestuous relationship between the media and politics can no longer be refuted in the post-Gulf War era, it seems wrong to see the Muhammad cartoons, and several others of their ilk, as merely accidental, or as more or less transparent vessels for transmitting evil messages. To paraphrase McLuhan, it is the medium of the cartoon that matters and that bears blame for the consequent course of events (McLuhan 1967). Far from serving as accidental *triggers* in the escalation of the Middle East crisis, the cartoons, which were often liable to be used as a deceptive tool of racist discrimination, played a fundamental *role* in the conflict itself.

As Paul Gilroy, among others, has claimed, the 'cognition of "race" [has never been] an exclusively linguistic process, and has [always] involved … a distinctive visual and optical imaginary' (Gilroy 2004, p. 35). Taking the Danish cartoons as a case in point, and beginning with Kurt Westergaard's notorious image of the suicide bomber, this chapter examines visual strategies for the contemporary representation of Islam and Muslim societies, and argues for the constitutive role of *pictorial* representation, especially cartoons, in naturalizing 'self-evident truths' about Islam and its alleged obscurantism and fanaticism, intolerance

---

contributors' names, including some articles in academic publications, and the virtual pages of the *Guardian* (www.guardian.co.uk/world/muhammad-cartoons) list subsequent news items. For a good spread of facts and contradicting opinions, see the special issue of *International Migration* (2006), 44(5), *The Danish Cartoon Affair: Free Speech, Racism, Islamism and Integration*.

and violence. It argues that cartoons, as an established technique for both the 'overloaded' and the 'liberated' image, and for the implementation of an 'evil eye' or a 'keyhole gaze', constitute an especially relevant medium for the study of visuality and its imbrication with language, power and the racially marked body.

The particular forms of caricature to be found in cartoons are a deceptive instance of stereotyping and of the naturalization of 'scopic regimes' (Jay 1988). Cartoons are considered transparent, trivial and entertaining precisely because of their opacity, because of their multiple intertextual references and semiotic density, as well as their close interaction with desires and anxieties that are repressed in the unconscious. Manoeuvring between piercing insight and worn-out cliché, blatantly subjective and yet parading as a more 'truthful' or 'rebellious' vision of reality than 'unmediated' camera images, cartoons tend to be perceived as instruments of subversion, even as they police established boundaries and preserve the status quo. Instrumental in the past in playing the 'race card' by exaggerating biological pointers of difference, cartoons continue to be deployed in the 'new racist' present, where the focus has arguably shifted from individual bodies to entire cultures, including their religious affiliations and their socio-cultural taboos.[3] It is no coincidence that the conflict, which owes its origins to the 'freedom to speak/freedom to offend' principle, was provoked by twelve cartoons that broke the Islamic ban on depicting the face of the Prophet Muhammad. For the 'cartoon war', ranged against a disadvantaged Muslim minority in a western state, broke out precisely because of the established properties of cartoons themselves, which are capable of excluding the other while parading at the same time as a celebratory exercise in free speech. Taking its cues from Freud, McLuhan and Baudrillard, the remainder of this chapter seeks to examine some of the ways in which the Danish cartoons functioned, and poses the question as to whether a medium that has historically been so effective in practising and/or perpetuating racial discrimination can also be used as a positive tool for re-signification in contemporary cultural debates.

As the crisis evolved, accusations of blasphemy, Islamophobia and racism on the Muslim side were countered by inflammatory waving of the freedom-of-the-press flag as an inalienable achievement of western liberal democracy, as well as a naming of religious fundamentalism and terrorism as its capital threats. A seemingly irresolvable dilemma of 'incitement to religious hatred versus right to offend' or, in another guise, 'cultural racism versus freedom of speech' emerged as the dominant binary, serving to generate contradictory meanings and assessments of the conflict, and also acting as a catalyst for its disastrous events. As already suggested, however, the 'racism versus freedom' binary is built into the very structure and mechanism of the cartoon as a visual medium. Operating primarily by distortion and substitution, caricatures and cartoons comprise a special category of persuasive visual representations. They appeal to

---

3   For an argument on various manifestations of anti-Muslim racism in Britain, which includes hostility to Islam, see Modood (2005, 2006b).

their viewers not by offering 'objective views' of reality but, on the contrary, by proclaiming subjectivity as an ultimate guarantee of reaching the 'hidden truth'. Moreover, they present aggressive distortion as an act of rebellion against the prevailing authority. Although commonly perceived as weapons of liberation, capable of toppling tyrants, cartoons have always been used against the powerless, deployed as particularly effective tools to mock, degrade, exclude and vilify social outcasts and minorities (Banta 2003; Curtis 1971; Wonham 2004). The 'right to offend', the defining feature of the cartoon, is a double-edged sword that can be either emancipatory or discriminating and is often both at the same time. Neither liberation nor denigration fully determines its ideological disposition. Whether cartoons act as 'weapons' targeting the powerful, or whether they serve as 'sermons' chastising the powerless and maintaining the existing social and political order, depends exclusively on their relations with power at any given time. What makes cartoons even more politically useful, and also particularly deceptive, is their liminal position between ritual and subversion, which allows them to parade as subversive or rebellious even as they cling to, and reinforce, the power/knowledge of the status quo.

At least since the European Reformation, satirical prints, caricatures and cartoons, disseminated in large numbers, have taken an active part in wars and conflicts, provoking anger, vilifying and humiliating the enemy and, most of all, degrading the represented 'other' while claiming the spiritual, moral and cultural superiority of the representing self. Caricatures and cartoons articulating and naturalizing racist discourse about Jews, Irish, blacks, eastern Europeans, suffragettes or gays have been a common feature in illustrated magazines and newspapers, from *Punch* to *Krokodil* and the *Daily Mail*, as well as in comics, from *Tintin* to *The Flintstones*. And yet, despite the stigmatizing propensities of the medium, throughout the last two centuries, cartoons, together with their 'older sister', caricature, have mainly been categorized as the subversive instruments of social and political intervention (see, for example, Gombrich 1963); it is only relatively recently that they have been examined as ritualized tools of the myth-making procedures that maintain the social and political order (Banta 2003; Edwards 1997; Gombrich 1999; Medhurst and DeSousa 1981).

In the mid-nineteenth century, the development of an illustrated press, along with the writings of Charles Baudelaire and the art of Honoré Daumier, staged caricature as a romantic rebellion against the classical canons of beauty; as a defiant valorization of ugliness as well as an agent of the oppressed, a weapon against social and political power. The most memorable images visualizing the free press as an instrument of the underprivileged, for example as a weapon in the class struggle, were created, predictably, by cartoonists themselves, and Daumier himself authored quite a few of them. Daumier's name stands to this day for the uncompromised rebellion of the free press against the ruling classes, censorship and the corrupted government of Louis-Philippe. Not only was Daumier jailed for his offensive caricatures, but some of his drawings, such as a memorable pear, which in a few strokes of the pen reduced the king's face to a 'fathead' (one of the slang meanings of *la poire*), also reputedly inspired rebellious crowds to agitate against the government, leading eventually to the re-imposition of censorship in France under the July Monarchy (Goldstein 1989).[4] However, despite a superficial analogy between the visual strategies and the inflammatory potential of Daumier's pear and Kurt Westergaard's suicide bomber, there is a fundamental difference between them. If Daumier's pear was targeted at the powerful, Muhammad's turban with a lit fuse was aimed rather at a disempowered immigrant minority. And yet, despite this blatant ideological contrast, the residual identification of caricature with rebellion and freedom still underscores current debates about the cartoons and the freedom of the press (see for example Dalgaard and Dalgaard 2006).

The same essentially modernist belief in revolt against the canon and the authority that sustains it must have inspired Freud's insights into the mechanisms of caricature, which are particularly interesting for an enquiry into the debasing strategies that are specific to satire, including visual satire. In his book *Jokes and Their Relationship to the Unconscious*, first published in 1905, Freud saw caricature as a vehicle of aggression, which, by sublimating anxieties and desires that have previously been repressed in the unconscious, is empowered to subvert the inflated ego of a person or a group, to degrade authority by making it comic.[5] Seemingly oblivious to racism, Freud links caricatures with dreams and jokes, justifying aggression by aligning it with rebellion: as he says of the joke, it 'represents rebellion against … authority, a liberation from its pressure. The charm of caricatures lies in the same factor: we laugh at them even if they are unsuccessful simply because we count rebellion against authority as a merit' (Freud 1991, p. 149). Freud's assertion of a 'far reaching analogy between the technique of jokes and the dream-work', both of which share the same cognitive mechanisms of condensation, displacement, faulty reasoning and indirect representation (62, 130), allows for an extension to the operational mechanisms of the cartoon, which deploys similar strategies of condensation and displacement, and which Gombrich, among others, has likened, following Freud, to 'cartoon work' (Gombrich 1963, p. 130). Explaining the mechanism for obtaining comic pleasure, Freud writes further:

> Caricature, parody and travesty (as well as their practical counterpart, unmasking) are directed against people and objects which lay claim to authority and respect…. *Caricature*, as is well known, brings about degradation by emphasising in the general impression given by the exalted object a single trait which is

---

4   For an alternative view of the agency of caricature under the July Monarchy, see Kerr (2000).
5   Although in his writing on caricature, Freud never used the English term 'cartoon', we can safely assume that he was an enthusiast of the genre; not only did he have a couple of Wilhelm Busch's satirical drawings displayed on the wall of his Vienna study, but after his escape from Vienna to London in 1938 he also declared himself an admirer of cartoons by David Low. The latter quotes in his autobiography a spontaneous letter of appreciation he received from Freud: '20 Maresfield Gardens, London, N.W. 3, Nov. 12th, 1938, A Jewish refugee from Vienna, a very old man personally unknown to you, cannot resist the impulse to tell you how much he admires your glorious art and your inexorable, unfailing criticism. Sigmund Freud' (Low 1956, p. 315).

comic in itself but was bound to be overlooked so long as it was only perceivable in the general picture. By isolating this, a comic effect can be attained which extends in our memory over the whole object. This is subject to the condition that the actual presence of the exalted object himself does not keep us in a reverential attitude. If a comic trait of this kind that has been overlooked is lacking in reality, a caricature will unhesitatingly create it by exaggerating one that is not comic in itself; and the fact that the effect of the caricature is not essentially diminished by this falsification of reality is once again an indication of the origin of comic pleasure. (Freud 1991, pp. 261–62, original emphasis)

Freud's analysis is helpful in deconstructing the workings of Westergaard's image. Westergaard's infamous cartoon, commissioned and published as an image of Muhammad, takes direct aim at the Prophet as an authority figure, revered and exalted by all Muslims. The cartoon begins its process of degradation by identifying 'a single trait which is comic in itself but was bound to be overlooked': here the stress is put on the angry expression on Muhammad's face, articulated in the image by dense eyebrows, dark beard and moustache, furrowed forehead and intense gaze cast down on an invisible object. The tangle of black hair also hints at the phenotypical features of an Arab face, based on the old oriental stereotypes, and the image obviously does not comply with idealized representations of the Prophet that occasionally appear in, say, Persian miniatures.[6] What alters the message of the cartoon dramatically is the substitution of Muhammad's white turban by a black bomb with a burning fuse and with an inscription in Arabic in front of it, which ironically declares 'Peace'. The image of the bomb, as diagnosed by Freud, may serve as the missing comic trait which, 'lacking in reality', has been added by the cartoonist to achieve his desired effect. The metaphorical displacement of the turban with a bomb, however, goes far beyond the mechanism for arriving at comic pleasure outlined by Freud, and does much more than attach a clown's nose to the face of a respected authority figure. Brutally and arbitrarily, it identifies the Prophet with a suicide bomber, implying the reduction of Islam to terrorism, and wilfully imposing this identity onto the global religious community of Muslims as a whole. Although the cartoonist, when interviewed, tried to distance himself from this reading of his work by claiming that he was targeting religious fundamentalists and not Islam in totality, his explanation could not reverse the way in which his image had already been received by followers of the Prophet and non-Muslims alike, some of the latter choosing to deploy it as their favourite icon in a series of high-profile anti-Islamic protests.[7] The harm (or, in Gayatri Chakravorty Spivak's

---

6   The ethnic ambiguity of Muhammad's face as drawn by Westergaard has been cleverly pointed out by a Jewish cartoonist Doron Nissimi in his entry in the Israeli anti-Semitic contest (discussed below, p. 159), who changed that into the familiar image of the Jewish other, by replacing the turban with a Hasidic hat, adding Jewish side locks and black dress. Easily obtainable on the Web, both images are also reproduced by Spiegelman (2006, p. 51).
7   Reform Minister in Italy, Roberto Calderoli, had to resign after being blamed for sparking clashes in Libya – which killed eleven people – by wearing a T-shirt on television bearing Westergaard's cartoon (Hooper *et al.* 2006).

words, the 'epistemic violence') had already been done, setting in motion the familiar protocols of cartoons' mechanism of representation. The cartoon thus not only supplied a visual regime for the dissemination of 'truths' about violence, terrorism and hypocrisy that were associated with Islam but also provided a memorable frame through which millions of viewers might look (down) at any Muslim person with a turban. The cartoon showed, in other words, how, in the 'new racism' era, phenotypical differences have been effectively displaced onto hairstyle and dress, or satirical stage props drawn from political actuality.

Westergaard's cartoon might appear ingenious, even witty, in its use of a visual pun derived from the parallel between the roundness (and cultural otherness) of the turban and the spherical shape of the bomb.[8] However, witty metaphors are not necessarily of the artist's invention and are often borrowed from others. Rather, intertextuality – deliberate references to well known tropes and visual metaphors that are already in circulation, and specific to the medium – serves as a token of the visual literacy of the maker, as an assurance of accessibility, and as a confirmation of his or her familiarity with the dominant discourses of the day. Repetition does not undermine the cartoonist's effort; rather, what counts is his or her choice of a convenient sign or a quotation, and a meaningful transposition of its original meaning. Westergaard does not score high, however, as a master of semiosis. Probably the closest reference to 'his' Muhammad is an image of Osama Bin Laden by the British cartoonist Scott Clissold, using the same concept of the turban with a burning fuse, and the same manic gaze. Clissold's cartoon, published in the *Sunday Express* on 23 August 1998, was a comment on Clinton's cruise missile attack on Osama bin Laden in response to the al-Qaeda bombing of two American embassies in East Africa. However, it matters less whether Westergaard was influenced by this particular image or another; what is more significant is the articulation of a general visual regime, set as a 'standard' frame for the representation of a Muslim body, whether that body belongs to a mass murderer or a religious leader or, by implication, as one might expect, to an ordinary citizen wearing a turban.

I have chosen to focus here on Westergaard's cartoon, but at least seven other of the twelve images published by *Jyllands-Posten* also draw clearly on orientalist clichés. To satisfy the expectations of the non-Muslim majority in Denmark against the Muslim minority, these images reproduce established regimes of truth about violence, promiscuity, patriarchalism, evil and backwardness as the defining features of Islam. The remaining five cartoons refer directly to the circumstances of their own commissioning, and are preoccupied largely with the dissemination of an image of a professional, urban and benign (white) Danish self, in marked contrast to its antithetical Muslim other. A total exception, however, is an image by Lars Refn, who, instead of featuring the Prophet, shows

---

8   Interestingly, and this detail has escaped attention in the unending debates on the cartoon, the bomb portrayed has little to do with the ammunition used by terrorists, and its generic form resembles rather an old cannonball, betraying in this way the essentially European framework of the cartoonist's references.

a seventh-grade Muslim boy named Mohammed, a pupil at the Valby school in an immigrant district of Copenhagen, with the term 'Future' emblazoned on his local football shirt. Not only is this the only cartoon which recognizes the existence of the Muslim community in Denmark, but the Arabic text written by the boy on the school blackboard, 'The *Jyllands-Posten* journalists are a bunch of reactionary provocateurs', may also serve as a surprising assessment of the commission as well as a diagnosis of the reaction it was likely to provoke.

Although its message is partly lost on a non-Arabic-speaking reader, who would be unable to understand the caption written on the blackboard, and is further compromised by the dominant context of the frame into which it is put, Refn's image deserves to be much better known. It is the one cartoon in the group which stands out from the rest, and which clearly manifests its links with the Daumier tradition of the interventionist caricature: concerned with social inequality, siding with the oppressed, representing and, literally, voicing their concerns.[9] Even if the remaining eleven cartoons commissioned by *Jyllands-Posten* merely serve to corroborate the conservative leaning inherent in the medium, Refn's cartoon single-handedly breaks with the unanimity of the other voices, reminding sceptics that cartoons are still capable of becoming agents of change. This confirms the ambiguous nature of the medium, suspended between ritual and subversion, and operating within both of these discursive practices. It also confirms the role of the reader, who, in interpreting both ritual and subversion, may well prove capable of turning the one into the other.

Cartoon war and the World Wide Web

So far, I have been examining the representational strategies specific to cartoons and assessing their ideological impact; I have paid far less attention, however, to the *physical* properties of the medium, and have assumed that its natural environment is the printed page. In this section of the chapter, I would like to focus on the ways in which the impact of the Danish cartoons and the character of the whole controversy have been utterly transformed by their dissemination on the World Wide Web.[10] According to the pioneer of media studies, Marshall McLuhan, cartoons belong to the category of the 'cool media', which are characterized by their 'low definition' and as such engender a 'hot' response from the viewer, who engages with them more intensively than with highly defined 'hot media', such as oil painting or film. When McLuhan formulated this opinion in 1964, he could not have predicted the extent to which the arrival of the World Wide Web would alter the reception of cartoons, at once intensifying their stigmatizing capacities and incendiary properties, but also heightening their liberating potential for the viewer.

---

9   Unfortunately, this has not been recognized by Islamic protesters.
10   I am grateful to Graham Huggan for suggestions pointing me in this direction.

Although there can be no argument that the 'cartoon war' did not happen, the crisis displayed all the features of a distinctly Baudrillardian media event (Baudrillard 1995). Like the Gulf War of 1990–91, the 'cartoon war' of 2006 was a media spectacle *par excellence*, primarily accessible on newspaper pages, television and computer screens, and generated, censored and disseminated within the disembodied and digitized realm of discursive representation. Even if it was labelled a 'war', it was far removed from the traditional realm of warfare, involving neither armies nor direct disputes about territory and resources. Unlike the Gulf War, the 'cartoon war' was fought entirely by civilians and was almost exclusively *about* the media and their representational codes. And indeed, both for the west and for Islam, the 'Muhammad cartoons controversy' was neither a war nor a 'clash' between secularism and spiritualism, but rather a particularly intense and disastrous episode in the long-running battle for signification itself. Safe and relatively easy to play as long as it was enclosed within the media circuit, it acquired apocalyptic dimensions when it 'turned real', and when the represented object, which, for centuries, had been locked into derogatory stereotypes, rose bodily against its own imprisoning visual regime.

The World Wide Web, with its instant access to information and imagery and its high potential for interaction, raised the mediaticity of the 'cartoon war' to an unprecedented level. The manifest virtuality of the 'war' was epitomized by the fact that it could now be shaped not only by the institutionalized media, with their diverse but largely predictable political agendas,[11] but also by any number of individual bloggers, producing and disseminating their own chronology, their own geography and their own heavily biased chronicles of events. As a result, a whole range of private versions of the 'war' began to appear in blogs, composed of news, reports and images downloaded from the Net, and often including a generous supply of entirely new cartoons.[12] Accessible to all-comers, these subjective narratives of the 'war' bore an uncanny resemblance to interactive games, free and open, with ready-made sets of black-and-white characters. The most comprehensive version, which was visited by millions of users, was offered by Wikipedia, as its constantly updated and revised digital entry '*Jyllands-Posten* Muhammad Cartoons Controversy'. Edited by individual users, each controlling and correcting the others' errors, it reproduced the cartoons at the very early stages of the controversy and kept expanding as the ideological temperature rose. Aspiring to rise above individual biases and to include arguments from all possible sides, Wikipedia not only became the primary source of contradictory knowledge about the affair and its shifting evaluations, but, vandalized many times and even frozen at particularly difficult moments, it also turned into a fractured site of violent tensions and forceful confrontations, becoming another battlefield in the Great (Cartoon) Game.

---

11   See for example the *Guardian*'s online 'Muhammad Cartoons Row 2006' (www.guardian. co.uk/world/muhammad-cartoons) or the BBC's 'Muslim Cartoon Row Timeline' (http://news. bbc.co.uk/1/hi/world/middle_east/4688602.stm).
12   See for example the Michelle Malkin site, http://michellemalkin.com.

As in the Gulf War, there was a profound inequality between western and Muslim stakes and strategies. Muslims entered the battle with their own bodies (or at least this is how it tended to be reported in the western media), flooding the streets and brandishing placards with florid slogans against Europe, desecrating Danish flags and setting fire to embassies. The 'west', by contrast, opted for remote control, mass reproduction and virtuality, pushing the 'cool' cartoons into the limelight and elevating them to the status of signifiers (if not fetishes) of freedom and enlightened secularism, golden nuggets of western democracy itself. Cartoonists, quick to capitalize on this newly acquired aura of respectability, flooded the Web with huge numbers of new cartoons about the 'war', vying with each other in the production of witty visual comments on the freedom of press and the constitutive heroism of their profession, as well as intensifying their production of visual metaphors about Islamic violence, Islamic terrorism, Islamic backwardness and Islamic anti-Semitism. The old cliché identifying cartoons with weapons, which had been exploited in earlier revolutionary propaganda, now took on a new lease of life, bringing with it a whole range of visual metaphors that either warned against taking 'dangerous' cartoons onto the plane, seeing them as alternative 'weapons of mass destruction', or conversely presented them as an 'innocent' form of western retaliation for the atrocities of 9/11.[13]

Even if, in the eyes of the (western) world, Muslim responses to the cartoon challenge were often reduced to tribal rituals and irrational violence, a significant number of cartoons commenting on the 'war' appeared in the Muslim media as well, and circulated freely on the Web. The editorial cartoon, after all, is not foreign to the Middle East either, and its stigmatizing potential has been widely deployed by Muslims for their own occidentalist vendetta against the Jews and the 'corrupt west', no less venomous and shocking than that produced by Islamophobia. The most conspicuous example of this vendetta was the so-called 'international Holocaust cartoons contest', announced by the Iranian newspaper *Hamshahri* and devised as an outright challenge to the limits of western tolerance of freedom of speech.[14] The contest confirmed the astonishing belief in the agency of cartoons expressed by the Muslim media and authorities, as well as signalling their readiness to take over the western rules of the game. The winning entries, judged by the author of *Maus*, a graphic novel about the Holocaust, Art Spiegelman (2006, p. 52), to be sharp and graphically competent, have since been published on the Web.

Finally, a brief look at some the visual arguments presented by Muslim cartoonists commenting on the 'war' seems necessary to redress the imbalance caused by the attention given almost solely to the Danish works. Freedom of

---

13   For a large collection of non-Islamic cartoons on the Danish 'cartoon war', see the Website run by the American cartoonist Daryl Cagle, www.cagle.com/news/Muhammad/1.asp.

14   See Wikipedia, 'International Holocaust Cartoons Competition' (http://en.wikipedia.org/wiki/International_Holocaust_Cartoon_Competition) and 'The Results of Holocaust Cartoon Contest' at http://irancartoon.com/120/holocaust/index.htm.

expression was again the favourite topic, and was presented graphically as either hypocrisy or hate speech. One interesting visual commentary was that provided by Amjad Rasmi in the Palestinian-edited Arabic paper *Alquds*, which showed a large newspaper page, full of blank images, being used by a white man to cover western atrocities in the Middle East. This image conveys a pertinent message on the mechanism of representation, implying that the Danish cartoons, which equated Islam with terrorism, were acting as a projection of the terror inflicted by the west, and suggesting more generally that any image, or indeed any representation, is likely to tell us more about the representing subject than the object it represents.

The 'cartoon war' inspired a huge output of cartoons all over the world, in both non-Islamic and Islamic countries, with a whole plethora of aggressively racist images being produced on both sides. Unsurprisingly, it also amplified individual cartoonists' egos, awakening or consolidating their belief in their power over world affairs. At the same time, their realization of the agency of the image, its enormous potential for persuasion, could also be used to succour marginalized and/or disempowered communities, and to articulate their alternative values to the wider world. One way of doing this has been suggested by Homi Bhabha, who, in writing about the Shoah, has pointed to the liberating potential of self-critical jokes, identifying them as a 'mode of minority utterance', a strategic tool of cultural resistance available to minority communities and groups (Bhabha 1998). As Bhabha suggests, by incorporating the conditions of exclusion and difference into their jokes, minorities can work 'othering' mechanisms of representation into their own critical narratives of self-recognition. Indeed, this particular strategy has been deployed by Jewish people for a long time, and the recent Israeli contest for anti-Semitic cartoons, held in response to the previously mentioned one in *Hamshahri*, represents one of its most striking applications. Although this strategy might appear to be culturally specific, I would argue that cartoons, which are capable of manoeuvring between ritual and subversion and of serving both racism and freedom, offer new transcultural sites for resistance, dialogue and re-significations of all kinds.

Works cited

Ali, T. (2006) 'This Is the Real Outrage'. *Guardian*, 13 February. Available at www.guardian.co.uk/world/2006/feb/13/muhammadcartoons.comment (accessed February 2006).

Banta, M. (2003) *Barbaric Intercourse: Caricature and the Culture of Conduct, 1841–1936*. Chicago, IL, University of Chicago Press.

Baudrillard, J. (1995) *The Gulf War Did Not Take Place*. Bloomington, IN, Indiana University Press.

Bech Thomsen, P. (2006) *Muhammedkrisen*. Copenhagen, People's Press.

Bhabha, H. K. (1998) 'Joking Aside: The Idea of a Self-critical Community'. In: Cheyette, B. and Marcus, L. eds. *Modernity, Culture and the 'Jew'*. Cambridge, Polity Press, pp. xv–xx.

Bleich, E. (2006) 'On Democratic Integration and Free Speech: Response to Tariq Modood and Randall Hansen'. *International Migration*, 44(5), pp. 17–22.

Bronner, S. E. (2006) 'Incendiary Images: Blasphemous Cartoons, Cosmopolitan Responsibility, and Critical Engagement'. *Logos*, 5(1). Available at www.logosjournal.com (accessed 28 May 2006).

Curtis, L. P., Jr (1971) *Apes and Angels: The Irishman in Victorian Caricature*. London, Newton Abbot.

Dalgaard, S. and Dalgaard, K. (2006) 'The Right to Offend: The Causes and Consequences of the "Danish Cartoon Affair"'. *RUSI Journal*, 151(2), pp. 28–33.

Edwards, J. L. (1997) *Political Cartoons in the 1988 Presidential Campaign: Image, Metaphor, and Narrative*. New York, Garland.

Freud, S. (1991) *Jokes and Their Relations to the Unconscious*. Translated by J. Strachey. Harmondsworth, Penguin.

Ghazi, M. T. (2006) *The Cartoons Cry*. London, Author House.

Giddens, A. (2006) *Europe in the Global Age*. Oxford, Polity Press.

Gilroy, P. (2004) *Between Camps: Nations, Cultures and the Allure of Race*. London, Routledge.

Goldstein, R. J. (1989) *Censorship of Political Caricature in Nineteenth-Century France*. Kent, OH, Kent State University Press.

Gombrich, E. H. (1963) 'The Cartoonist's Armoury'. In: *Meditations on a Hobby Horse and Other Essays on the Theory of Art*. London, Phaidon, pp. 127–42.

—— (1999) 'Magic, Myth and Metaphor: Reflections on Pictorial Satire'. In: *The Uses of Images: Studies in the Social Function of Art and Visual Communication*. London, Phaidon.

Hansen, R. (2006a) 'The Danish Cartoons Controversy: A Defence of Liberal Freedom'. *International Migration*, 44(5), pp. 7–16.

—— (2006b) 'Free Speech, Liberalism and Integration: A Reply to Bleich and Carens'. *International Migration*, 44(5), pp. 42–51.

Henkel, H. (2006) 'The Danish Cartoon Controversy and the Self-image of Europe'. *Radical Philosophy*, 137, pp. 2–7.

Hooper, J., Harding, L. and Walsh, D. (2006) 'At Least Nine Killed in Libya as Cartoon Protests Escalate'. *Guardian*, 18 February. Available at www.guardian.co.uk/world/2006/feb/18/muhammadcartoons.libya (accessed 28 January 2009).

Huntington, R. (1996) *The Clash of Civilizations: And the Remaking of World Order*. New York, Simon and Schuster.

Jay, M. (1988) 'Scopic Regimes of Modernity'. In: Foster, H. ed. *Visions and Visuality*. Seattle, WA, Bay Press, pp. 3–28.

Kerr, D. S. (2000) *Caricature and French Political Culture 1830–1848: Charles Philipon and the Illustrated Press*. Oxford, Oxford University Press.

Low, D. (1956) *Low's Autobiography*. London, Michael Joseph.

McLuhan, M. (1964) *Understanding Media: The Extensions of Man*. London, Routledge.

—— (1967) *The Medium is the Message*. Harmondsworth, Penguin.

Medhurst, M. J. and DeSousa, M. A. (1981) 'Political Cartoons as Rhetorical Form: A Taxonomy of Graphic Discourse'. *Communication Monographs*, 48, September, pp. 197–235.

Modood, T. (2005) *Multicultural Politics: Racism, Ethnicity and Muslims in Britain*. Minneapolis, MN, University of Minnesota Press.

—— (2006a) 'The Liberal Dilemma: Integration or Vilification'. *International Migration*, 44(5), pp. 4–7.

—— (2006b) 'Obstacles to Multicultural Integration'. *International Migration*, 44(5), pp. 51–62.

Nederveen Pieterse, J. (1992) *White on Black: Images of Blacks in Western Popular Culture*. New Haven, CT, Yale University Press.

—— (2006) 'Multiculturalism Conflicts: The Danish Cartoons'. *JUST Commentary*, 6(5) (www.just-international.org).

Ramadan, T. (2006) 'The Danish Cartoons, Free Speech and Civic Responsibility'. *New Perspectives Quarterly*, 23(2), pp. 17–18.

Rose, F. (2005) 'Muhammeds ansigt'. *Jyllands-Posten, Kulturweekend,* 30 September, p. 3.

Sifaoui, M. (2006) *L'affaire des caricatures: dessins et manipulations*. Paris, Privé.

Soyinka, W. (2006) 'Psychopaths of Faith vs. The Muse of Irreverence'. *New Perspectives Quarterly*, 23(2), pp. 12–16.

Spiegelman, A. (2006) 'Drawing Blood. Outrageous Cartoons and the Art of Outrage'. *Harper's Magazine*, June, pp. 43–52.

Wonham, H. B. (2004) *Playing the Races: Ethnic Caricature and American Literary Realism*. Oxford, Oxford University Press.

Part IV
Towards the future?

CHAPTER 11

Violence in France: crisis or towards post-republicanism?

Michel Wieviorka

To the observer, particularly the foreign one, the image of France is that of a country in a time warp, incapable of reforming, resolutely turned towards the past and a mythical golden age, as sometimes cited in the expression coined by economist Jean Fourastié, the *'Trente Glorieuses'* (the thirty golden years), the years 1945 to 1975. For other observers, especially those in France itself, the country has entered a period of historical decline or even decadence, an age of crisis that is periodically subject to spasms of violence. One illustration of this were the urban riots in the autumn of 2005, in which action was taken against the CPE, the *Contrat Première Embauche* (First Employment Contract), a law voted through without parliamentary debate in March 2006. (The CPE was a new work contract for those aged under twenty-six years with a two-year trial period, during which employers could terminate the contract without having to offer an explanation.)

In order to understand what is at stake here, we must start with two main features: on the one hand, the huge transformation of social relations in France and the passing from an industrial to a post-industrial society; and on the other, the general crisis of all French institutions today. After the Second World War, France entered into a thirty-year period when industry was the very core of society. This industrial society offered full employment to its members, including numerous migrants, more and more of whom in the 1950s and 1960s came from North Africa: the Maghreb. During this period, which at the beginning was considered to be one of 'reconstruction', housing was a very important issue and social housing a distinct challenge. In industrial areas, large-scale programmes launched by the public sector, sometimes also by private investors, were supposed to bring a solution, albeit an imperfect one, to the huge demand for housing. From the 1950s to the mid-1970s, there were still jobs for almost everyone, mostly unskilled jobs, and adequate housing was provided for millions of families who had previously lived in slums and other awful conditions. This was not a golden age, of course, and life was difficult for the workers. The main social issue was social exploitation, including low salaries, but at least everyone was participating in society at large.

Then, in the mid-1970s, several important changes happened. The masters of industry introduced new forms of organization, in which unskilled work was deemed unnecessary and unemployment became a structural reality, but many migrants decided nevertheless to stay in the country and to bring the rest of their families from abroad. Social housing – the 'HLM' (*Habitations à Loyers Modérés*) – which had previously been a real bonus, became in many neighbourhoods a source of serious problems: violence, delinquency, lack of security, racism. The main social issue in the post-industrial era appeared to be exclusion, with high rates of unemployment for some categories of the population (for instance, young people of migrant origin), and this phenomenon could be seen, first and foremost, in the populous suburbs, the *'banlieues'*. In such a situation, trade unions appeared less and less able to represent the main victims of these changes, who were no longer workers, but rather people being excluded from the workplace as a whole.

At the same time, and at least partly due to this development, the whole French system of institutions began to face new and huge difficulties of its own. The French version of the welfare state entered into a fiscal crisis. The school system now had to deal with many more pupils than it had done in the past, and its new mixture of democratization and massification led to problems such as violence within schools, or strong feelings of downward mobility and loss of status for teachers. The *police nationale* lost the quasi-monopoly that had formerly made it a key actor in the Republican model, due to the rapid increase of *polices municipales* and, even more significantly, to the development of the private sector (for security in France, as in many other countries, is now a real business). Some public services – a solid tradition in France – were privatized, at least partially, while military conscription, also an important element in the French Republican model, was suppressed. Meanwhile, the Catholic Church became weaker and weaker, and Islam became the second religion in the country.

Looking at these elements, it is tempting to speak in 'pure' terms of crisis. However, I would like to suggest a more cautious, or at least a more discerning, approach. My argument here will consist of an examination of those aspects in the recent development of France that might be attributed to crisis, and those that might alternatively lead us to consider that France is entering a new era in which new ways of living together are gradually taking shape. To put it even more succinctly, the breakdown in the French style of integration that is currently to be found in all spheres of community, social, institutional, political, cultural and intellectual life should not prevent us from noting the existence of change.

The violence of autumn 2005

Let me begin by briefly recalling the facts. When the death in Clichy-sous-Bois was officially announced of two youths 'of immigrant origin' who, believing themselves to be pursued by the police, took fatal refuge in an electricity transformer, other youths in this same small town, then in other Parisian *banlieues*, and finally throughout France, inaugurated a cycle of violence which was to last for three weeks. Every night, hundreds of private cars and, at times, public amenities (state schools, nurseries and buses) were torched. The phenomenon was not new: since the end of the 1970s, France has been shaken by violence of this type (Wieviorka 1999), but it had never attained this degree of intensity, lasted as long, or extended to the whole country. Two kinds of explanation were put forward for the violence: the first, by commentators who had very little actual knowledge of the terrain and who interpreted it as the expression of 'ethnic-religious' problems, as an 'anti-republican pogrom' (e.g. Alain Finkielkraut), or even as the outcome of polygamy (e.g. Carrère d'Encausse); and the second, by social science researchers who knew the 'working-class' *banlieues* well, and who agreed fairly unanimously that the violence was down to a crisis or failure of integration of young people who were expressing their rage at being excluded, who were victims of racism and all manner of discrimination, and who were being rejected by the very society that had ordered them to integrate into its midst. On several occasions, I have suggested an inclusive explanation which, on one hand, sets out three time periods and, on the other, takes into account the various facets of the crisis. Let me briefly rehearse this argument here, beginning with the latter.

1 The crisis is *total*. In the first instance, it is social because these young arsonists live in areas which are well on the way to becoming ghettos, do not have access to jobs, are systematically harassed by the police and, in Robert Castel's words, are prime victims of processes of 'disaffiliation' (Castel 2000).
2 The crisis is *institutional*, because the institutions which are supposed to transform the promises of the Republic – liberty, equality, fraternity – into actuality are not working. This begins with state schools, which clearly do more than just *reproduce* the inequalities in society (the previous accusation of the 1970s sociologists Baudelot and Establet). Rather, the education system *reinforces* social inequality, as Georges Felouzis's 2005 survey of school apartheid convincingly shows (Felouzis 2005). This explains why there is nothing surprising about the fact that the young arsonists have sometimes attacked the very state schools that have contributed to their exclusion.
3 Furthermore, the crisis is *cultural*, especially because the nation, which in French political culture is the only collective identity that theoretically has the right to exist in the public sphere, is increasingly being challenged by all sorts of specific identities that demand recognition in this public arena: a recognition, and I shall return to this, which clashes with the classical conceptions of the Republic *per se*.
4 The crisis is also *political*, and at two levels. At the *national* level, the political system is finding it increasingly difficult to be representative, as witnessed for example in the figures for abstention from voting over the last thirty years or so, or in the vote for parties of the extreme right or the extreme left. One of the reasons for this crisis resides in the abiding incapacity of the

traditional parties to include people of immigrant origin, in particular from North Africa or sub-Saharan Africa, among their leaders or elected representatives. At the *local* level, we need to understand how working-class areas have evolved since the 1970s. In the past, at grass-roots level, two types of political actors were the driving force. One of these was the Communist Party, which ensured that social demands were taken up at a political level, particularly in the so-called *banlieues rouges* ('red suburbs'), which, today, the Party has either deserted or definitively lost. The other was a network of associations functioning largely 'from below', but often under the leadership of militants of middle-class origin. These former leaders no longer live in working-class areas, the associations have gone under and, with them, their crucial role as political operators of social demands has disappeared. And what do we find in their place? Frequently a vacuum, sometimes initiatives from the town hall or perhaps an imam who, initially offering school assistance at the local mosque, builds up a new association or network that at least helps to keep the area alive. But the social workers paid by such associations tend to come from elsewhere, to be paid by public institutions and, in many cases, to be responsible to them; less frequently, they might be paid by humanitarian non-governmental organizations. As such, they personify an approach from the outside, not a 'bottom up' approach.

5 Finally, the crisis is *intellectual*, in particular due to the involvement of a sizeable section of the intelligentsia in what I have called, perhaps slightly polemically, 'republicanism', a contemporary perversion of the original which consists of appealing to a republican ideal that is increasingly artificial, and that calls on immigrants to adopt the values of the Republic without realizing that the concrete means towards this integration are effectively being refused. 'Republicanism' is an ideology the invocation of which can only discourage all those who see that their individual fates can never conform to its generalizing discourse. I shall come back to this below.

If we want to analyse the process that has resulted in this situation historically, we need, as I have said, to distinguish between three time periods. The first, also the longest, takes us from the mid-1970s to the present day. This is the most important: it is the period during which, in each of the dimensions I have listed above, the crisis took shape and was set up and generalized, gaining momentum in the last few years. (At the outset, there were hardly any ghettos: these developed from the end of the 1990s. Didier Lapeyronnie (2008) has written a book that demonstrates this in spectacular fashion.) The second period is short term and highly political. The government elected in 2002 not only failed to pursue the efforts of the previous governments, particularly in the domain of urban policy (inadequate, it is true, but perhaps avoiding the worst), but it in fact undid what little existed, cutting the neighbourhood police force that the left-wing government had previously set up, putting an end to *emplois-jeunes* or 'youth jobs', and reducing grants to the social work associations I referred to above. This social 'unravelling' was to exacerbate the crisis. Finally, the third time period is the present economic climate, which has had a considerable impact. The death of the two youths in Clichy-sous-Bois was certainly experienced as hugely unjust, and it is well known that riots are often triggered by realities, or rumours, of this type of injustice (recall the riots in Los Angeles in 1992, when it was learnt that the police officers who had savagely beaten a black van driver, Rodney King, filmed by an amateur, had been acquitted by the courts). At the same time, the behaviour of the then Minister of the Interior (and now President of the Republic), Nicolas Sarkozy, actively contributed to setting the *banlieues* on fire, be it through his conspicuous mismanagement of the actual events[1] or through the provocative vocabulary he used to during the period immediately leading up to them, in which such phrases as *nettoyage au Kärcher* (cleaning up with a Kärcher, a pressure-washer deployed for heavy cleaning jobs), used in relation to the working-class estates, or *racaille* (riff-raff), used to describe a certain category of youth, could hardly be perceived as anything other than deeply offensive in the working-class areas and, particularly, by the young people who lived there.

The post-republican model

Three months later, the full glare of the media was to be trained on an event that was more limited but much more tragic (for the riots, though dramatic, did not involve any fatalities): the kidnapping then, three weeks later, the revolting assassination of Ilan Halimi, a young Jewish man. The facts are as follows. A gang of *barbares* ('barbarians') – to use the actual term of some of its members – kidnapped Halimi for loathsome reasons, being convinced that 'Jews have money' and that the ransom they were demanding would be quickly paid. Nothing of the sort happened and, after having been held prisoner for a long time and tortured, Halimi was eventually left, at the edge of a forest, to die. What concerns me here, over and above the barbarity of the crime, is the way in which general indignation took shape and was publicly expressed. To begin with, the highest powers in the state went to a synagogue – a gesture which was, in the main, well received but still open to criticism, including from myself: for would it not have been better, in a country which is so concerned with secularism and in which not all Jews necessarily practise their religion, if the public gesture of the political leaders had been made in a building other than a religious one? Then, the following Sunday, an impressive demonstration was held in Paris, organized by the Jewish institutions, led by the CRIF (Conseil Représentatif des Institutions juives de France; Representative Council of French Jewish Institutions), and also attended by participants who had come to demonstrate their republican and democratic rejection of anti-Semitism.

---

1   The lawyers of the families of the two victims from Clichy-sous-Bois have published an edifying book (Mignard and Tordjman 2006).

This demonstration had two major implications. The first was that the Jewish community presented itself as both visible and active in the public sphere, in conflict with the classical republican model in which Jews are visible only in the private sector. The second was that the Jewish community presented itself as being anxious to be understood and supported by the Republic, with high expectations of its institutions and their representatives. This mobilization can therefore be taken as evidence of minorities' capacity to begin to outline a new model, which I would call post-republican, in which their aim is *both* to constitute themselves as a minority in the public sphere *and* to continue to adhere to the Republic.

This is by no means the first instance in which this type of observation has been made: we can go back to the mid-1960s to find the foundations of this movement, which has gained particular momentum in the last few years. Moreover, the Jews are not the only people to have advanced a post-republican formula. Islam, for example – especially in France – has taken some steps in this direction. Thus, when two French journalists were kidnapped in Iraq by a group whose primary demand was that France repeal the March 2004 law on the 'ostensible signs of religion' in schools, a delegation of Muslim dignitaries was dispatched. These dignitaries explained that, in the name of Islam, they were requesting the kidnappers to release the hostages, adding that they were also there as French citizens who respected the laws of the Republic and considered that the law in question should be observed: a good example of French Islam's public support for the Republic. Similarly, during the riots of autumn 2005, neither Islamism nor Islam were used as reference points for the young arsonists; on the contrary, on several occasions Muslim leaders turned to young people in the working-class areas and requested them to stay at home and not take part in the violence. Here again, Islam acted very openly in the public sphere in support of the republican order that was being treated with such obvious disrespect. It therefore seems legitimate to say that a way out of the classical republican model is currently taking shape and that we are moving towards a post-republican formula, open to religious identity in the public sphere.

The national narrative

In France, there is little distinction between the nation and the Republic, at least in the case of the classical French-style model of integration. In principle, the Republic does not tolerate any specific expression of identity in the public sphere, where only individuals free and equal in rights are recognized; but there is, nonetheless, a collective cultural identity, the nation. Intellectually, the move from the universal – the rule of law, republican reason applicable to each individual – to the nation, an identity which is by definition specific, is extremely simple; all that is required is to declare that the French nation is universal. Thus, all French people are supposed, at one and the same time, to be citizens and nationals, individuals who are free and equal in law and 'French'.

From this point of view, the nation is a collective entity to which each individual belongs and which has a narrative that is specific to it: the national, historical narrative. Traditionally, to assert its unity, the nation is required to appear in the best possible light. This, for example, is what led Ernest Renan to state, in his celebrated lecture 'What Is a Nation?' (1882), that the nation must forget its crimes, the barbarism which had accompanied its foundation; since everyone must be able to identify with the nation, it must not be portrayed as the outcome of the violent domination of one group by another. But here again, the classical model is showing signs of crumbling. The first cracks were to appear at the end of the 1960s. On one hand, the regionalist movements – in particular, the Breton and Occitan movements – began to challenge the French nation state, accusing it of being responsible for their cultural decline and of being politically too centralized. On the other, Jews in France, spurred on in part by foreign historians like Marrus and Paxton, but mostly by their own individual and collective memories, pressed increasingly for the recognition of the responsibility of the Vichy regime in the eradication of French Jews during the Second World War. Turning to the state, they demanded that the national narrative be revised, a feat that was eventually to be accomplished in a speech made by President Jacques Chirac in July 1995, just after he had been elected for the first time.

Thereafter, other groups pressed for their respective pasts to be recognized, with two major implications. First, they were concerned with obtaining state recognition of the existence of a particular historical event, such as genocide or a mass crime, and its inclusion in history. Thus, for example, Armenian communities in France were to obtain official recognition by parliament of the Turkish genocide in 1915. But there was also the question of mobilizing collective memory in the name of a past that had to some extent been corrupted, and of being acknowledged in the public sphere without necessarily attempting to impact on history itself. Similarly, over the past few years, initiatives have developed around the slave trade, slavery and colonization that offer evidence either of a specific concern to impact on history or of a mobilization of collective memories for political ends. This debate continues to gain momentum, driven by the descendants of the groups concerned, but also by political and intellectual militants. We have evidence of this in such interventions by 'natives of the Republic' as the publication of a collective book about *la fracture coloniale* ('the colonial fracture'), which was a huge success. Another example is the founding of the CRAN (Conseil Représentatif des Associations Noires de France; Representative Council of Black Associations in France), a federation of about a hundred associations joined in a campaign against racism and for reparative justice to victims of the slave trade and slavery. Similarly, when the then leaders of the country, in an abortive attempt to put an end to the riots in autumn 2005, resorted to a 1955 law enabling them to set up a curfew by decree, many people voiced their indignation at the use of a text originally voted in during the time of the wars of decolonization, when the Vietnam War was ending and the Algerian war had just begun. The measure, aimed at areas populated in the main by people of immigrant origin from the former colonies, smacked of colonialism.

Discussions about these issues are now extremely heated in France, forcing history to open up to realities that have often been underestimated and transforming the national narrative. This not only means that the narrative is changing but that its very conception is moving away from the classical model and the 'Renan-style' ideal, towards proposing an image of the nation which is more precise but also more troubled and violent – and distinctly less glorious. As a result, history teachers have become the bearers of a subject that has lost the legitimacy it once had, when it represented the national narrative and was one of the core subjects. For their part, professional historians, whose role is to produce knowledge, are now caught in a situation in which they may be publicly challenged. They have had to take a stand vis-à-vis the government, which, for example, votes in laws depriving them of their theoretical monopoly over the historical truth. They have had to sign petitions or to mobilize to defend fellow historians, like Olivier Pétré-Grenouilleau, the author of a remarkable global history of the slave trades, which involved him in a series of virulent attacks, including in the courts (Pétré-Grenouilleau 2005). Memory impacts on history and a power struggle ensues; we saw this when, some months after its promulgation, a February 2004 law was suddenly attacked by historians, who quite rightly denounced one of its articles stipulating that school curricula should present pupils with the positive role of colonization. (In another sign of the present cultural fragmentation, a member of parliament had introduced this article to satisfy a specific group, the *pieds noirs*, who consider themselves on the whole to be poorly treated in France.)

This same fragmentation provides the source of an intense competition between victims that can become racist in tone. One of the outstanding examples here is the comedy actor Dieudonné, who, on several occasions, has rounded on Jews, whom he accuses of having played a decisive role in the slave trade – which is demonstrably false. He has also accused the Jews of attempting to monopolize historical suffering, via the Shoah, to prevent discussion of other tragedies, like the slave trade and slavery – which is equally false. On the contrary, numerous Jewish historians have played, and continue to play, an important role in opening discussions about these questions. Here, memory is not being mobilized to have an impact on history but rather to put forward questionable or disturbing ideas that have found an echo among their specific target groups.

Intellectuals in the storm

Contemporary French historians, as we have just seen, are often ill at ease with changes that have forced them to distance themselves from those concepts that make of their subject if not a hagiographic element in the national narrative then at least a core subject from the point of view of national integration. They are not the only intellectuals to be faced with this transformation, which also involves the emergence of new figures, in particular of immigrant origin, who claim to be followers of Islam. Of course, some intellectuals have no desire to undertake, or are simply incapable of undertaking, major revisions and are extremely reluctant to confront these transformations. This has especially been the case for those who represent the republican idea in its most classical formulations, or the national narrative in its most traditional versions. In this respect, Alain Finkielkraut is a particularly interesting case, though perhaps an extreme rather than a characteristic example.

Finkielkraut is a philosopher very much to the fore in public discussions. At the time of the violence in late 2005, he gave an interview to the Israeli daily *Haaretz*, in which he made remarks that were racist in connotation. He said that the behaviour of the young arsonists was of an 'ethnico-religious' type – whereas, apart from the colour of their skin, there was nothing to indicate the slightest religious dimension or demand in ethnic terms. He then went on to suggest that they were indulging in an 'anti-republican pogrom', as if their violence had an anti-Semitic dimension, and as if it was murderous in the same manner as the past pogroms in central Europe or Russia – whereas they never acted in a bloodthirsty way. Finally, he referred to the national football team as being, to his regret, 'black-black-black'. These verbal blunders on the part of a recognized and influential intellectual gave rise to a vast discussion. This is how I read it.[2]

Finkielkraut is one of those intellectuals who, since the end of the 1980s, have been most actively involved in the 'pro-republic' campaigns. He has frequently pleaded in favour of the republican ideal in terms that appear in the last resort to be elitist, for example in relation to state schools, but also in support of a public sphere where only free and equal individuals should be recognized. For several years now, Finkielkraut's discourse has appeared to his critics to be increasingly artificial and contrary to reality: how, for example, can individuals be invited to integrate by following the republican model if republican institutions are not fulfilling their role correctly and are going against this ideal? The riots in the autumn of 2005 brought to light the profoundly ideological nature of a discourse that no longer had any connection with reality. This is the first explanation for Finkilekraut's verbal blunders. But we have to add another.

Finkielkraut is clearly committed to the defence of the classical republican model – a commitment that shines through in his weekly broadcast on the France Culture national radio station. But he is also an important person in the Jewish community: with airtime on a Jewish radio station and a column in the community publication *L'Arche*, he is an influential Jewish intellectual, known and recognized as such. Now, as I have suggested, this community is breaking with the classical, republican model and is currently involved in a post-republican approach. From this point on, Finkielkraut represents a myth, the imaginary reconciliation of two contradictory demands, one republican and the other post-republican. When this myth meets with reality, the outcome is uncontrolled forms of behaviour – like the blunders that interest us here.

---

2 For further details, I refer the reader to the article I published in *L'Arche* (Wieviorka 2006) in reply to Alain Finkielkraut, who, in the previous issue, had attacked Pierre Vidal-Naquet and myself.

In intellectual life we can find many similar expressions of innovation, but also tension, verbal violence and difficulty, in discussing issues on the part of an intelligentsia that has been made subject to concrete changes, but also to ideas for which they have not always been well prepared. (This tends especially to be the case when newcomers arrive on the scene, such as Tariq Ramadan, who, in 2003, published a widely cited article with anti-Semitic overtones criticizing Jewish intellectuals who, according to him, had moved from universalism to communitarianism.) The main point here is to understand that intellectual life is also affected by this general transformation and that intellectuals hesitate between or are divided between those who remain attached, whatever happens, to the old model and those who are seeking a way to project themselves into the future.

Return to the social dimension

In March 2006, widespread mobilization, which had started in a few universities the month before, demanded the abandonment and then, when the bill became law at the beginning of April, the abrogation of the CPE, which the Prime Minister defended. Students and high-school pupils occupied an increasing number of universities and schools and rapidly received the support of the trade unions, whose members were also unanimous in demanding the withdrawal of the CPE. As stated above, the CPE included two main provisions: it enabled employers to take on people aged under twenty-six years with a two-year trial period, during which they could terminate the contract without having to offer any explanation. If this important event in social history demands our consideration here, it is because it also confronts us with a further change in the 'French model' of integration.

For the government of the day, the CPE was part of a neo-liberal approach clearly aimed at introducing flexibility to the employment market to the sole advantage of employers. It therefore constituted an endeavour, if a somewhat limited one, to undermine social relations by eliminating important forms of social protection, and can rightly be conceived as having put a number of young wage earners at risk. It aimed at accelerating the decline of the classical model of integration, this time in its social dimensions. However, it offered nothing constructive, nothing suggesting a new model apart from a belief in the virtues of the market and the capacity of growth to restore employment. The trade unions, for their part, were concerned with rescuing what could still be saved of the old model and the protection it afforded, in this instance in matters of labour law. The support of the trade unions for the youth movement is understandable if one takes into consideration the state of trade unionism in France today: outside the public or similar sectors and a few large-scale firms in which employment is still protected, trade unionism is weak. However, in this instance, trade union mobilization was not self-seeking, corporatist or neo-corporatist; it could only be defensive, the expression of a fundamental refusal with little capacity to articulate counter-projects or a realistic vision of the future.

Finally, the mobilization of the young anti-CPE protesters was in no way related to the riots in the autumn; rather, high-school pupils and students were demanding reassurance in the face of a future that appeared to be offering them only uncertainty. In the general assemblies of their movement, these protesters frequently endeavoured to project themselves into the future, to think about the future of the education system or public policies concerning research as a whole. But all of this was stifled, so to speak, by what appeared to be the only realistic aim of the movement: obtaining the withdrawal of the CPE. The young people in question were demonstrating their desire for a future that distanced them both from the classical model and from the government's neo-liberal projects. But they were incapable of expressing anything other than the slogan that seemed to solve everything: 'No to the CPE'. The result is that we are confronted with a situation that remains socially blocked.

In the final reckoning, the contemporary image of France is one of a highly complex situation. The country is paralysed by blockages, of which the most obvious are social and political in nature, epitomized by an inability to undertake reform. But in cultural matters it is also modernizing, with the beginnings of a model I call post-republican, a model that affords a possible way out of the institutional blockage in which, ever since the 1970s, it has lived. So France, it seems, is falling apart on the intellectual plane, while, at the same time, inventing new and arresting themes for discussion and new paradigms for itself.

Works cited

Castel, R. (2000) 'The Routes to Disaffiliation: Insecure Work and Vulnerable Relations'. *International Journal of Urban and Religious Research*, 24(3), pp. 519–35.

Felouzis, G. (2005) *L'apartheid scolaire*. Paris, Seuil.

Finkielkraut, A. (2005) 'Interview with Alain Finkielkraut'. *Haaretz*, November.

Lapeyronnie, D. (2008) *Ghetto urbain*. Paris, Robert Laffont.

Mignard, J. and Tordjman, E. (2006) *L'affaire Clichy: morts pour rien*. Paris, Stock.

Pétré-Grenouilleau, O. (2005) *Les traites négrières: essai d'histoire globale*. Paris, Gallimard.

Ramadan, T. (2003) 'Les (nouveaux) intellectuels communautaires'. Oumma.com. Available at http://oumma.com/article.php3?id_article=719 (accessed 28 January 2009).

Renan, E. (1996) '"What Is a Nation": Lecture at the Sorbonne, 11 March 1882'. In: Eley, G. and Grigor Suny, R. eds. *Becoming National: A Reader*. Oxford, Oxford University Press, pp. 41–55.

Wieviorka, M. (1999) *Violence en France*. Paris, Seuil.

—— (2006) 'Reply to Alain Finkielkraut'. *L'Arche*, February.

CHAPTER 12

The politics of imperial nostalgia

Robert Spencer

> We must take stock of the nostalgia for empire, as well as the anger and resentment it provokes in those who were ruled, and we must try to look carefully and integrally at the culture that nurtured the sentiment, rationale, and above all the imagination of empire. (Said 1994, p. 12)

In Tanzania in January 2005, Britain's Chancellor and future Prime Minister turned his thoughts to the British Empire: 'I've talked to many people on my visit to Africa', Gordon Brown told the *Daily Mail* before adding, in a telling *non sequitur*, that 'the days of Britain having to apologize for its colonial history are over.... And we should talk, and rightly so, about British values that are enduring, because they stand for some of the greatest ideas in history – tolerance, liberty, civic duty – that grew in Britain and influenced the rest of the world'.[1] Leaving aside his curious assertion that Britons have been going round apologizing for their imperial crimes, I want to argue that Brown's nostalgia for Empire is best understood as part of the assertion of a new national, even national*ist* ideology that associates the British state's domestic and foreign policy with values and practices that are made to appear altruistic but are actually parochial, humanly destructive and very far from uncontested.

This ideology seeks, first, to justify Britain's belligerent and, as Mark Curtis has shown, both elite-driven and elite-serving system of priorities at the international level (Curtis 1998, 2003, 2004). Those priorities include, most obviously, the disastrous war in Iraq. They also encompass Britain's support for a neo-liberal model for the European Union, its role in imposing an extreme form of economic 'liberalization' (for which read corporate control) on underdeveloped countries, and its pusillanimous part in what Philippe Sands has called the United

---

1 'It's Time to Celebrate the Empire, Says Brown', *Daily Mail*, 15 January 2005.

States' 'war on law' (Sands 2005, p. xii). The association of the state with nebulously defined values like tolerance and liberty serves a second function. It is further employed to exonerate this invidious structure of diplomatic, economic and military aims of any blame for the deeply felt (even, as in the case of the bombings in London in July 2005, violent) discontent of religious and ethnic minorities and others, a discontent that is actually occasioned in part by Britain's actions abroad, particularly in relation to the Middle East (Ali 2005; Nairn 2006).

The name I have given to this ideology is imperial nostalgia, a concept originally developed, with somewhat different inflections, by Renato Rosaldo (1993), although I have taken the term from a recent article by Seamus Milne in *Le Monde Diplomatique* (Milne 2005). Imperial nostalgia, as I define it, is a form of nationalism. In *Imagined Communities*, his celebrated study of the origin and appeal of nationalism, Benedict Anderson claims that the imaginative construction of praiseworthy national histories or narratives serves to endow nations with the, for many, bewitching qualities of unity, continuity, even immortality. By inciting attachment to the idea of the nation, these narratives give rise among citizens to a sense of community and comradeship, notwithstanding inequality, exploitation and various other forms of internal division (Anderson 1983). Strictly speaking, therefore, and despite the fact that Anderson himself prefers the far less pejorative term 'imaginary', the idea of the nation is in fact *ideological*: whatever else it does, the idea of the nation fosters an atmosphere of unity that obfuscates relations of power.

I want to argue, however, that British nationalism is also ideological in another sense, one that is peculiar to the British state's continuing insistence on playing a particular kind of global role. That is, unity and conformity are engendered by camouflaging the, to say the least, invidious and divisive malefactions perpetrated by the British state abroad. What makes British nationalism objectionable is not just, as Stuart Hall (1997) has noted, that it responds in a narcissistic and exclusionary way to Britain's loss of formal colonies, deindustrialization, immigration, the traumatic readjustment to new regimes of accumulation, production and consumption, ecological interdependence, the fissiparousness of Britain itself (Nairn 2000, 2003), and the loss of power to multinational corporations (Monbiot 2001) and undemocratic supra-national entities like NATO, the EU and the IMF. This, of course, is dangerous enough. Such nationalism smoothes away class conflicts within Britain with the spurious notion of national interest; it acts as if power has not been ceded to unaccountable bodies and organizations beyond the reach of the nation's democratic sovereignty; and, perhaps most importantly, it fails to appreciate the considerable opportunities offered by immigration and international interdependence. But I want to add to this analysis by arguing that imperial nostalgia is an especially damaging and even insidious form of nationalist ideology because it camouflages the parochial priorities of the British state with cosmopolitan rhetoric. Imperial nostalgia is a form of nationalism masquerading as internationalism.

My aim here is to show that politicians' imperial longings and, in particular, the conservative historian Niall Ferguson's revisionist defence of British and contemporary American imperialism entail an unjustified (even counter-intuitive) faith in these states' ability and willingness to perform what they champion as philanthropic cosmopolitan tasks, such as overseeing economic development, toppling despots and upholding human rights. As my title makes clear, my focus is primarily on the *politics* of imperial nostalgia, and only second-arily on its negligible merits as an interpretation of history. The increasingly unabashed celebration of British imperialism in popular historical writing and political rhetoric has a series of identifiable political goals.

First of all, the effort to whitewash the brutality of British imperialism is misleading and harmful because it has the effect of making us complacent about the motivations and consequences of Britain's political system: constructions of a philanthropic past are obviously intended to cast a favourable light on the state's current commitments. Second, it leaves us slow to learn the lessons of the history of imperialism: that imperialism is hypocritical, exploitative, reliant on racist justifications and conducive to the commission of despicable deeds on an enormous scale. Third and not least in importance, the nostalgic distor-tion of the British Empire is designed to offer a ready-made alternative to the democratic, grass-roots forms of global governance being articulated by radical thinkers and movements. It is their unwarranted dismissal of these alterna-tives (a dismissal that is political in origin) that makes the likes of Brown and Ferguson nostalgic: unable to make out contemporary solutions to problems of deprivation and disaffection, they look back wistfully to an era in which such inconveniences could be tackled (or at least could appear to be tackled) by the unilateral projection of British and American power.

Imperial nostalgia needs to be resisted, therefore, because it works to deprive us of the capacity to criticize and develop alternatives to the selfish priorities of powerful states. Most prominent among these alternatives is the cosmopoli-tan perspective, by which I intend to designate a sort of grass-roots solidarity with mistreated peoples outside the confines of one's national community. Cosmopolitan allegiances can result, as Paul Gilroy has argued on many occa-sions (Gilroy 1991, 1993, 1994, 2000, 2002, 2004, 2005), from membership of or, alternatively, identification with a diasporic community. Frequently, this cosmopolitan disposition begins with the attachment of many Muslims in Britain to the *ummah* or community of believers. Engendering sensitivity to the often unseen effects of Britain's violent, elitist and in the main unaccountable foreign policy, such ties can lead to constructive dissent from the established powers' effectively racist disparagement of peoples who either do not share their com-placent estimation of the virtues of British and American power or are excluded from that power's benefactions.

As Ron Greaves has argued, the discourse of social justice that has informed, for instance, protests against the war in Iraq 'not only links Muslims in a global resistance to perceived injustices, bringing together disparate alliances of moderates and radicals, but also creates bridges to non-Muslim organisations concerned with similar issues of inequality, neo-colonialism, ecological concerns or other imbalances between the world's powerful and less powerful nations'

(Greaves 2005, p. 73). I will claim that attention to (rather than revision of) the ongoing history of imperialism can encourage us to adopt something of this dissenting viewpoint. Indeed, it is a notable irony that it is in Europe that the presence of diasporic communities as a result of the continent's imperial history is leading to the elaboration of such anti- and post-imperial perspectives. Those perspectives call for Europeans to continue to constitute and embed ever more far-reaching cosmopolitan allegiances and arrangements. Hence the eradication of imperial nostalgia falls to thinkers and movements with a global and postcolonial remit. They must emulate displaced communities and embattled minorities by encouraging what Bruce Robbins and Pheng Cheah have called 'thinking and feeling beyond the nation' (Robbins and Cheah 1998).

7/7

In a statement to parliament on 11 July 2005, Prime Minister Tony Blair presented the recently perpetrated bombings as unprovoked attacks on a united multicultural society: a cohesive nation would emerge 'from this horror with our values, our way of life, our tolerance and respect for others, undiminished'.[2] This recourse to the cliché of a Blitz-spirited nation united in support of the principled actions of its government elides the considerable and increasing opposition to government policy (particularly in relation to the Middle East), opposition which found the government wanting precisely in its warped or hypocritical commitment to ideas such as 'tolerance' and 'respect' for the citizens of other countries. Time after time in the wake of the bombings, a complacent image of Britain as a hospitable place with altruistic foreign policy objectives was conjured up in order to exonerate the state of all responsibility for the crimes. Commentators and politicians shifted responsibility for minorities' disaffection from racism to a widespread refusal to 'integrate'; from the invidious, unresponsive and unself-conscious practices of the state to the incorrigible separateness and wilful marginalization of minority groups.

In the *Daily Telegraph* on 3 August 2005, shadow Home Secretary David Davis, then campaigning for the leadership of the Conservative Party, endorsed the view of the chair of the Commission for Racial Equality, Trevor Phillips, that multiculturalism was 'outdated', while acclaiming Britain's 'proud history of tolerance and respect towards people of different views, faiths and backgrounds' (Davis 2005). A month later, the ubiquitous Phillips himself, tellingly deploying the first-person plural, told the Conservative Party conference that 'we can look at our own history to show that the British people are not by nature bigots. We created something called the empire where we mixed and mingled with people very different from those of these islands' (Phillips 2005b). Loosely defined

---

2 'Statement to Parliament on the London Bombings', 11 July 2005. Available at www.number10.gov.uk/Page7903 (accessed 28 January 2009).

virtues such as tolerance and fair-mindedness that might previously have been associated with a multicultural challenge to the status quo were being appropriated as unchanging attributes of the British state.

A year after the bombings, Blair compounded this simplistic opposition between Britain's mixing-and-mingling national polity and its antagonists when he told the House of Commons Liaison Committee that, in order for the state to defeat terrorism, it must persuade 'the Islamic community' (defined already by this appellation as a separate grouping) 'to address the completely false sense of grievance against the West', a point he had made several times in the weeks following the bombings (see Rai 2006, pp. 7–14). Blair thus sought to rally support for his failing agenda by appropriating the rhetoric of diversity and tolerance for the unpopular actions of the state and by associating principled criticism of British and American foreign policy with murder. To exonerate the state, the government went to great lengths to deny the connection between events in Iraq and London, rejecting calls for a public inquiry into the causes of the atrocities and opting instead for a cursory 'narrative' of events. Contradicting the contents of secret intelligence documents that had warned ministers of the likelihood that an invasion of Iraq would increase the risk of terrorist outrages (Rai 2006, pp. 15–20), the response of the government in the weeks following the July bombings was to deny any link between the perpetrators' grievances and events in the Middle East. Working groups were set up instead on mosques, foreign imams and 'community cohesion'. Plans to outlaw religious hatred sought to separate 'good' from 'bad' Muslims. At every turn, the complexity of the bombers' motivations was effaced and Blair's simplistic opposition reinforced.

But to say that the actions of the British state in relation to, most obviously, the Middle East are a crucial factor in promoting violent radicalization is not, as Blair has repeatedly alleged, to claim that the bombings were justified, but rather to engage with them, as John Tulloch, the sociology professor and survivor of the Edgware Road bomb, has insisted on doing: as a citizen (one opposed to the war in Iraq and to the government's crackdown on civil liberties) and not as a combatant in a conflict between good and evil (Tulloch 2006). The principal obstacle to 'community cohesion' or collective solidarity is not, as Blair and Phillips maintain, the obstinacy of minorities who are, in the latter's infelicitous phrase, 'sleepwalking into segregation' (Phillips 2005a). The real obstacle, as Tom Nairn has argued, is the vast wall that the state has erected between itself and its citizens: that separates many young Muslims from the rewards of free-market capitalism and thus increases the allure of political Islam; that obliges new arrivals to imbibe a fantasy version of Britishness before they are allowed to become 'subjects' and, in so doing, forestalls the articulation of a more meaningful definition of citizenship; that fosters disaffection by preventing all but a handful of uncommitted voters in marginal constituencies from influencing the priorities of the government; and that prevents concerned citizens from holding to account the state, a difficulty that is experienced in almost all aspects of British life in relation to the nation's dilapidated constitution and its unresponsive and 'modernity'-infatuated political culture (Nairn 2006) but that is manifested most significantly in relation to what Milan Rai has called, in his important study of the causes of the London bombings, the government's 'foreign policy fundamentalism' (Rai 2006, p. 134).

Blair's elaboration of a reductive dichotomy between a unanimous, blameless national community and a fifth column of traitors and malcontents perpetuates this situation. It traduces conscionable opposition to, for example, the war in Iraq and Israeli conduct in Lebanon and the occupied territories. It also works to prevent understanding of the bombings by portraying them either as baseless strikes against a guiltless national consensus or as products of some deep-rooted defect in the religion or culture of the bombers. What is more, Blair's conflation of dissent with subversion and treachery both provides a rationale for the restriction of basic civil liberties (Kennedy 2005) and, because it endeavours to suppress principled objections to unpopular policies, makes additional attacks more rather than less likely.

Almost as damagingly, in its invocation of a national community united against outsiders and renegades, Blair's dichotomy encourages nationalistic sentiments, emboldens parties of the far right, and provides an excuse for racism and Islamophobia. Finally, therefore, when he hails Britain's tolerance and respect, Blair reduces the multicultural idea to nothing more than a platitude. Whereas Britain's multiple cultures tend to view themselves both as citizens of the state and as affiliates of an international community (and therefore as proponents of differently situated critiques of national policies and institutions), Blair sees them as outsiders who must demonstrate their loyalty, or even as recreants who are obliged, for fear of accusations of treachery, to act in their communities as emissaries for British foreign policy (Kennedy 2005). Multiculturalism is thus hollowed out until it is reduced to little more than a signifier for multi-coloured conformity to the priorities of the British state.

What Ben Pitcher calls the 'multicultural nationalism' to which the Prime Minister gave voice after the bombings is, as Pitcher (2006) points out, an oxymoron. For, as Gilroy has shown, minority cultures tend, rightly, to think in international rather than national terms. They articulate their protests against the state in a global language of human rights that disassociates pieties like tolerance and respect from the national context and translates them into a cosmopolitan language of, among other things, hospitality towards new arrivals, protest against British foreign policy and solidarity with mistreated peoples in other states. This language communicates directly to minorities 'and their supporters all over the world asking for concrete help and solidarity in the creation of organisational forms adequate to the pursuit of emancipation, justice and citizenship, internationally as well as within national frameworks' (Gilroy 2002, p. 205).

History from above

It is, I suspect, for its wish to discredit these organizational forms, just as much as for its unwavering faith in the virtues of British and American power, that Niall Ferguson's work has received such widespread notice and approval. Ferguson sets out in his 2005 study *Colossus: The Rise and Fall of the American Empire* to rehabilitate the idea and practice of imperialism. *Colossus* breathes hardly a word of criticism of US institutions, economic doctrines and military clout. The only objection that could fairly be ventured (and Ferguson ventures it incessantly) is that the United States, unlike its predecessor (at least until what Ferguson sees as Britain's loss of nerve after the First World War), is too reluctant to use its power. Like Michael Ignatieff, the prominent polemicist and now Canadian Liberal politician, Ferguson bemoans what both see as the United States' preference for 'empire lite', for a kind of imperialism on the cheap, in which the willingness to employ overwhelming military force is not matched by a comparable commitment of personnel, money and time to help turn round what Ignatieff refers to as the world's 'barbarian zones' (Ignatieff 2003, p. 21). American citizens and their representatives are, Ferguson suspects, too pusillanimous to countenance the human and fiscal costs of nation building. A determined and self-conscious American empire, Ferguson writes, is therefore the world's only hope, since the alternative is not, as bleeding hearts like Gilroy might anticipate, a 'pacifist utopia' but, on the contrary, 'an anarchic new Dark Age' (Ferguson 2005, p. xxiii). The significance of Ferguson's title is thus apparent. He views the American Empire as Thomas Hobbes once viewed the sovereign: the imperial Colossus or Leviathan is a bulwark against chaos. Ferguson draws his battle lines very clearly: on the one side is the sometimes indelicate but ultimately advantageous institutional form of imperialism; on the other, the ruinous, impracticable aspirations of its opponents.

Ferguson's earlier volume, *Empire: How Britain Made the Modern World* (2003) (accompanied, as usual, by a lavish television series), begins with a passage from Joseph Conrad's *Heart of Darkness* (1899). But not only does Ferguson overlook the element of satire in Conrad's apparent celebration of British colonialism – for he does not, as they say, do irony – he also misses (assuming he has read the novel) both Conrad's impressive depiction of the sheer cruelty of colonialism and the account of the narrator, Marlow, in a slightly later passage, of the ideology that seeks to finesse and excuse this cruelty:

> They were no colonists; their administration was merely a squeeze, and nothing more, I suspect.... They grabbed what they could get for the sake of what was to be got. It was just robbery with violence, aggravated murder on a great scale, and men going at it blind – as is very proper for those who tackle a darkness. The conquest of the earth, which mostly means the taking it away from those who have a different complexion or slightly flatter noses than ourselves, is not a pretty thing when you look into it too much. What redeems it is the idea only. An idea at the back of it; not a sentimental pretence but an idea; and an unselfish belief in the idea – something you can set up, and bow down before, and offer a sacrifice to.... (Conrad 1995, p. 20)

This familiar passage, needless to say, does not make it into the book. Indeed, Ferguson sets out, as Marlow puts it, to 'redeem' robbery and murder by bending his knee to what he calls 'Anglobalization'. Ferguson has none of Conrad's insight into the constitutive defects of European imperialism and the duplicity of its perpetrators: 'what the British Empire proved', he states, although proof is not something that Ferguson really bothers with in his glossy chronicle, 'is that empire is a form of international government that can work – and not just for the benefit of the ruling power' (Ferguson 2003, p. 362).

Ferguson finds in Britain's supposed authorship of the modern world a useful precedent for the kind of virtuous power that can engineer the economic development that 'backward peoples' (Ferguson 2005, p. xxvi) are too feckless to accomplish alone. Indeed, their fecklessness is one of Ferguson's favourite subjects, a result, he suspects, of the sultry climate (197). A sort of non-fiction Naipaul,[3] his talk in these books, bestsellers both, is of the ancient hatreds that bedevil the globe's backward zones (xvii) and of the hash the natives have made of independence (27). It is with insights such as these that he seeks to persuade his readers of the quaint proposition that British colonialism is the best model for contemporary global governance. Ferguson lists the rewards to which those ruled by the British Empire could look forward, endowments so splendid that even when set alongside slavery, genocide, indentured labour and famine, they make the British Empire an example for future generations.

In no particular order, these bequests are: the dissemination of the English language, banking, common law, Protestantism, the limited state, representative assemblies, English forms of land tenure, the idea of liberty and, most curiously of all, team sports (Ferguson 2003, p. xxii). Amazingly, Ferguson seems unconcerned that the Empire's legatees might consider some of these benefactions to be, at best, mixed blessings. Nor has it yet dawned on him that the putative advantages of British occupation might have been outweighed, at least for those to whom the occupying was done, by the very considerable disadvantages – that, in other words, teaching the natives to play cricket might not have made up for the countless millions of Indians who died in famines. Ferguson's slanted approach is simply not equipped to weigh the (arguable) pros of, say, the incorporation of the Hong Kong and Shanghai Banking Corporation or the belated arrangement of elections to Kenya's Legislative Council against the (incontestable) cons of the Opium Wars and Britain's brutal incarceration – searingly described by Caroline Elkins (2005) and David Anderson (2005) – of hundreds of thousands of Kenyan men, women and children during the Mau Mau uprising in the 1950s.

Happily, many of Ferguson's readers will be less willing to take imperialists at their word. They would wish to question whether the dominance of

---

3 In his *Among the Believers* (1982) and *Beyond Belief* (1999) the Trinidadian writer V. S. Naipaul chides Indian, Iranian, Malaysian and Pakistani Muslims for their parasitic but resentful dependence on 'our [i.e. Europe and North America's] universal civilization', a resentment that for Naipaul manifests itself in rage and a militant attachment to an aggressive and backward religion. As Rob Nixon (1992) has shown, Naipaul's presentation of himself as an exile (an unaffiliated and uncompromising intelligence) conceals his work's orthodox, even Eurocentric, preconceptions about Islam and the postcolonial world.

English is an unmitigated godsend, whether misgivings about the dogma of transubstantiation are a prerequisite for economic development, and whether the Empire's subjects might have developed an attachment to the concept of liberty in spite rather than because of its avowal by the British. Ferguson also glosses over the fact that British-style legislatures and legal systems were largely restricted to the settler colonies of Australia, Canada and New Zealand, hardly a great record for a power that (as Ferguson keeps reminding us) once covered a quarter of the globe's surface. He has no idea (or perhaps would rather not let on) that for decades most of the Empire's subjects in, for example, India and the Caribbean looked in vain for a representative assembly and for the rule of law, and that they certainly never set eyes on a limited state. Only the reference to English forms of land tenure gets close to the truth, though the similarity of the dispossession of Kenya's Gikuyu people (and the expropriation of their land by a handful of settlers) to the brutal clearances of the population of the Scottish Highlands or the enclosure of English common land might not strike many as a point in imperialism's favour.

Ferguson's tone is too querulous for us to fail to notice his conservative or, more accurately, *neo*-conservative agenda. That he is equal parts historian and polemicist is clearly revealed when in *Colossus* he grumbles that Medicare and social security are absorbing money that could better be spent on small wars, or better still, given the tendency of small wars to leave the job half done, big ones (Ferguson 2005, pp. 269–74). Ferguson poses as a brave opponent of 'conventional wisdom' (Ferguson 2003, p. xiii) but in fact he is little more than a partisan of power. Nowhere in these books can be found the obvious insight that the British Empire was a mechanism for systematically exploiting the labour of countless millions of men and women whom it deemed racially inferior and, consequently, expendable. Instead, Ferguson portrays the victims of imperialism as beneficiaries of a benign subjugation and, where he cannot ignore the evidence of their mistreatment, presents their sufferings as nugatory exceptions to the rule that (to paraphrase the synopses of both volumes) British and American imperialism is a good thing. Transparently tendentious, Ferguson's approach to the writing of history necessitates a series of evasions and half-truths. Though he admits the culpability of British rulers' 'dogmatic' policies (2003, pp. 249–50), the Great Hunger in Ireland merits a mere two sentences in *Empire*. Kenya (surely an instructive case study for anyone wishing seriously to weigh British imperialism's boons against its drawbacks) is mentioned only twice in passing. Admittedly, Ferguson dwells a little longer on Kenya in his introduction, but there it is to relate tales of the 'magical' childhood he spent in that country in the late 1960s, not to inform readers of the unspeakable tortures inflicted during the Emergency a few years earlier.

The colonizers that people Ferguson's books, though occasionally maladroit, are rarely anything less than well intentioned. The word 'Empire' – or, more grandiloquently, 'the transforming power of the imperial dream' (Ferguson 2003, p. xv) – conjures for him the family Fergusons' sepia photographs of their broad-shouldered Scottish forebears, picturesque farming folk who waved goodbye to drizzly old Fife in order to cultivate the fertile prairies of Canada. As well as giving Ferguson the chance to crack jokes about 'friendly' 'Indians' (xv), these figures, alongside Livingstone, the Old Carthusian 'Steve' Baden-Powell, the chartered companies, the London Missionary Society, and the abolitionists of the Clapham Sect, allow him to distort the deeds and motivations of the Empire's protagonists. Almost invariably presented as pioneers and philanthropists, the British and their North American brethren are distinguished in Ferguson's texts from low-rent imperialists like the French and the Belgians. Ferguson soft-pedals the atrocities committed in Kenya and mistakes a gargantuan system of human exploitation for a kind of travel agency for Victorian adventurers because his transatlanticist agenda demands that Anglo-Saxon imperialism be made to appear more humane and less violent than that of its rivals. *Empire* overlooks the behaviour of the Black and Tans, who fired into the crowd at Croke Park, of the British Indian Army commander who ordered his men to shoot down the people gathered at Amritsar, and of the torturers who operated with impunity in numerous counterinsurgency operations in the Empire's dying days (Tulloch 2005). Not even a footnote is given over to the colonial administrators whose negligence and inhumanity, when they were faced with the catastrophic droughts and famines in nineteenth-century India, led to one of the most appalling events in human history and, as Mike Davis has shown, sowed the seeds of the third world's enduring underdevelopment (Davis 2002). *Empire* simply passes over the similarity between these abominations and the crimes perpetrated by the troops of Thomas Bugeaud, who burned and asphyxiated civilians in Algerian caves, and by the mercenaries of Leopold's *Force Publique*, who imposed the king's rubber quotas by lopping off hands, *pour encourager les autres*.

It is very apt that imperial cartographers should have shaded Britain's possessions in red. But for Ferguson the centuries of bloodletting are, in a sense, beside the point. Though he contests their prevalence, has no inkling of their systematic nature and plainly lacks the imaginative resources necessary to think his way into the experiences of their victims, Ferguson is prepared to concede that atrocities took place, bemoaning, for example, Elizabethan 'plantations' in Ireland as early forms of 'ethnic cleansing' (2003, p. 63). He does not always deny that atrocities happened. He merely asserts that their victims would have been even worse off if they had been ruled by other powers or (a possibility that Ferguson cannot really countenance) if they had been left to rule themselves. The same Ferguson who elsewhere urges historians to construct counterfactual historical scenarios (visions of what might have happened), to 'attach equal importance to all the possibilities which contemporaries contemplated' (Ferguson 1998b, p. 87), and to use 'Virtual history [as] a necessary antidote to [historical] determinism' (89), shows himself in these texts to be rather more deterministic about the inevitability of imperialism and rather less ready to attach any importance whatsoever to the alternatives developed over the years by socialists and anti-colonial nationalists. Though it is receptive to, say, the implausible idea that Britain might have stayed out of the First World War (Ferguson 1998a), Ferguson's 'imagination reels from the counterfactual of modern history without the British Empire' (2003, p. xxi), just as it disregards contemporary thinkers' and movements' development of an alternative to American power. In short, there was and is no alternative. Ferguson bears each abomination with equanimity because in every case there is the (counterfactual and evidence-free) mitigation that if the British had not been present the natives would have fared no better; which means, for instance, that the extermination of the population of Tasmania should not be allowed to affect our judgement of British imperialism because the genocidal depopulation of Australasia would have been even worse if the British authorities had not 'restrained' the settlers (2003, p. 111).

The key to understanding the purpose of Ferguson's revisionist approach, therefore, is to realize that, despite his weakness for the myths and rhetoric of Empire, his agenda is not so much to glorify imperialism or to deny its shortcomings as it is to discredit alternatives (Blackburn 2005). He wants to refute liberal, nationalist and especially socialist critiques of imperialism by showing that there is no globalization without gunboats (Ferguson 2003, p. xix). Notwithstanding the sporadically fruitful but for a variety of reasons usually thwarted attempts of postcolonial peoples to negotiate independent paths to development, Ferguson assumes that a world without imperialism would be a world standing still (xxi). 'The question', he writes, 'is not whether British imperialism was without a blemish. It was not. The question is whether there could have been a less bloody path to modernity. Perhaps in theory there could have been. But in practice?' (xxv). The question is, of course, rhetorical: dispossession and murder are the necessary price of economic development. One might, after the saying, call this the eggs-and-omelette view of history.

More even than his uncritical celebration of British and American power, it is therefore his quite appalling blindness to that power's human consequences that indicts Ferguson's work. It leads him to pen the sort of sweeping historical narratives that, though admirable in their attempt to shed light on economic and other long-term trends, frequently pass over the ordinary human existences wherein history is decided and lived. Ferguson has none of, say, Eric Hobsbawm's knack for educing general theses from the astute observation of representative experiences (Hobsbawm 1995). On the contrary, the monotonous chronicle of American virtue served up by *Colossus* is virtually unalleviated by any humane sympathy for those at imperialism's receiving end. Ferguson prefers to relate history with the numerous figures, graphs and tables compiled by his research assistants (on everything from projected Iraqi oil revenues to the box office receipts of Vietnam War movies). Still the best corrective to this way of thinking is Aimé Césaire's magnificent expostulation in his *Discourse on Colonialism* of 1950:

> They talk to me about progress, about 'achievements', diseases cured, improved standards of living. I am talking about societies drained of their essence, cultures trampled underfoot, institutions undermined, lands confiscated, religions smashed, magnificent artistic creations destroyed, extraordinary possibilities wiped out. They throw facts at my head, statistics, mileages of roads, canals

and railroad tracks. I am talking about thousands of men sacrificed to the Congo–Ocean railroad. I am talking about those who, as I write this, are digging the harbour of Abidjan by hand. (Césaire 1995, pp. 21–22)[4]

I quote this passage in order to stress the extremely serious drawbacks of Ferguson's cosmic book-keeping, an approach that allows him to weigh millions of lives blighted, cut short and endured in torment against unexamined abstractions like modernity, the free movement of capital and, most bizarrely of all, 'global peace' (Ferguson 2003, p. 359). Another way of putting this is to say that unlike, say, E. P. Thompson, Ferguson is practising a sort of 'history from above'. Whereas Ferguson is capable of describing the Berlin Conference of 1884–85, which went a long way to partitioning up Africa between European powers, as 'the biggest game of Monopoly in history' (2003, p. 235), a more perspicacious historian like Adam Hochschild has called this gathering of potentates 'the ultimate expression of an age whose newfound enthusiasm for democracy had clear limits, and slaughtered game had no vote' (Hochschild 1999, p. 84). Ferguson pens Whiggish chronicles of great men and warrior states leading mankind towards the light, written at such a towering elevation that he loses sight of (or, rather, does not even bother to look for) the human costs of empire. Whereas Thompson, famously, saw it as the historian's task to rescue ordinary people from 'the enormous condescension of posterity' (Thompson 1986, p. 12), Ferguson evidently sees it as his to heap the condescension back on. '[P]robably a good deal of ill' (Ferguson 2005, p. 216), he concedes in a revealingly dispassionate aside, came about as a result of America's intercessions since the Second World War in the Caribbean and Central America, as though the murderousness of those depredations is still at issue and as though that 'ill' were a negligible matter and constituted a mere botched dry run for a further attempt – albeit this time with more men, material and money – to magically rearrange these backwaters into proper countries.

The best way to refute Ferguson's case, therefore, is not just to point out that imperialists do bad things (he has done that already, at least in some cases) but to show that these deeds are far worse than he pretends and, just as crucially, to demonstrate that they need not take place. The most important lesson to draw from Ferguson's celebrity is that the political and cultural establishments are receptive to the, in my view, invidious and doctrinaire assumption that there is no alternative to imperial power. Despite his vaunted intolerance of fixed ideas and although, as Terry Eagleton has said (1998, p. 320), revisionist historians ought logically to be alert to the possibility that their own conclusions are arguable and revisable, Ferguson's books betray two sweeping, unsubstantiated but, alas, widely held preconceptions: that imperialism was and is *not* systematically maleficent, and that we did and do *not* possess any alternatives to it. The first of these assumptions can be disputed by careful scholarship. The second is a

---

4 I must thank Neil Lazarus for drawing this passage to my attention.

hypothesis being put to practical test by a number of what Immanuel Wallerstein has called 'antisystemic movements' (Wallerstein 2002).

Capitalist globalization is currently revealing the fragility of existing democratic arrangements at the level of the nation state. It raises the spectre of a system in which decisions are made not by democratically elected representatives in the interests of their citizens but by states and corporations. The risks and perils of this system are increasingly borne by those least able to influence its direction. What Richard Falk has called 'predatory' capitalism (1999) moves across borders and triggers a 'race to the bottom' as states seek to outdo each other as profitable fields of investment by ditching constraints on big business, lowering wages, impairing environmental protections, inhibiting organized labour and slashing social spending (Amin 1997; Arrighi 1994; Bourdieu 1998; Harvey 1999; Mann 2001; Sassen 1996). Ferguson falls back on imperialism as the only feasible means of assuming the political functions once expected of the nation state: 'liberal empire', he writes, is 'the political counterpart to economic globalization' (Ferguson 2005, p. 183). But many movements (Kingsnorth 2004) and thinkers (Brecher and Costello 1998; Callinicos 2003; Monbiot 2003) under the banner of the Global Justice Movement have in different ways sought not just to analyse the gulf between the great majority of the world's people and a global and unrepresentative political and economic system, but also to envision new arrangements that might serve to correct the current imbalance between people and power. The problem with Ferguson's work is that, although it correctly diagnoses the drawbacks of the current dispensation of failing and impoverished states, it appeals as a solution to pre-existing and more or less totally discredited arrangements and authorities. What are actually required, however, are new ways of imagining those arrangements from democratic and cosmopolitan perspectives.

Alternative histories and alternative futures

What this brief examination of Ferguson's work intends to illustrate is that the revisionist account of the British Empire is politically motivated. Revisionism seeks to legitimize contemporary imperialism and to discredit alternatives to the lawless hegemony of powerful states. Nonetheless, the movements and thinkers who are articulating those alternatives insist that diversity, equality and so on should be thought of not as national values, and least of all as benefactions dispensed by empires, but as civic or, better still, cosmopolitan principles. Freed from disarming notions of national loyalty they are capable of channelling widespread grievances into politically constructive forms of protest. We should therefore radicalize multiculturalism by viewing it not as a marketing strategy or a weapon in the rhetorical armoury of the state, but as a principled and practical challenge to the ideologies of domination that structure the globe.

However, embedded in the very shape and nature of our institutions and forms of economic and social life, racism persists. It endures because it provides an idea of hierarchy that can be used to justify forms of domination, namely the omission from Britain's prosperous 'modernity' of what Salman Rushdie (1992) once called 'the new Empire within Britain' (including scapegoated minorities). More broadly, racism explains the official unconcern both for captives who are deprived of their rights and abandoned to a secretive archipelago of 'black sites' and for the millions of 'unpeople' (Curtis 2004) who are governed and exploited from afar without recourse to representative institutions and without the protection nominally afforded by numerous covenants, treaties and charters that enshrine their human rights. Put simply, my argument has been that a kind of racism underpins the ruling priorities of domestic and foreign policy. It is racism that takes the form not of conventional colour prejudice, though that too is far from dead, but rather of a more insidious though equally noxious variant: civilizationism, the belief that cultures, not races, are absolute and incompatible. Blair's uncritical affirmation of the 'British way of life' and Ferguson's transatlanticist advocacy of the Anglo-Saxon world role have both given rise to an erroneous and profoundly destructive and invidious demarcation between Anglo-American values, on the one hand, and, on the other, the troublesome minorities and 'backward' peoples who are said to stand in need of these.

We have urgent need of dissenting scholarship that is capable of examining these received ideas. At its best, postcolonial criticism fits this bill. It sets the ideals of democracy and human equality against the civilizationist dogma that cultures are unalterably discrete, a belief that once widespread academic discourses of anti-humanism and identity politics have done far too little to contest. If it is to be effective at promoting democracy and equality, then postcolonial criticism must, in the first instance, take aim at racism. It should endeavour to refute mainstream justifications for imperialism, explain imperialism's connections to capitalism, expose imperialism's violent history and elaborate those ideas, commitments, dispositions and arrangements that are necessary to bring imperialism to a close. What Edward Said has called postcolonial studies' 'intellectual and interpretative vocation to make connections' (Said 1994, p. 115) involves but hardly limits itself to investigations of the links between imperialism and European culture, as well as analyses of how literature and other forms of art have been used to articulate alternative modes of thought and feeling. This aesthetic counter-articulation, as C. L. Innes (2002), John McLeod (2004) and Sukhdev Sandhu (2003) have demonstrated, is now taking place within as well as beyond Europe's borders. It is an agreeable irony evident in many of the works of the novelists, poets, artists and musicians examined by these three critics that European colonialism has engendered its opposite: the importation of lives (alongside that of materials and commodities) has created in Europe communities in which racism is being contested by a new cosmopolitan consciousness first articulated by minorities and those in solidarity with them. I am arguing, therefore, for a form of post-colonial work that is not restricted to a narrowly academic exercise of censuring Eurocentrism or documenting the cultural and political means by which colonized populations express their resistance to that ideology, but that is expanded to include a distinctive type of intellectual intervention in a First World setting.

This is a way of repeating what I have stressed already: that if dissatisfaction with patriotic moods and with the undemocratic political systems that are driving forward neo-liberal globalization is what occasions the impulse to think and feel beyond the confines of the nation state, then postcolonial criticism logically entails a decision to situate oneself as far as possible outside of, or, much better, *in opposition to* the state. Criticism behoves a form of action that is directed against the nation state but which acknowledges that, even though the repressive and ideological apparatuses of state power occupy much of one's practical and intellectual energy, the society in which one resides does not exhaust one's allegiances and, in addition, political action does not end with the criticism and reform of national institutions. A serviceable definition of postcolonial critical work is provided by Gilroy's call for 'the cultivation of cosmopolitan disloyalty and the practice of systematic estrangement from the over-integrated culture of belligerent national states' (Gilroy 2004, p. 92). What both he and I are trying to say is that postcolonial criticism must emphasize its radical and even subversive character, and that without this element it tends, as Benita Parry has noted, to trail off either into a kind of cynical detachment or, more often, into a premature celebration of desirable cosmopolitan situations that do not yet exist for the world's majority and that can be brought about only by intentional, dedicated and painstaking practical work (Parry 2004).

Of course, an awareness of the pitfalls of the sort of glib or precipitate cosmopolitanism that one finds in some postcolonial thinkers – what Tom Nairn (2000, p. 148) has called their 'departure-lounge internationalism' – does not mean forfeiting cosmopolitan aspirations. Rather, it means avoiding the sort of elitist or precipitate cosmopolitanism that excludes (or at least fails to heed) those impoverished communities that continue to live in bounded spaces, for whom travel usually means the desperate pursuit of sanctuary or employment, and from whose perspective the oft-maligned nation state constitutes the first stratum of governance they must conquer if their grievances are to be addressed (Brennan 2003). In other words, as Nestor García Canclini (2000) has argued, it is as important not to conceptualize our cosmopolitan aspirations too amorphously and abstractly as it is to avoid conceptualizing them too parochially or ethnocentrically. To this end, postcolonial studies should be a form of scholarship that looks inwards and outwards at the same time, at the continuing power of the nation state as well as at the prospect of cosmopolitan forms of life.

In emphasizing the potentially salutary aspect of the idea and experience of diaspora, I have followed Edward Said (2000) and especially Paul Gilroy in arguing that sometimes 'What was initially felt to be a curse – the curse of homelessness or the curse of enforced exile – gets repossessed. It becomes affirmed and is reconstructed as the basis of a privileged standpoint from which certain useful and critical perceptions about the modern world become more likely' (Gilroy 1993, p. 111). But diasporas should not always be celebrated. Hindus in North America who bankroll sectarian violence in India, Zionists in the United States who defend Israeli atrocities in the occupied territories, and

Cuban expatriates in Florida who crave the overthrow of Cuban socialism are hardly embodiments of self-sacrificing cosmopolitan virtue. Nor is the fate of exile always, or even usually, voluntary or serendipitous: witness the experiences of countless refugees, migrants and seekers of asylum. But I want to insist on making use of this concept because many, though by no means all, of those who consider themselves to be part of a diaspora embody what the cosmopolitan theorist David Held has called 'multiple citizenships', in which individuals are 'citizens of their immediate political communities, and of the wider regional and global networks which impact upon their lives' (Held 1996, p. 233). As well as giving rise, in some people, to what Benedict Anderson calls 'long-distance nationalism' (Anderson 2001, p. 42), membership of a diaspora engenders in others a principled rejection of national loyalties. What I am advocating here, then, is a comparable scholarly commitment to the broad allegiances and the acute critical consciousness that can result from membership of a diaspora. We need to hold fast to the concept's discomfiting connotations, to the use of diaspora to denote a form of subversive, principled and politically efficacious commitment to supranational groupings.

I have been arguing in this chapter that the reactions of the government and the media to the London bombings have shown that the British state and the social and economic set-up that it protects depend upon the construction of a rigid opposition between the blameless practices and values of a native majority and the baseless disaffection of outsiders. Perspectives need to be found that problematize this dichotomy, that reveal the real costs of Britain's intransigent status quo, and in so doing entreat the need to subject the status quo to criticism and change. Analysis of our usually forgotten or nostalgically distorted imperial past is one such perspective, not least because it exposes disturbing continuities in the priorities and exploits of the state, because it illustrates the appalling human consequences of these, and because it draws our attention to the parallels between the European empires and the activities of their American successor. That past offers incentives for self-criticism and corrective political action. For example, lessons learnt from a critical scrutiny of Europe's colonial history include the insight that high-flown humanitarian sentiment has been used many times before to excuse blood-soaked colonial ventures. Such lessons can be used to interrogate Europe's (and particularly Britain's) present closeness to what David Harvey has called the United States' 'new imperialism' (Harvey 2003). Ultimately, a searching examination of Europe's previous misdeeds can embolden its pursuit of the kind of exemplary cosmopolitan arrangements of which the world's most recent and overwhelmingly unself-conscious imperial power has not yet shown itself capable.

For better and for worse, Europe is what it is today – a multifarious if at times appallingly inhospitable place, one characterized as much by extraordinarily promising experiences of equality between people of diverse origins as it is by chauvinism, exploitation and the fear of outsiders – *because of* the history of imperialism. Enrique Dussel has shown that Europe itself was inconceivable until in 1492 Columbus's voyage to the Americas and the *Reconquista* that brought to an end Islamic rule in Andalucía made it possible for Europeans to contrast themselves with others (Dussel 1995). Since its inception, in other words, the idea and the very existence of Europe have been secretly dependent on those whom Europe excludes and disparages: 'Europe', in Frantz Fanon's memorable phrase, 'is literally the creation of the Third World' (Fanon 1990, p. 81). Tackling racism at a deep rather than a superficial level will involve recognition, not avoidance, of this fact. Europe's past is inseparable from its racism, and likewise its future (or at least a future that is not characterized by exclusion, cultural hierarchy and an endlessly perpetuated political and economic status quo) cannot be addressed without also addressing and expunging racism. To become aware of these facts, through a critical examination of Europe's colonial history, is to begin explaining, criticizing and offering alternatives to the enduring power of racism as an ideology. It is, in post-imperial societies like Britain and France, to transform guilt and self-awareness into a sense of moral responsibility; it is to bid farewell to a Europe characterized by its hostility towards refugees, minorities and strangers and to a Europe complacently enamoured of its own unchanging domestic and foreign priorities; it is to realize that 'integration' is ineffective if cultures and races are not invited to integrate on terms of equality; and it is, conceivably, to initiate in a nearly discredited continent institutions and allegiances that are open, hospitable and no longer indifferent to those peoples blighted by racist imperialisms past and present.

A sceptical meditation on Europe's past is thus one way of promoting cosmopolitan aspirations, of reviving democratic politics and, ultimately, of reconstituting European economic, social and political life with the aid of cosmopolitan forms of thinking and modes of action (Bourdieu 2003; Watkins 2005; Žižek 2005). For instance, Jürgen Habermas contends that a critical engagement with their nation's history can persuade Germans of the need to base citizenship not on homogeneous ethnic or cultural origins but on constitutionally guaranteed political rights. To disremember that history, is, he writes, for Germans to close their eyes to the consequences of racism, of insularity and of an economic set-up that fails to appreciate the humanity of its victims (Habermas 1989). For example, the attempt by recent governments to use the relocation of the federal government to Berlin and other symbols to present modern Germany as, effectively, a reconstitution of Bismarck's Second Reich serves to normalize the nation's catastrophic past, to present National Socialism as a freak interregnum, and to excuse modern Germans from the responsibility to learn from the period of fascism (Habermas 1998a). Germans, Habermas argues, should instead learn, by reflecting on the shattering cost of racism, to view and construct their nation as *Einwanderungsland*, a hospitable habitation for all arrivals, including migrants and guest workers. Careful reflection on the nation's past will thus become a source of strength and progress.

Hence Habermas's important conviction that, in the opportunities for social, political and economic transformation offered by the 'inter-cultural' encounter with immigrants and others, 'world history has offered a unified Europe a second chance' (Habermas 1994, p. 75). Free of imperialistic ambitions and narcissistic self-absorption, Europeans can show themselves capable of learning from their past by developing rational, democratic and inclusive institutions.

> Occidental rationalism must go back into itself and overcome its own blindnesses in order to open up dialogically what it can learn from the traditions of other cultures. An inter-cultural encounter worthy of the name would also demand that the submerged elements of our own tradition be brought to light. Europe must use one of its strengths, namely its potential for self-criticism, its power of self-transformation, in order to relativize itself far more radically vis-à-vis the others, the strangers, the misunderstood. That's the opposite of Eurocentrism. But *we* can overcome Eurocentrism only out of the better spirit of Europe. (Habermas 1994, p. 96)

Others may find different resources that enable them to confront this past and overcome it. But, as well as uncovering examples of domination and inhumanity, Europeans will find in their history democratic and egalitarian principles, along with resources for self-criticism, that might form the basis of exemplary institutions at the trans- and even supranational level. Such institutions will hopefully amount to an enlightened cosmopolitanism and not just a self-protective and undemocratic consortium competing for a global market share (Habermas 1998b, 2006). A model of public participation in an international public sphere must therefore replace the technocratic pursuit of neo-liberal goals. That would mean listening to the French and Dutch voters who rejected the constitution for the European Union and it must involve, as Pierre Bourdieu has argued, restoring politics to Europe's currently undemocratic institutions: in particular, to its unaccountable Central Bank, to its immensely powerful but largely unanswerable Commission, to its toothless legislative body, to the rigid fiscal restrictions of its single-currency system, and to the subordination of its defence and foreign policy to Washington.

> If they are genuinely to be transformed, it can only be by a vast European social movement, capable of elaborating and imposing an open and coherent vision of a political Europe, rich with all its past cultural and social achievements and armed with a generous and lucid project of social renewal, resolutely open to the entire world. (Bourdieu 2003, p. 15)

If the postcolonial discipline is to help free minds from subordination to a system of violent and racist exploitation, then it has no more appropriate target today than what I have dubbed imperial nostalgia, which in the works of historians like Ferguson and the pronouncements of politicians like Blair, Brown and Davis betokens a barefaced enthusiasm for the actions and for the social and economic forms of British and American power. Imperial nostalgia not only bowdlerizes the historical record of imperial violence; it also uses that distortion to write off the possibility of any political alternatives to imperial rule. On the other hand, critical examination of the history of imperialism can be a source for the ideas, convictions and motivations necessary to put in place a cosmopolitan solution. One aspect of that solution will be the construction of a genuinely postcolonial Europe. Rarely has Walter Benjamin's great insight – that thinkers and movements dedicated to effecting fundamental social change must apprehend ruling powers' past as well as current misdeeds – been more apposite (Benjamin 1992). 'Critical theory', in Herbert Marcuse's useful dictum, 'must concern itself to a hitherto unknown extent with the past – precisely insofar as it is concerned with the future' (Marcuse 1972, p. 158). Postcolonial studies' role, then, is to provide a counter-memory to the official narrative of imperial power, to make clear that narrative's invidiousness and its provinciality, to lay emphasis on the resistance and humanity of its victims and, not least of the discipline's responsibilities, to show that simplifications about national missions are nowhere near sufficient to prevent alternative histories from being written and alternative futures from coming into being.

Works cited

Ali, T. (2005) *Rough Music: Blair/Bombs/Baghdad/London/Terror*. London, Verso.

Amin, S. (1997) *Capitalism in the Age of Globalization: The Management of Contemporary Society*. London, Zed Books.

Anderson, B. (1983) *Imagined Communities: Reflections on the Origins and Spread of Nationalism*. London, Verso.

—— (2001) 'Western Nationalism and Eastern Nationalism'. *New Left Review*, 9, pp. 31–42.

Anderson, D. (2005) *Histories of the Hanged: The Dirty War in Kenya and the End of Empire*. New York, Norton.

Arrighi, G. (1994) *The Long Twentieth Century: Money, Power and the Origins of Our Times*. London, Verso.

Benjamin, W. (1992) 'Theses on the Philosophy of History'. In: Arendt, H. ed. *Illuminations*. Translated by H. Zohn. London, Fontana, pp. 245–55.

Blackburn, R. (2005) 'Imperial Margarine'. *New Left Review*, 35, pp. 124–36.

Bourdieu, P. (1998) *Acts of Resistance: Against the New Myths of Our Time*. Translated by R. Nice. Oxford, Polity Press.

—— (2003) *Firing Back: Against the Tyranny of the Market 2*. Translated by L. Waquant. New York, New Press.

Brecher, J. and Costello, T. (1998) *Global Village or Global Pillage: Economic Reconstruction from the Bottom Up*. Cambridge, MA, South End Press.

Brennan, T. (2003) 'The Italian Ideology'. In: Balakrishnan, G. ed. *Debating Empire*. London, Verso, pp. 97–120.

Callinicos, A. (2003) *An Anti-capitalist Manifesto*. Cambridge, Polity Press.

Césaire, A. (1995) *Discourse on Colonialism*. Translated by J. Pinkham. New York, Monthly Review Press.

Conrad, J. (1995) *Heart of Darkness* [1899]. Harmondsworth, Penguin.

Curtis, M. (1998) *The Great Deception: Anglo-American Power and World Order*. London, Pluto Press.

—— (2003) *Web of Deceit: Britain's Real Role in the World*. London, Vintage.

—— (2004) *Unpeople: Britain's Secret Human Rights Abuses*. London, Vintage.

Davis, D. (2005) 'Why Cultural Tolerance Cuts Both Ways'. *Daily Telegraph*, 3 August. Available at www.telegraph.co.uk/opinion/main.jhtml?xml=/opinion/2005/08/03/do0302.xml (accessed 28 January 2009).

Davis, M. (2002) *Late Victorian Holocausts: El Niño Famines and the Making of the Third World*. London, Verso.

Dussel, E. (1995) *The Invention of the Americas: Eclipse of 'the Other' and the Myth of Modernity*. New York, Continuum.

Eagleton, T. (1998) 'Revisionism Revisited'. In: *Crazy John and the Bishop and Other Essays on Irish Culture*. Cork, Cork University Press, pp. 308–27.

Elkins, C. (2005) *Britain's Gulag: The Brutal End of Empire in Kenya*. London, Pimlico.

Falk, R. A. (1999) *Predatory Globalization: A Critique*. Cambridge, Polity Press.

Fanon, F. (1990) *The Wretched of the Earth* [1961]. Translated by C. Farrington. Harmondsworth, Penguin.

Ferguson, N. (1998a) *The Pity of War*. London, Penguin.

—— (1998b) 'Virtual History: Towards a "Chaotic" Theory of the Past'. In: Ferguson, N. ed. *Virtual History: Alternatives and Counterfactuals*. London, Pan, pp. 1–90.

—— (2003) *Empire: How Britain Made the Modern World*. London, Allen Lane.

—— (2005) *Colossus: The Rise and Fall of the American Empire*. Harmondsworth, Penguin.

García Canclini, N. (2000) 'The State of War and the State of Hybridization'. Translated by K. Pesola. In: Gilroy, P., Grossberg, L. and McRobbie, A. eds. *Without Guarantees: In Honour of Stuart Hall*. London, Verso, pp. 38–52.

Gilroy, P. (1991) 'It Ain't Where You're From, It's Where You're At: The Dialectics of Diasporic Identification'. *Third Text*, 13, pp. 3–16.

—— (1993) *The Black Atlantic: Modernity and Double Consciousness*. London, Verso.

—— (1994) 'Diaspora'. *Paragraph*, 17(3), pp. 207–12.

—— (2000) *Against Racism: Imagining Political Culture Beyond the Colour Line*. Cambridge, MA, Harvard University Press.

—— (2002) *There Ain't No Black in the Union Jack: The Cultural Politics of Race and Nation* [1987]. London, Routledge.

—— (2004) *After Empire: Melancholia or Convivial Culture?* London, Routledge.

—— (2005) 'A New Cosmopolitanism'. *Interventions*, 7(3), pp. 287–92.

Greaves, R. (2005) 'Negotiating British Citizenship and Muslim Identity'. In: Abbas, T. ed. *Muslim Britain: Communities Under Pressure*. London, Zed Books, pp. 66–77.

Habermas, J. (1989) 'On the Public Use of History'. In: Nicholsen, S. W. ed. *The New Conservatism: Cultural Criticism and the Historians' Debate*. Cambridge, MA, Harvard University Press, pp. 229–40.

—— (1994) 'Europe's Second Chance'. In: Pensky, M. ed. *The Past as Future: Interviews by Michael Haller*. Cambridge, Polity Press, pp. 73–97.

—— (1998a) *A Berlin Republic: Writings on Germany*. Translated by S. Rendall. Cambridge, Polity Press.

—— (1998b) 'The European Nation-State: On the Past and Future of Sovereignty and Citizenship'. In: Cronin, C. and De Greiff, P. eds. *The Inclusion of the Other: Studies in Political Theory*. Cambridge, Polity Press, pp. 105–27.

—— (2006) 'Euroskepticism, Market Europe, or a Europe of (World) Citizens?' In: Cronin, C. and Pensky, M. eds. *Time of Transitions*. Cambridge, Polity Press, pp. 73–88.

Hall, S. (1997) 'The Local and the Global: Globalization and Ethnicity'. In: McClintock, A., Mufti, A. and Shohat, E. eds. *Dangerous Liaisons: Gender, Nation, and Postcolonial Perspectives*. Minneapolis, MN, University of Minnesota Press, pp. 173–87.

Harvey, D. (1999) *Limits to Capital*. London, Verso.

—— (2003) *The New Imperialism*. New York, Oxford University Press.

Held, D. (1996) *Democracy and the Global Order: From the Modern State to Cosmopolitan Governance*. Stanford, CA, Stanford University Press.

Hobsbawm, E. (1995) *Age of Extremes: The Short Twentieth Century*. London, Abacus.

Hochschild, A. (1999) *King Leopold's Ghost: A Story of Greed, Terror, and Heroism in Colonial Africa*. London, Macmillan.

Ignatieff, M. (2003) *Empire Lite: Nation-Building in Bosnia, Kosovo and Afghanistan*. London, Vintage.

Innes, C. L. (2002) *A History of Black and Asian Writing in Britain, 1700–2000*. Cambridge, Cambridge University Press.

Kennedy, H. (2005) *Just Law: The Changing Face of Justice – Why It Matters To Us All*. London, Chatto and Windus.

Kingsnorth, P. (2004) *One No, Many Yeses: A Journey to the Heart of the Global Resistance Movement.* London, Free Press.

Mann, M. (2001) 'Globalization and September 11'. *New Left Review*, 11, pp. 51–72.

Marcuse, H. (1972) 'Philosophy and Critical Theory'. In: *Negations: Essays in Critical Theory.* Translated by J. J. Shapiro. Harmondsworth, Penguin, pp. 134–58.

McLeod, J. (2004) *Postcolonial London: Rewriting the Metropolis.* London, Routledge.

Milne, S. (2005) 'Britain: Imperial Nostalgia'. *Le Monde Diplomatique*, May. Available at mondediplo.com/2005/05/02empire (accessed 28 January 2009).

Monbiot, G. (2001) *Captive State: The Corporate Takeover of Britain.* London, Pan.

—— (2003) *The Age of Consent: A Manifesto for a New World Order.* London, HarperCollins.

Naipaul, V. S. (1982) *Among the Believers: An Islamic Journey.* Harmondsworth, Penguin.

—— (1999) *Beyond Belief: Islamic Excursions Among the Converted People.* London, Abacus.

Nairn, T. (2000) *After Britain: New Labour and the Return of Scotland.* London, Granta.

—— (2003) *The Break-Up of Britain: Crisis and Neo-Nationalism.* London, Common Ground.

—— (2006) 'The New Furies'. *New Left Review*, 37, pp. 130–40.

Nixon, R. (1992) *London Calling: V. S. Naipaul, Postcolonial Mandarin.* Oxford, Oxford University Press.

Parry, B. (2004) 'The Institutionalization of Postcolonial Studies'. In: Lazarus, N. ed. *The Cambridge Companion to Postcolonial Literary Studies.* Cambridge, Cambridge University Press, pp. 66–80.

Phillips, T. (2005a) 'After 7/7: Sleepwalking into Segregation'. London, Commission for Racial Equality, 22 September. Available at http://83.137.212.42/sitearchive/cre/Default.aspx. LocID-0hgnew07s.RefLocID-0hg00900c002.Lang-EN.htm (accessed 28 January 2009).

—— (2005b) 'We Need a Highway Code for the Multiethnic Society'. Proceedings of the Conservative Party Conference Muslim Forum (unpublished), 4 October.

Pitcher, B. (2006) 'Multicultural Nationalism: Race and the War on Terror'. Unpublished paper.

Rai, M. (2006) *7/7: The London Bombings, Islam and the Iraq War.* London, Pluto Press.

Robbins, B. and Cheah, P. eds. (1998) *Cosmopolitics: Thinking and Feeling Beyond the Nation.* Minneapolis, MN, University of Minnesota Press.

Rosaldo, R. (1993) *Culture and Truth: The Remaking of Social Analysis.* Boston, Beacon Press.

Rushdie, S. (1992) 'The New Empire Within Britain'. In: *Imaginary Homelands: Essays and Criticism, 1981–1991.* Harmondsworth, Penguin, pp. 129–38.

Said, E. W. (1994) *Culture and Imperialism*, London: Vintage.

—— (2000) 'Reflections on Exile'. In: *Reflections on Exile and Other Literary and Cultural Essays.* London, Granta, pp. 173–86.

Sandhu, S. (2003) *London Calling: How Black and Asian Writers Imagined a City.* London, HarperCollins.

Sands, P. (2005) *Lawless World: America and the Making and Breaking of Global Rules.* London, Penguin.

Sassen, S. (1996) *Losing Control? Sovereignty in an Age of Globalization.* New York, Columbia University Press.

Thompson, E. P. (1986) *The Making of the English Working Class.* Harmondsworth, Penguin.

Tulloch, J. (2005) 'Normalising the Unthinkable – The British Press, Torture, and the Human Rights of Terrorist Suspects'. *International Journal of Communication Ethics*, 2, p. 4.

—— (2006) *One Day in July: Experiencing 7/7.* London, Little and Brown.

Wallerstein, I. (2002) 'New Revolts Against the System'. *New Left Review*, 18, pp. 29–39.

Watkins, S. (2005) 'Continental Tremors'. *New Left Review*, 33, pp. 5–21.

Žižek, S. (2005) 'The Constitution Is Dead. Long Live Proper Politics'. *Guardian*, 9 May. Available at www.guardian.co.uk/comment/story/0,3604,1498989,00.html (accessed 28 January 2009).

CHAPTER 13

Afterword: Europe's racial crisis?

Ian Law

This volume is bound together by the twin intellectual and ethical goals of, first, seeking to promote a better understanding of the deep cultural roots of racism and its ideological, cultural and psychological foundations, processes and mechanisms within the European context; and, second, offering hope through the interrogation and shaping of narratives of opposition, celebration and humanity in order to provide signposts to alternative European futures. The necessity of understanding racial Europe in a postcolonial context has been a central theme here and, as Goldberg (2005, 2006) insists, there is much to be said for examining the power and persistence of racism in the context of geopolitical regions. Goldberg (2005, p. 88) identifies racial Europeanization as one of five dominant mappings of racism, the others being Americanization, Palestinianization, Brazilianization and South Africanization. This approach points to the significance of locating European racism in a global context, the importance of categorizing and exposing the historical logic of racism in specific time/space conjunctions, and the quest for universally adequate theories and concepts. This project of regionalizing European racism is akin to the analytical process of 'provincializing' postcolonial Europe (Chakrabarty 2000), referred to in the Introduction to this volume by Graham Huggan.

The addressing of such issues and the development of global approaches to racism are an increasing trend in this field (Bhattacharya *et al.* 2002; Bowser 1995; Macedo and Gounari 2006; Winant 2006). In international politics, global approaches to tackling racism and ethnic violence have been led by the United Nations and the Third World Conference Against Racism, Racial Discrimination, Xenophobia and Related Intolerance (WCAR), held in 2001. The WCAR declaration set out international standards for tackling racism and provides one attempt to grasp the complexity and variety of competing and contested claims for recognition of global racisms. However, the 'calamity' that this event represented

(Banton 2002) arose from the failure to manage the many axes of conflict over these claims, and also the failure to pursue effective action as a result (European Network Against Racism 2006). An easier task has been to elaborate some key working principles, as set out in a number of conventions and statements from the United Nations (UN) and its Educational, Scientific and Cultural Organization (UNESCO), including the recognition of common humanity, the right to difference and the claim that racism has no justification. Although these approaches have been criticized for understanding racism as being primarily driven by individual prejudice and for ignoring the intrinsic racialization of liberal democracies (Lentin 2004, p. 310), this is not borne out by more recent activities. For example, the 2001 WCAR report makes a specific recommendation on the link between the prevention of racist violence and democratic governance:

> We recognize that democracy, transparent, responsible, accountable and participatory governance responsive to the needs and aspirations of the people, and respect for human rights, fundamental freedoms and the rule of law are essential for the effective prevention and elimination of racism, racial discrimination, xenophobia and related intolerance. We reaffirm that any form of impunity for crimes motivated by racist and xenophobic attitudes plays a role in weakening the rule of law and democracy and tends to encourage the recurrence of such acts. (World Conference Against Racism 2001, p. 19)

The WCAR programme is also being pursued by the UN special rapporteur (Doudou Diène for the period 2002–8, presently Githu Muigai) on contemporary forms of racism, racial discrimination, xenophobia and related intolerance. Reports on different countries across the globe arising from visits are also available on the Website of the Office of the UN High Commissioner for Human Rights (www.ohchr.org). Diène's assessment of strategic aims draws on the WCAR programme of action and identifies four key priorities:

- *monitoring and analysis* of old and new forms of racism, racial discrimination and xenophobia
- *political strategy* – the expression of a firm political will to combat racism by governments
- *legal strategy* – the adoption and implementation of national legislation against racism, discrimination and xenophobia
- *intellectual and ethical strategy* – seeking to promote better understanding of the deep cultural roots of racism, and its ideological, cultural and psychological foundations, processes and mechanisms.

Despite these rather general pronouncements, in both theory and politics the globalization of racism is still substantially to be addressed. Winant (2006, p. 999), confronting the hazards of prediction, suggests a coming 'global racial crisis' and argues that we are likely to see better theory and greater understanding of racial identity and related 'human waste', on the one hand, and deepening 'structural' racism and planetary racial stratification, on the other. This, for him, illustrates a central contradiction in the postcolonial era.

This contradiction is evident within the European politics of race. The establishment of the European Monitoring Centre for Racism and Xenophobia (EUMC) in Vienna in 1997/98, and the implementation of systematic surveillance of patterns and trends in racism and xenophobia across the increasing number of member states of the European Union (EU), both represent a significant advance. But this has also been accompanied by deepening structural racism across the region. Grounding an understanding of contemporary European racism requires a thorough examination of empirical evidence. The EUMC's mandate was extended in February 2007 and that organization is now part of the European Union Agency for Fundamental Rights (FRA). It has recently produced an evaluation of trends and developments in racism, xenophobia and anti-Semitism, drawing on the evidence it collected from 1997 to 2005 (FRA 2007). Surprisingly, these issues were not identified as a serious concern by the European Economic Community until the 1970s and concerted action to address racism did not really begin until the late 1990s, with legislative developments included in the Treaty of Amsterdam (1997), the declaration of the European Year Against Racism and the founding of the EUMC. A handful of key events have clearly marked this period and have served to intensify debates about, and generate awareness of, deep racial and ethnic divisions, many of which have been specifically addressed in this book. These events have included riots in Spain against Moroccan immigrants, terrorist attacks in the United States, Madrid and London, the murder of Dutch film director Theo van Gogh, the controversy over the cartoons depicting the Prophet Mohammed, and the urban disturbances and fires in immigrant apartment blocks in France.

Submissions by National Focal Points (NFPs) to the EUMC give empirical evidence of highly durable forms of racial and ethnic stratification. Patterns of labour market and unemployment inequality show migrants and minorities suffering worse employment conditions, lower wages and concentration in the most precarious, least desirable jobs. In housing, substantial cross-national evidence shows migrants and minorities experiencing poor housing conditions, homelessness and relative deprivation, all of which has compounded social and economic inequalities (Harrison *et al.* 2006). This is most evident for the Roma and Travellers, who, in many European countries, live in segregated neighbourhoods and settlements with extremely poor infrastructure, and are persistently subject to high levels of racial discrimination, evictions and forced displacements. Some NFP reports present a very bleak picture indeed. For Spain, housing experiences of migrants and minorities include homelessness, occupation of abandoned or wrecked buildings, and movement into overcrowded accommodation of poor quality and lacking basic facilities. One study of the homes of Moroccan migrants in Andalusia found 75 per cent with no hot water, 57 per cent with extreme dampness, 49 per cent with no toilet, 45 per cent with no kitchen and 40 per cent with no running water. Meanwhile, 80 per cent of the Roma are concentrated in shantytowns where 30 per cent of households live in sub-standard housing, exacerbated by poor facilities, overcrowding and poor local environments. Even more striking, in Greece, the housing conditions of the Roma are described as constituting a 'humanitarian emergency', with no access to sanitary facilities, refuse disposal, sewerage, water or electricity, and with discrimination in access to mortgages, price discrimination for rented housing, and direct and indirect discrimination by landlords. Furthermore, forced evictions and police raids on Roma camps have frequently been reported. Poor housing conditions have also been identified for the Muslim minority in Thrace, while high levels of homelessness have been noted among immigrants and asylum-seekers, with large numbers of nomadic Roma, asylum-seekers and undocumented migrants living in squatting environments of various types. In Thessalonica, 80 per cent of Albanian migrants have been identified as homeless, with others living in poor-quality housing with minimal facilities. Unacceptable living conditions in refugee reception centres have been recorded, with severe overcrowding and lack of basic sanitary facilities.

In Italy, the reported consensus among key actors is that migrants, refugees and asylum-seekers face great difficulties in securing accommodation, encountering barriers such as discriminatory residential qualifications applied by providers of low-rent public housing. Reports show that homelessness and high levels of overcrowding are key features of the housing histories of 'migrants'. Of those with no fixed abode, including those using abandoned industrial warehouses, old apartment blocks identified for demolition and empty warehouses and camps, 40.7 per cent have been identified as 'foreigners'. Nineteen such unauthorized settlements have been identified around Milan alone, inhabited by Roma, Moroccans, Albanians and Romanians. Almost all provinces of Italy have laws providing for Roma and Sinti camps, which are usually in industrial areas, highly overcrowded and with poor access to essential utilities, and they are the frequent target of racist eviction campaigns. Nationally, 27 per cent of squatters are authorized migrants with fixed jobs, with squatting resulting partly from barriers to accessing rented housing, including high rents, price discrimination and direct discrimination by landlords. In a recent national sample, 73 per cent of 'authorized immigrants' were found to be living in overcrowded conditions. In terms of quality of housing, one Italian study of the availability of facilities such as cooking, bathroom, drinking water and other utilities, found that over 15 per cent of 'migrants' did not have either drinking water or heating systems in their accommodation (Harrison *et al.* 2006).

Housing exclusion for these groups, as for many others, interconnects with discrimination and deprivation in access to education, health care and work. In many member states, including Britain, the Netherlands and France, growing concern over housing exclusion has been diverted into fruitless debates about segregation and integration, with most countries failing to implement specific measures that target improvements in housing conditions at migrants and minorities. In education, despite increasing political concern over discriminatory practices against the Roma, and growing awareness of the impact this discrimination has on Roma children, these processes remain at a significantly high level, leading to segregation, underperformance and violent attacks. Due to poor state practices in monitoring and documenting racist violence, non-governmental organizations

(NGOs) continue to play a key role in bringing this evidence to light, confirming three key trends in this field: first, increasing attacks against Muslim people and Muslim targets; second, increasing racist violence and crime against newer vulnerable immigrant groups, including irregular migrants, asylum-seekers and refugees; and third, continuing violence and abuse of the Roma, including abuse by state officials, for example the police, particularly in central and southern Europe. The 'racism of minor differences', which can easily escalate into both individual and mass violence, often drives such hostility, as analysed by Griselda Pollock in Chapter 2. Pollock echoes UN and UNESCO conventions in declaring the urgent need to acknowledge the right to recognition of difference and to construct social lives on that basis. Despite the political and social urgency of this task, globalization and Europeanization effectively 'thrive on the business of difference' (Bhattacharya *et al.* 2002, p. 164), commodifying ethnicities and specificities, constructing and mobilizing hierarchies of peoples, nations and regions, and remaking racial and economic inequalities and stratifications. Bhattacharya and her colleagues' 'call to arms' in response to these processes is similar to Pollock's: searching for alternatives, being innovative and unorthodox in our thinking, and diligently pursuing a multitude of solutions. However, the vagueness of these aspirations indicates some level of crisis in academic prescription. Lentin (2004), in a thorough examination of the nature of anti-racism in Europe, calls for renewed attention to be given to the mundane 'conveyor belt' of racist incidents, to the acts of discrimination and violence that anti-racist organizations deal with, and to the interrogation of the institutionalized roots of such actions in public political culture and in the governance of nation states.

The 2007 FRA report confirms the everyday persistence of the diverse racisms and exclusions that shape the lives of a complex range of migrant and minority groups across Europe. It also highlights ambivalent governance, which both exacerbates and reproduces many of these surface/overt and structural racialization processes, at the same time as it produces an increasingly bewildering array of unevenly developed strategic and practice responses, many of which fail outright. This is particularly evident in responses to racist violence. A 'crisis' exists in strategies to tackle racist violence, where legislation, techniques and approaches increasingly proliferate in the face of highly durable and resurgent patterns of attack. The NFP reports, all of which are available on the FRA Website, are full of examples of poor legislation, poor criminal justice practice and poor data collection, alongside limited evidence of practical actions and commitments by some governments and agencies to tackle the racist violence in their midst. Traditional criminal justice approaches appear to have made little headway in this area (Goodey 2005, 2007). Newer forms of restorative justice, which aim to resolve conflicts in informal settings with meetings between victim and offender, and which sometimes involve wider meetings with families and communities, are increasingly popular in many criminal justice jurisdictions, notably in Austria, Belgium, Germany and Britain, but these have been criticized for demoting racist violence to a form of 'secondary justice', or 'soft option', leading to intimidation of the victim and failure to recognize the history of repeated violence.

Franco Frattini, the former EU justice commissioner, recently confirmed that five EU member states have major problems with endemic right-wing extremism and associated racist violence: Belgium, Denmark, France, Germany and Italy. These comments were made after a gang of fifty drunken youths shouting racist slogans attacked eight Indians in the east German town of Mügeln, and two African men were beaten by right-wing extremists in the west German town of Mainz, together with concerns over the role played by the far-right Nationaldemokratische Partei Deutschlands (NPD, National Democratic Party of Germany) in inciting these two incidents (Beunderman 2007). Amil, a leading anti-Nazi group in the (east German) Saxony region, confirmed that there had been 137 neo-Nazi attacks on individuals in the first six months of 2007, and the Forsca research group found that half of east German youths (aged fourteen to twenty-five) currently believed that National Socialism had many good points (Paterson 2007). Meanwhile, the NPD, a nationalist anti-immigrant group, directly associated with neo-Nazi and skinhead groups, openly incites race hate on its Website. There has been much debate over the banning of the group, but to date this has been a legal fiasco, underlining the fact that Germany's response to such political racism and violence is in crisis, as it has been for many years. What is to be done? And what works?

Winant's pessimistic account of a coming 'global racial crisis' does appear, then, to characterize the contemporary European context. Admittedly, we may expect progress on a range of fronts: in international and national politics and policy, NGO activity, cultural and artistic affairs, and human interaction. But we may equally expect exclusion and discrimination, racial and ethnic conflict, and associated violence and murder to be happening across a wide range of European countries soon.

In Chapter 11, Michel Wieviorka specifically addresses the nature of the racial crisis in France, examining the institutional, cultural, political and intellectual dimensions of current events. For Wieviorka, the French Republic, following the violent confrontations in 2005, is paralysed and in high probability of terminal decline, though with some prospect of a post-republican future. More recent events indicate, however, that this post-republican future is unlikely to occur and, instead, the ongoing renewal of state racism is evident. This is epitomized in President Nicholas Sarkozy's speech at the University of Dakar on 26 July 2007, in which he conspicuously failed to address the French role in the Rwandan genocide and French support for vicious regimes in postcolonial Africa. He stated instead that: 'One cannot blame everything on colonization – the corruption, the dictators, the genocide, that is not colonization'. France might have made 'mistakes', he conceded, but they still believed in their 'civilizing mission' and 'did not exploit anybody'. Sarkozy also confirmed the durability of Eurocentric racism with these words:

> Africans have never really entered history. They have never really launched themselves into the future. In a world where nature controls everything, man has remained immobile in the middle of an unshakable order where everything

is determined. There is room neither for human endeavour, nor for the idea
of progress. (Quoted in Mbembe 2007)

Describing African urban youth as 'scum', talking up racist exclusion and immigration agendas, and presiding over the police harassment of African immigrants
have been key markers of Sarkozy's politics, all of which indicates a deepening
of the racial crisis in France. As Christophe Bertossi (2007) argues, the French
'liberal hour' has passed, and there is a lack of political will to implement anti-
discrimination and anti-racist policies despite the 2005 disturbances. Bertossi
confirms what many contributors to this volume have argued: that there is
a political crisis of national models of integration, whether the Dutch pillar
system, the French republican model or British race relations, with the prevailing
'European diagnosis' being that Islam is both the 'source and explanation' of the
politically constructed problem. This view skews and obstructs understanding
of the diversity and durability of racism in postcolonial Europe, and indeed
constitutes a core form of racialized governance that infects the heart of liberal
democracies. We must turn to non-governmental sources, such as ICARE (the
Internet Centre Anti Racism Europe, www.icare.to), for exposure of current trends
in racist hostility. Resurgent, ideologically driven race hate is being documented
in many European countries. Public political culture in the Netherlands has
become more hostile and aggressive, as Philomena Essed forcefully suggests in
Chapter 9, and this, combined with a focus on Islamic extremism rather than
right-wing extremism, has allowed organized race hate groups to flourish. The
Anne Frank Foundation documented a doubling of extreme-right acts of racist
violence from 2006 to 2007, and identified a small core of 100 ideologically
driven men in groups like Blood and Honour and Combat 18. The public formation of anti-Semitic, anti-Roma and homophobic paramilitary groups continues,
for which two recent examples will suffice. In Hungary, Jobbik, a far-right party,
and over 1,000 of its supporters inducted the founding members of its new paramilitary wing, the Magya Guard, in full public glare outside the Presidential Palace
in Budapest in August 2007. Meanwhile, in the Czech Republic, the extreme-right
National Corporativism movement, which mobilizes many skinheads, organized
a demonstration in Svitavy in July 2007 to support the cause of a twenty-three-
year-old skinhead who had been convicted of killing a Roma man.

For many European states, racism is all about the activities of the extreme
right. The central role played by the figure of 'the black', 'the Jew' and 'the
Muslim' in the racialized construction of Europe has been examined by David
Goldberg (2006), who argues that the rule and law of 'postcolonial distinction'
in Europe founds itself upon racial denial: both a masking of the causes of
institutionalized racial violence and a repeated exclusion through the fictitious
construction of panic-inducing postcolonial figures of vilification. As a result,
racial exceptionalism prevails, racism is reduced to the fringes of extremism and
European state institutions pronounce themselves 'guiltless'.

Continual diverse forms of mobilization by migrants and minorities, who are
living in the midst of local, national, European and international racial crises,

are evident across Europe. In reviewing the black diaspora in the context of globalization and what he calls the 'western spectacle', Hesse (1999) reminds us that three forms of reflexivity characterize the social construction of black identities: first, an anti-slavery reflexivity, which is concerned with restoring humanity and integrity to black people; second, an anti-colonial reflexivity, which makes claims for black people's 'lives, livelihoods and cultural heritage' in the context of national sovereignty; and third, an anti-racist reflexivity, which challenges racialized inequalities in material and political conditions in western societies. The need for action on this last point has recently been underlined by a wide-ranging review of ethnicity and poverty in Britain that draws on research evidence from 350 studies carried out from 1991 onwards (Platt 2007). According to the review, over half of Pakistani, Bangladeshi and black African children are growing up in poverty. Stark ethnic differences in poverty rates are determined by a variety of factors, including persistent discrimination, patterns of educational qualifications, labour market outcomes, housing locations, disabilities and ill health. Across Europe, the failure of nation states to engage with repeating patterns of racialized and ethnicized suffering and exclusion is abundantly clear. Instead, there is a marked preference for political rhetoric about integration, security and immigration and a corresponding failure to grasp the depth of racism and racialization. Weighing up the future for racial Europe needs particular care. John Stone and Polly Rizova (2007), in drawing attention to the perils of prediction, have pointed out the failure of social scientists to predict key historical events, such as the ending of apartheid. However, on the positive side, narratives of resistance, opposition, celebration and humanity continue to be found in a profusion of voices, social and political spaces and locations in Europe and beyond: a conversation to which this volume seeks to contribute, and which should inspire us to reflection and action in the face of Europe's racial crisis, both at the present moment and for times to come.

Works cited

Banton, M. (2002) *The International Politics of Race*. Cambridge, Polity Press.

Bertossi, C. (2007) *Distant Neighbours: Understanding How the French Deal with Ethnic and Religious Diversity*. London, Runnymede Trust.

Beunderman, M. (2007) 'Frattini Backs Calls to Outlaw German Far-Right Party'. Euobserver. com, 27 August. Available at http://euobserver.com/?aid=24637 (accessed 31 January 2009).

Bhattacharya, G., Gabriel, J. and Small, S. (2002) *Race and Power: Global Racism in the Twenty-First Century*. London, Routledge.

Bowser, B. ed. (1995) *Racism and Anti-racism in World Perspective*. London, Sage.

Chakrabarty, D. (2000) *Provincializing Europe: Postcolonial Thought and Historical Difference*. Princeton, MA, Princeton University Press.

European Network Against Racism (2006) *Durban's Legacy: National Action Plans Against Racism in the European Union*. Fact Sheet No. 29, October. London, ENAR.

FRA (European Union Fundamental Rights Agency) (2007) *Trends and Developments in Racism, Xenophobia and Anti-Semitism, 1997–2005*. Vienna, FRA.

Goldberg, D. (2005) 'Racial Americanisation'. In: Murji, K. and Solomos, J. eds. *Racialization: Studies in Theory and Practice*. Oxford, Oxford University Press.

—— (2006) 'Racial Europeanisation'. *Ethnic and Racial Studies*, 29(2), pp. 331–64.

Goodey, J. (2005) *Racist Violence in 15 EU Member States*. Vienna, EUMC.

—— (2007) 'Racist Violence in Europe: Challenges for Official Data Collection'. *Ethnic and Racial Studies*, 30(4) (*Racist Futures* special edition), pp. 570–89.

Harrison, M., Law, I. and Phillips, D. (2006) *Migrants, Minorities and Housing*. Vienna, EUMC.

Hesse, B. (1999) 'Reviewing the Western Spectacle: Reflexive Globalisation Through the Black Diaspora'. In: Brah, A., Hickman, M. and an Ghaill, M. M. eds. *Global Futures, Migration, Environment and Globalisation*. Basingstoke, Macmillan.

Lentin, A. (2004) *Racism and Anti-racism in Europe*. London, Pluto Press.

Macedo, D. and Gounari, P., eds (2006) *The Globalisation of Racism*. Boulder, CO, Paradigm.

Mbembe, A. (2007) 'Sacré bleu! Mbeki and Sarkozy?' *Mail and Guardian Online*, 28 August. Available at www.mg.co.za/article/2007-08-27-sacr-bleu-mbeki-and-sarkozy (accessed 31 January 2009).

Paterson, T. (2007) 'Merkel Under Pressure to Ban Neo-Nazi Party'. *Independent*, 25 August. Available at www.independent.co.uk/news/world/europe/merkel-under-pressure-to-ban-neonazi-party-462937.html (accessed 31 January 2009).

Platt, L. (2007) *Poverty and Ethnicity in the UK*. York, Joseph Rowntree Foundation.

Stone, J. and Rizova, P. (2007) 'Rethinking Racial Conflict in an Era of Global Terror'. *Ethnic and Racial Studies*, 30(4), pp. 534–45.

Winant, H. (2006) 'Race and Racism: Towards a Global Future'. *Ethnic and Racial Studies*, 29(5), pp. 986–1003.

World Conference Against Racism, Racial Discrimination, Xenophobia and Related Intolerance (2001) *Report of the World Conference Against Racism, Racial Discrimination, Xenophobia and Related Intolerance*. Durban, UN, WCAR.

Index

Emboldened page references denote complete chapters. *Italicized* page references denote illustrations.

Printed and bound by CPI Group (UK) Ltd, Croydon, CR0 4YY

07/07/2026